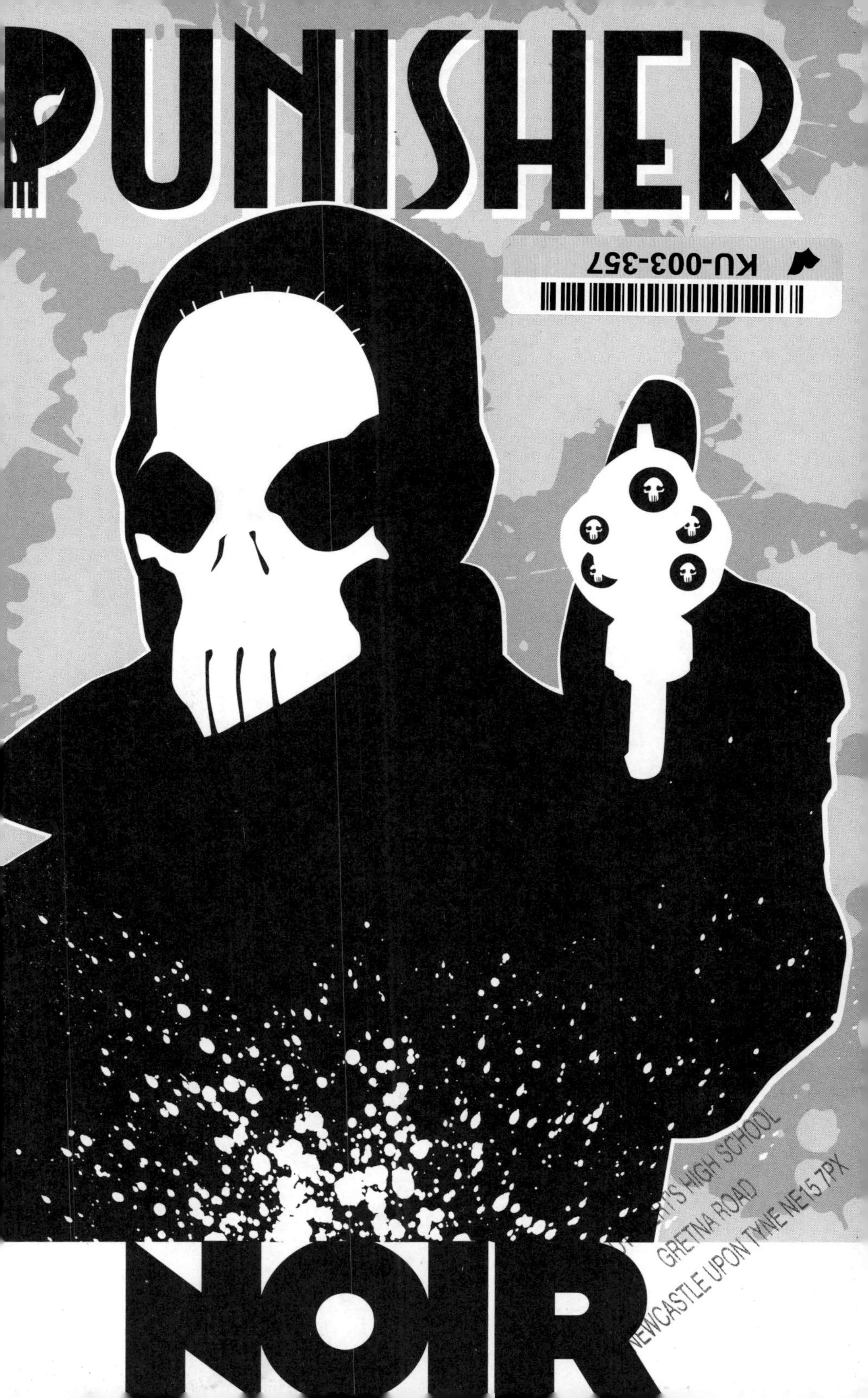
PUNISHER
NOIR

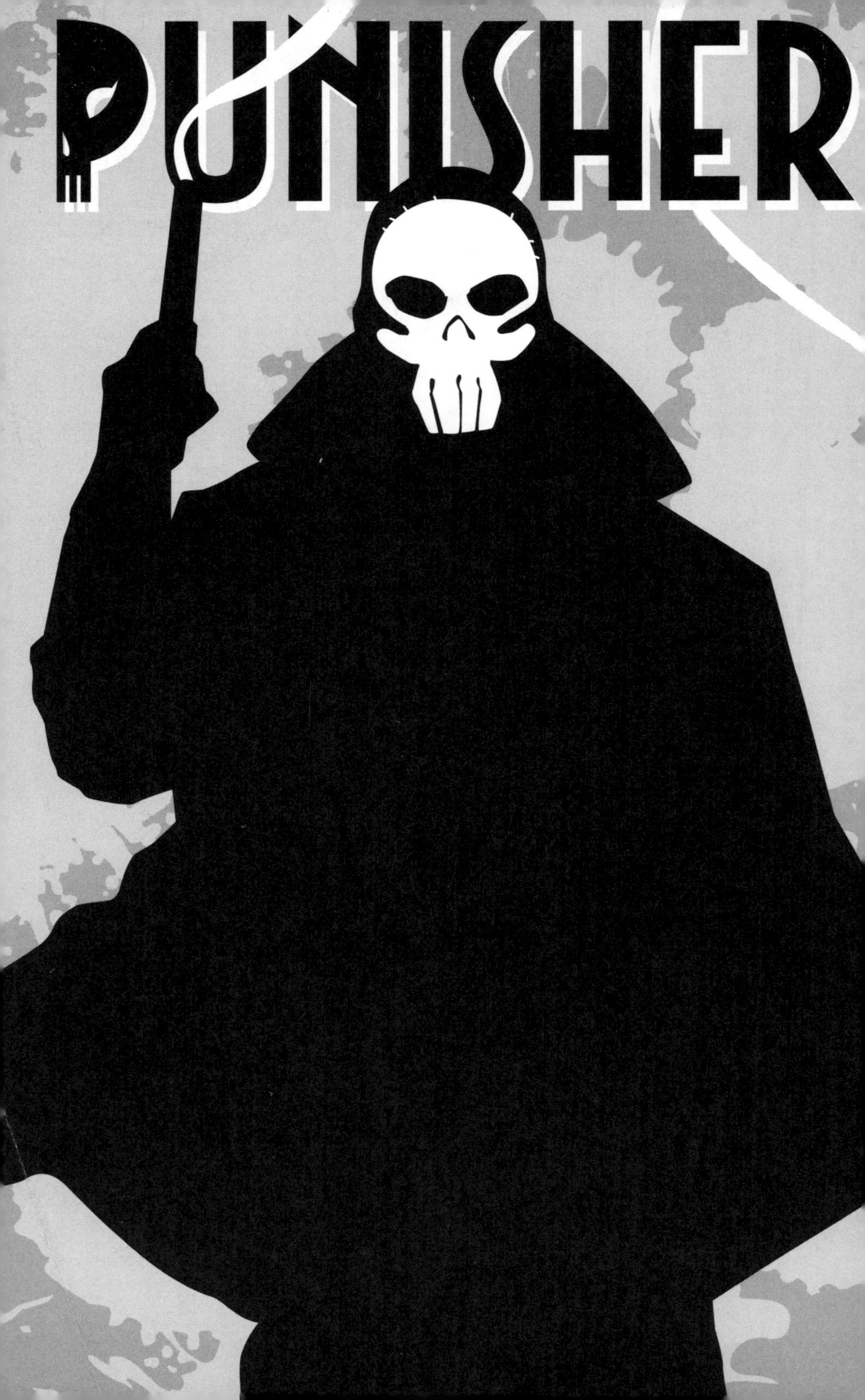
PUNISHER

WRITER
FRANK TIERI

ARTISTS
PAUL AZACETA AND
ANTONIO FUSO (ISSUE 4)

COLORIST
NICK FILARDI

LETTERER
VC'S JOE SABINO

COVER ART
TIM BRADSTREET

EDITOR
SEBASTIAN GIRNER

CONSULTING EDITOR
AXEL ALONSO

COLLECTION EDITOR
JENNIFER GRÜNWALD
EDITORIAL ASSISTANTS
JOE HOCHSTEIN & JAMES EMMETT
ASSISTANT EDITORS
ALEX STARBUCK & NELSON RIBEIRO
EDITOR, SPECIAL PROJECTS
MARK D. BEAZLEY
SENIOR EDITOR, SPECIAL PROJECTS
JEFF YOUNGQUIST
SENIOR VICE PRESIDENT OF SALES
DAVID GABRIEL
BOOK DESIGN
JEFF POWELL
EDITOR IN CHIEF
JOE QUESADA
PUBLISHER
DAN BUCKLEY
EXECUTIVE PRODUCER
ALAN FINE

PUNISHER NOIR. Contains material originally published in magazine form as PUNISHER NOIR #1-4. First printing 2010. ISBN# 978-0-7851-3276-9. Published by MARVEL WORLDWIDE, INC., a subsidiary of MARVEL ENTERTAINMENT, LLC. OFFICE OF PUBLICATION: 417 5th Avenue, New York, NY 10016. Copyright © 2009 and 2010 Marvel Characters, Inc. All rights reserved. $14.99 per copy in the U.S. and $16.99 in Canada (GST #R127032852); Canadian Agreement #40668537. All characters featured in this issue and the distinctive names and likenesses thereof, and all related indicia are trademarks of Marvel Characters, Inc. No similarity between any of the names, characters, persons, and/or institutions in this magazine with those of any living or dead person or institution is intended, and any such similarity which may exist is purely coincidental. **Printed in Canada.** ALAN FINE, EVP - Office of the President, Marvel Worldwide, Inc. and EVP & CMO Marvel Characters B.V.; DAN BUCKLEY, Chief Executive Officer and Publisher - Print, Animation & Digital Media; JIM SOKOLOWSKI, Chief Operating Officer; DAVID GABRIEL, SVP of Publishing Sales & Circulation; DAVID BOGART, SVP of Business Affairs & Talent Management; MICHAEL PASCIULLO, VP Merchandising & Communications; JIM O'KEEFE, VP of Operations & Logistics; DAN CARR, Executive Director of Publishing Technology; JUSTIN F. GABRIE, Director of Publishing & Editorial Operations; SUSAN CRESPI, Editorial Operations Manager; ALEX MORALES, Publishing Operations Manager; STAN LEE, Chairman Emeritus. For information regarding advertising in Marvel Comics or on Marvel.com, please contact Ron Stern, VP of Business Development, at rstern@marvel.com. For Marvel subscription inquiries, please call 800-217-9158. **Manufactured between 9/1/10 and 9/15/10 by IMPRIMERIES TRANSCONTINENTAL S.E.N.C., BEAUCEVILLE, QC, CANADA.**

10 9 8 7 6 5 4 3 2 1

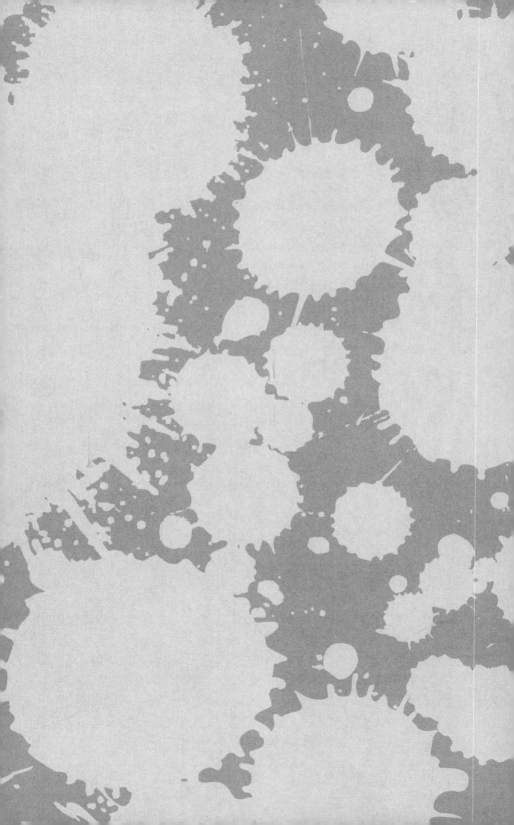

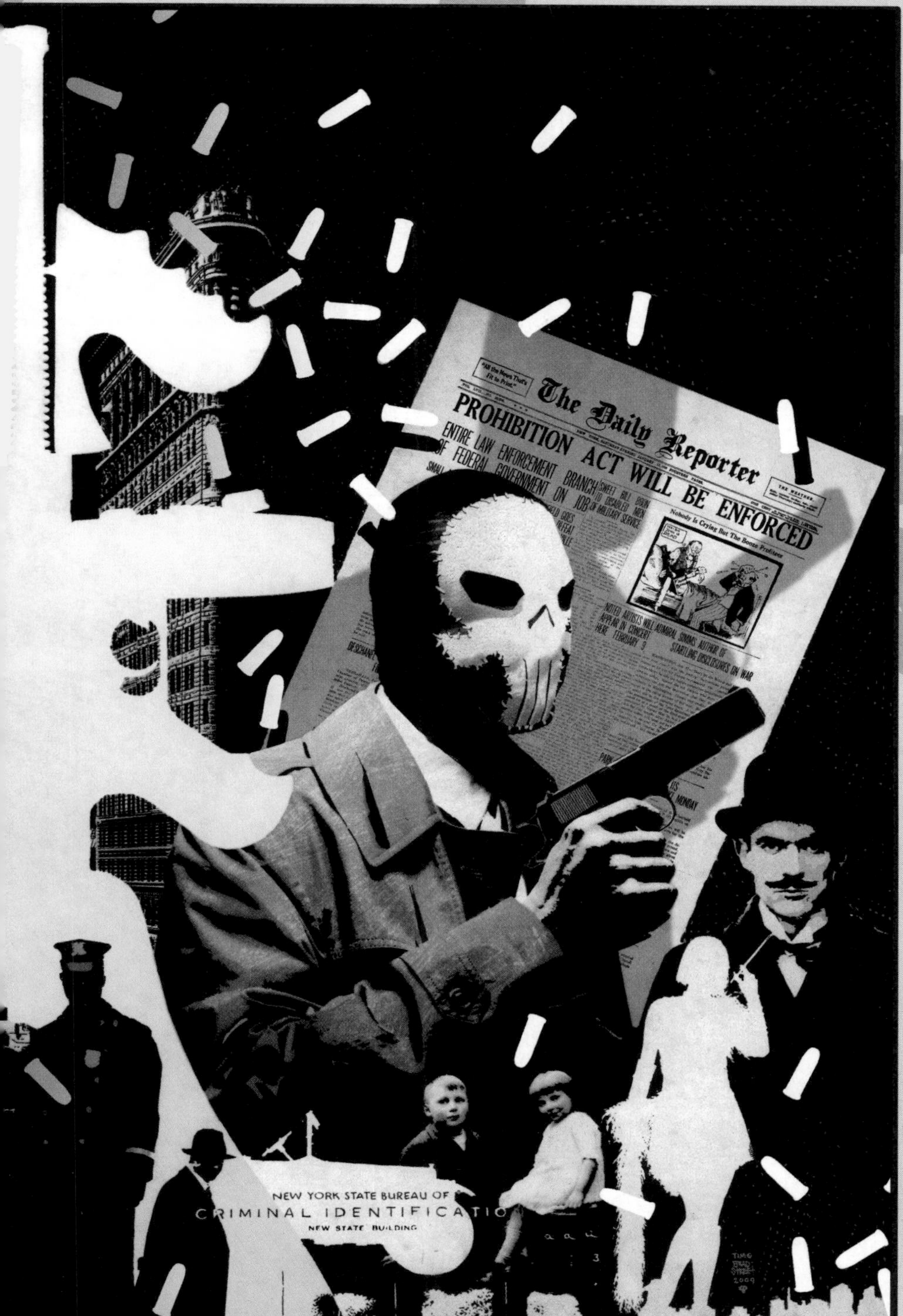
"All the News That's Fit to Print."
The Daily Reporter
PROHIBITION ACT WILL BE ENFORCED
ENTIRE LAW ENFORCEMENT BRANCH OF FEDERAL GOVERNMENT ON JOB
SWEET BILL BOON TO DISABLED MEN OF MILITARY SERVICE
Nobody Is Crying But The Booze Profiteer
NOTED ARTISTS WILL APPEAR IN CONCERT HERE FEBRUARY 9
ADMIRAL SIMMS AUTHOR OF STARTLING DISCLOSURES ON WAR
NEW YORK STATE BUREAU OF
CRIMINAL IDENTIFICATIO
NEW STATE BUILDING

ONE

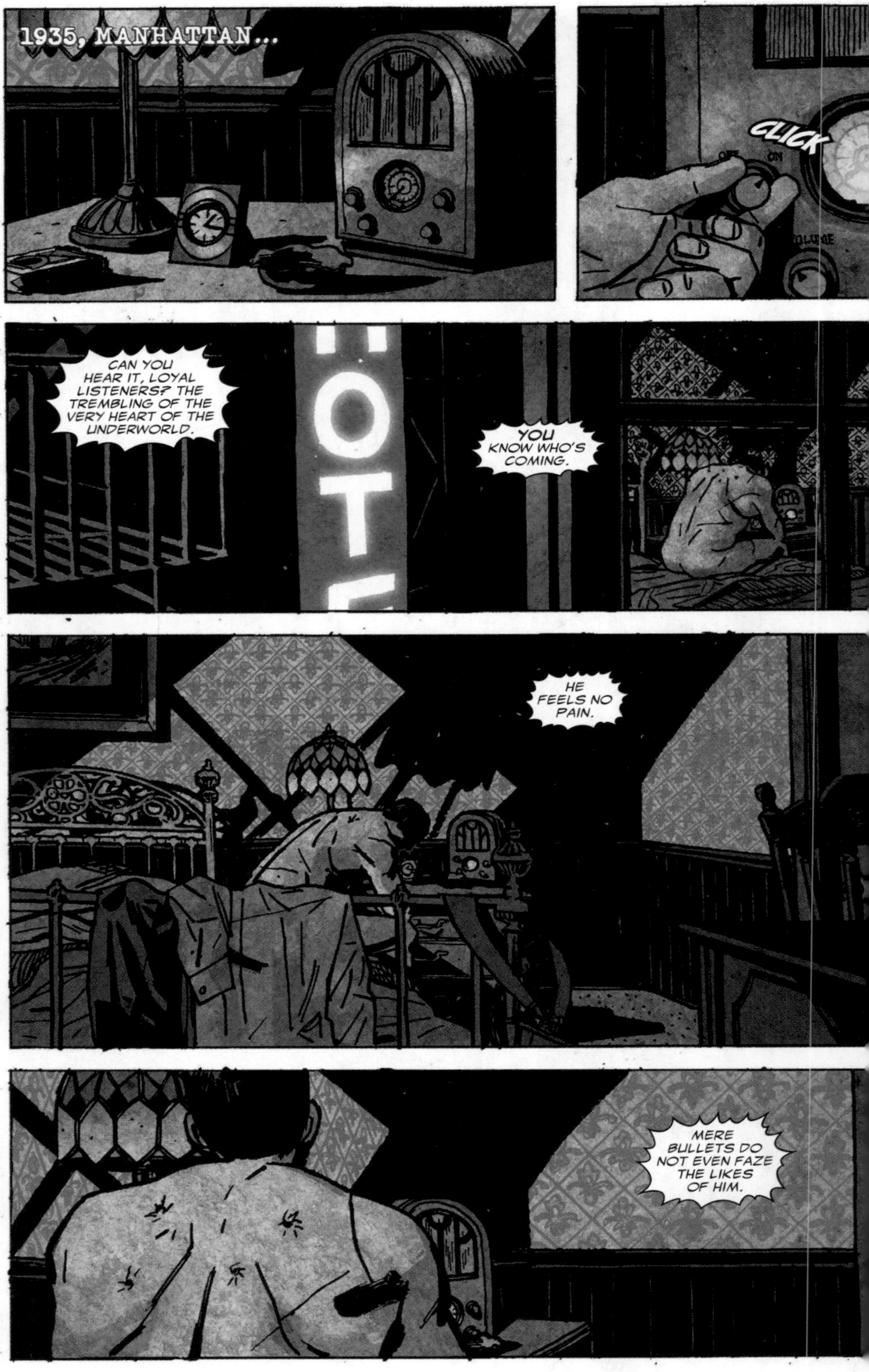
1935, MANHATTAN...
CLICK
OFF
ON
VOLUME
CAN YOU HEAR IT, LOYAL LISTENERS? THE TREMBLING OF THE VERY HEART OF THE UNDERWORLD.
YOU KNOW WHO'S COMING.
HE FEELS NO PAIN.
MERE BULLETS DO NOT EVEN FAZE THE LIKES OF HIM.

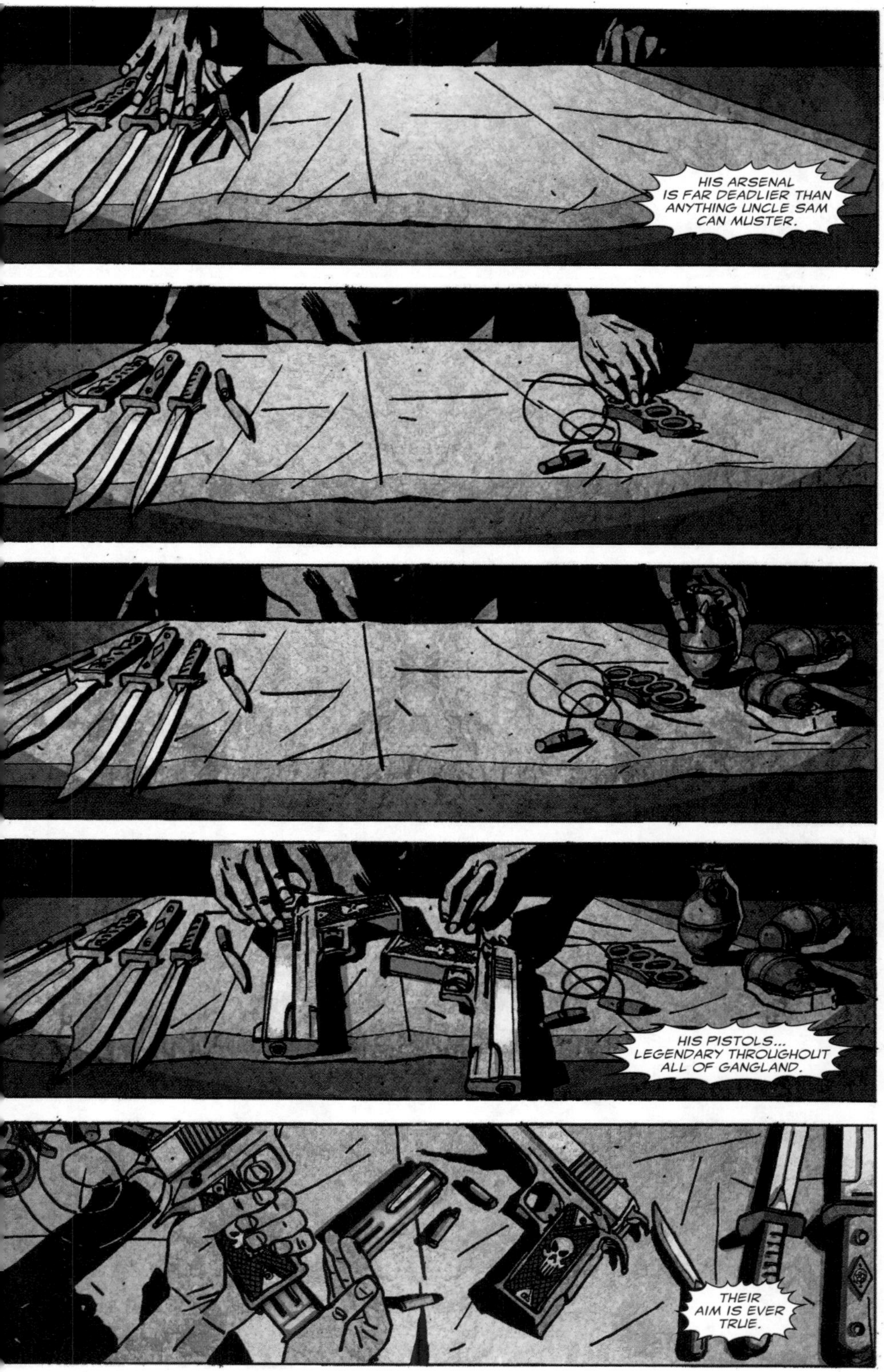
HIS ARSENAL IS FAR DEADLIER THAN ANYTHING UNCLE SAM CAN MUSTER.
HIS PISTOLS... LEGENDARY THROUGHOUT ALL OF GANGLAND.
THEIR AIM IS EVER TRUE.

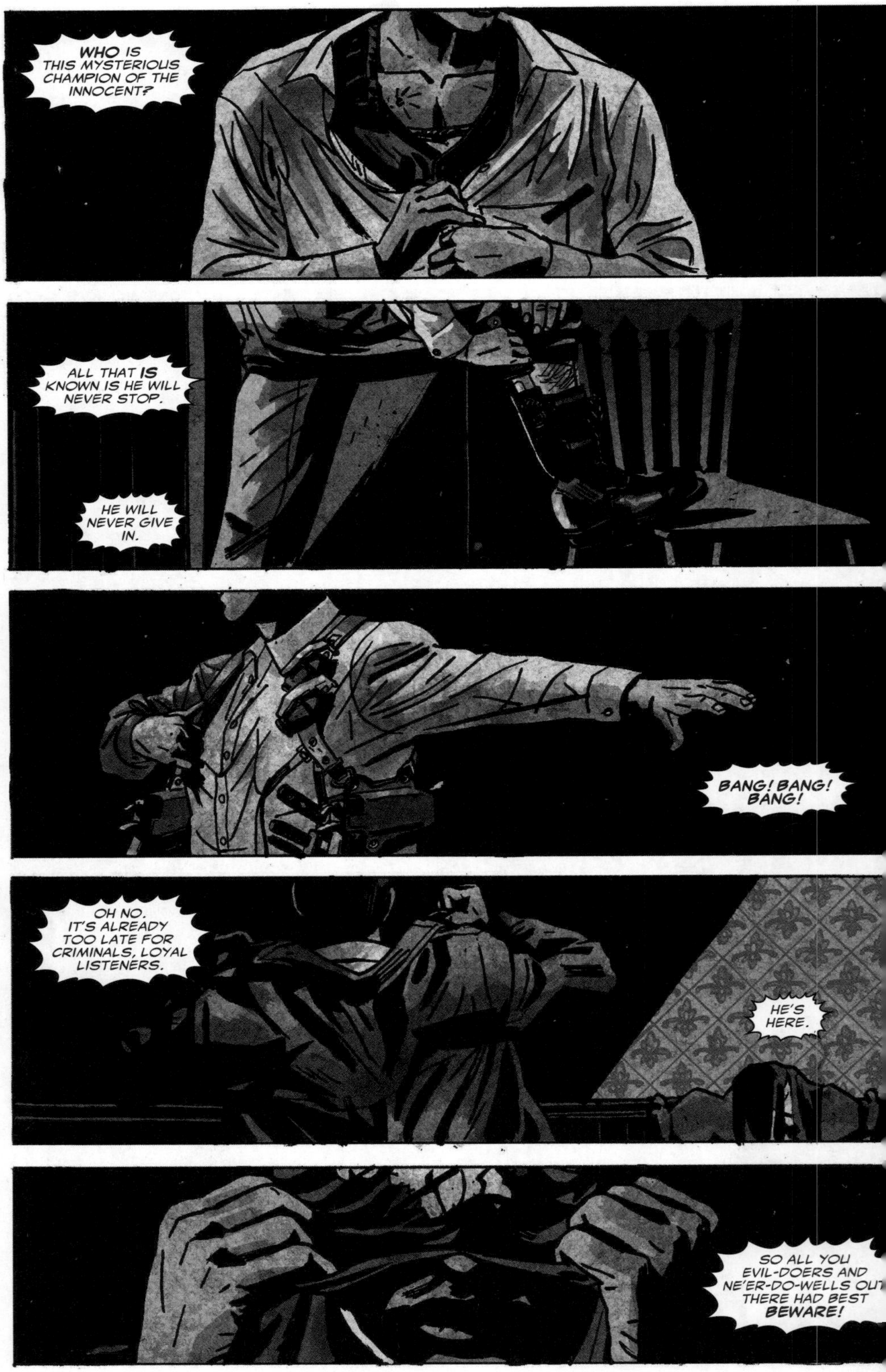
WHO IS THIS MYSTERIOUS CHAMPION OF THE INNOCENT?
ALL THAT IS KNOWN IS HE WILL NEVER STOP.
HE WILL NEVER GIVE IN.
BANG! BANG! BANG!
OH NO. IT'S ALREADY TOO LATE FOR CRIMINALS, LOYAL LISTENERS.
HE'S HERE.
SO ALL YOU EVIL-DOERS AND NE'ER-DO-WELLS OUT THERE HAD BEST BEWARE!

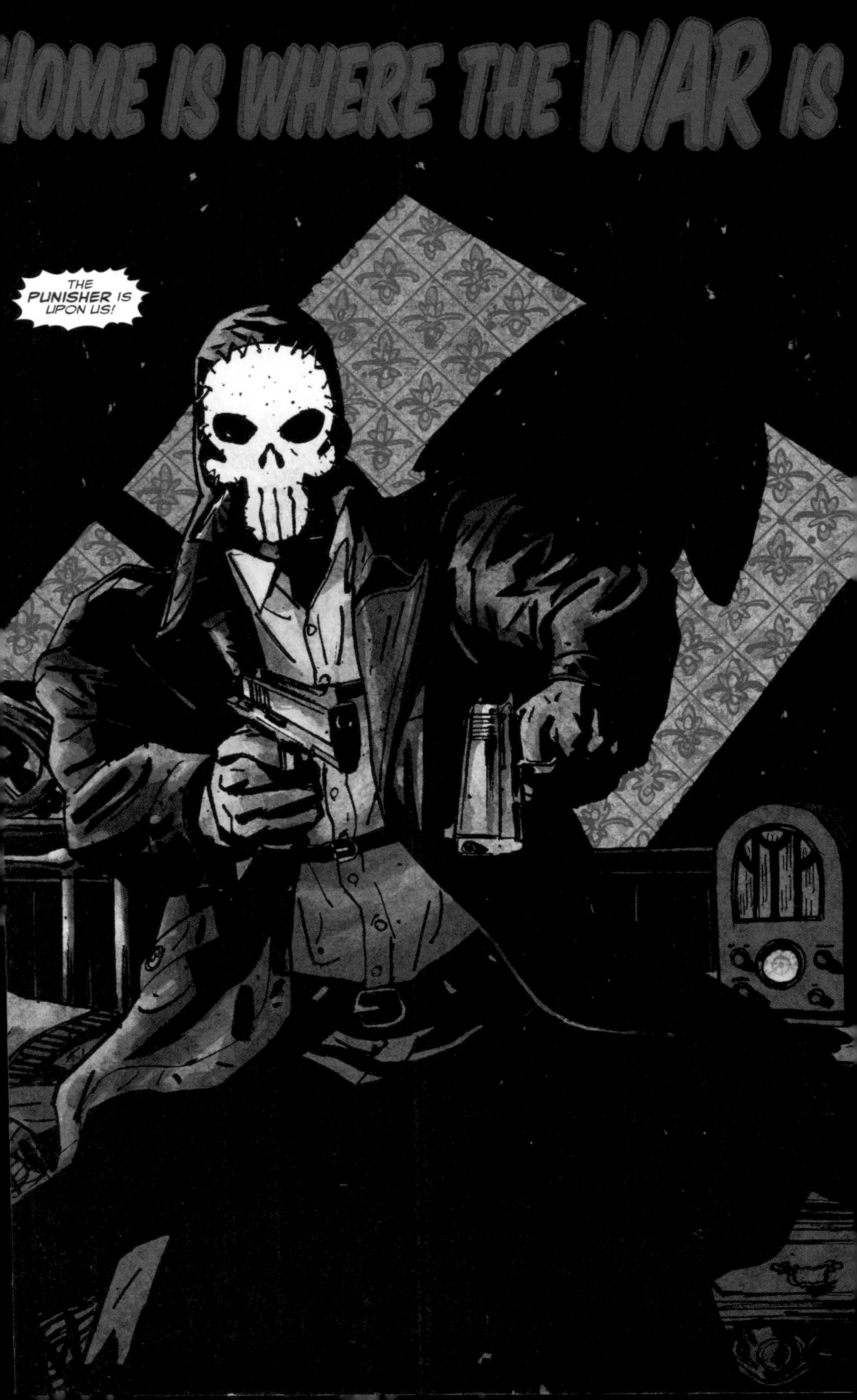
HOME IS WHERE THE WAR IS
THE PUNISHER IS UPON US!

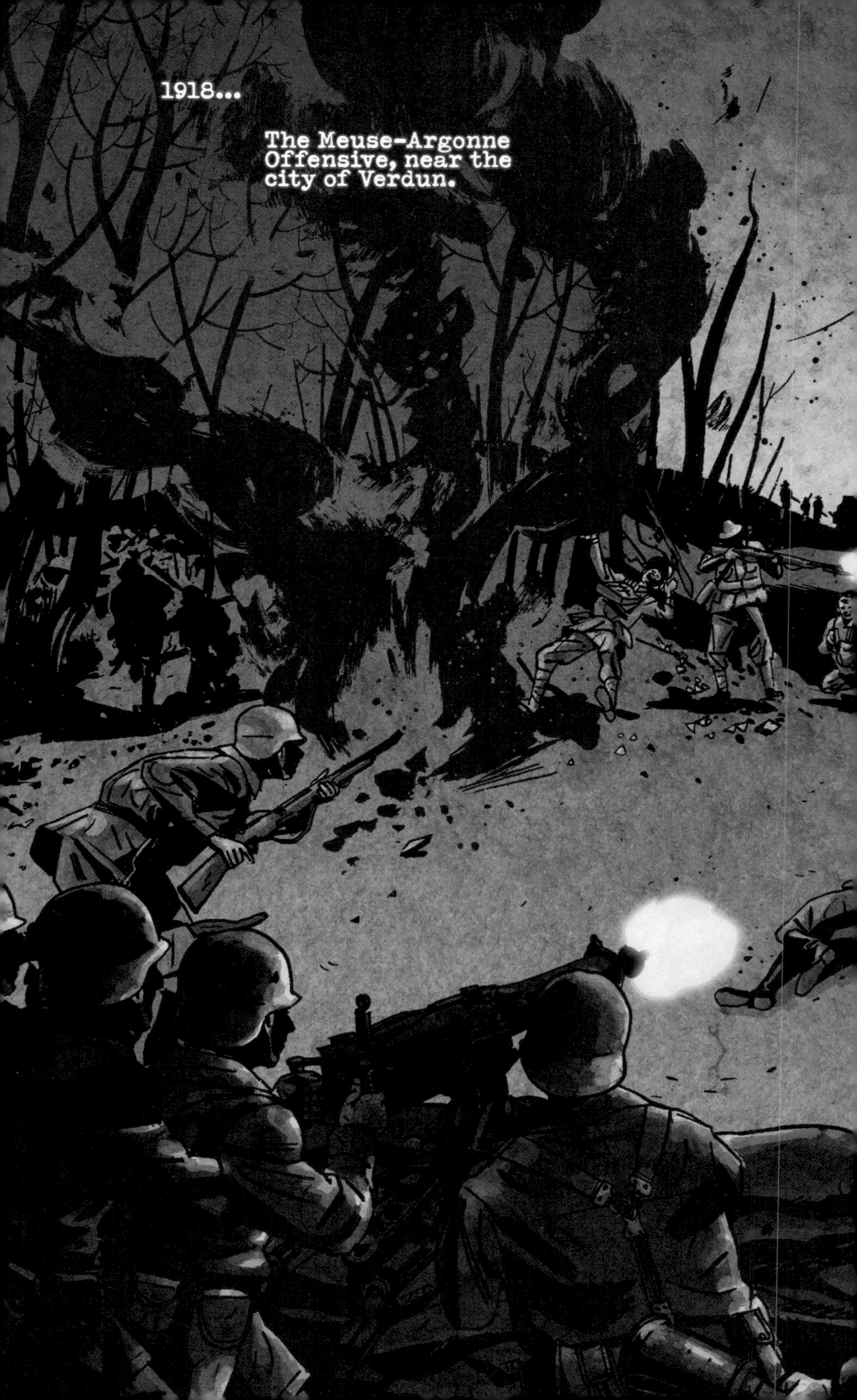
1918...
The Meuse-Argonne Offensive, near the city of Verdun.

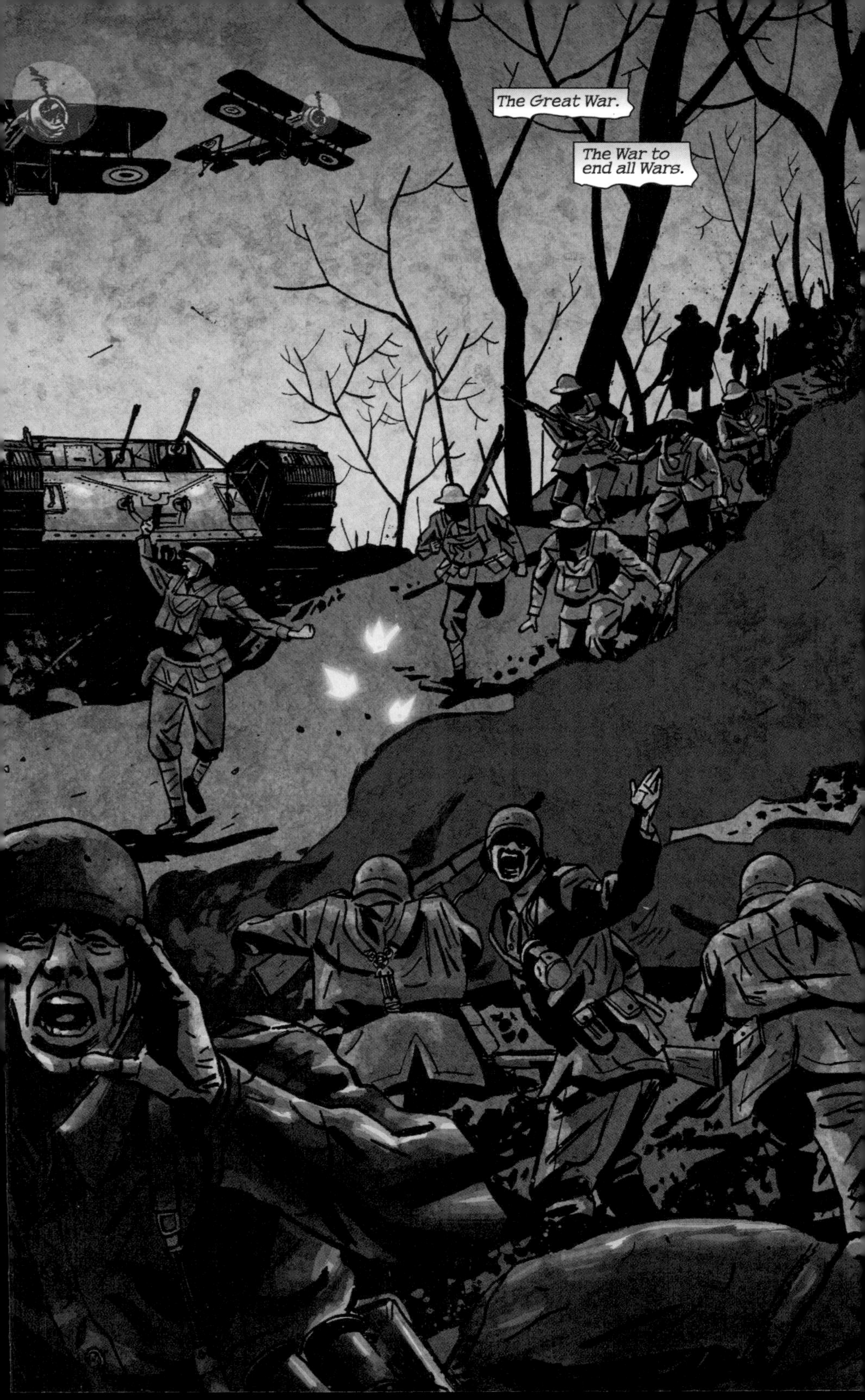
The Great War.
The War to end all Wars.

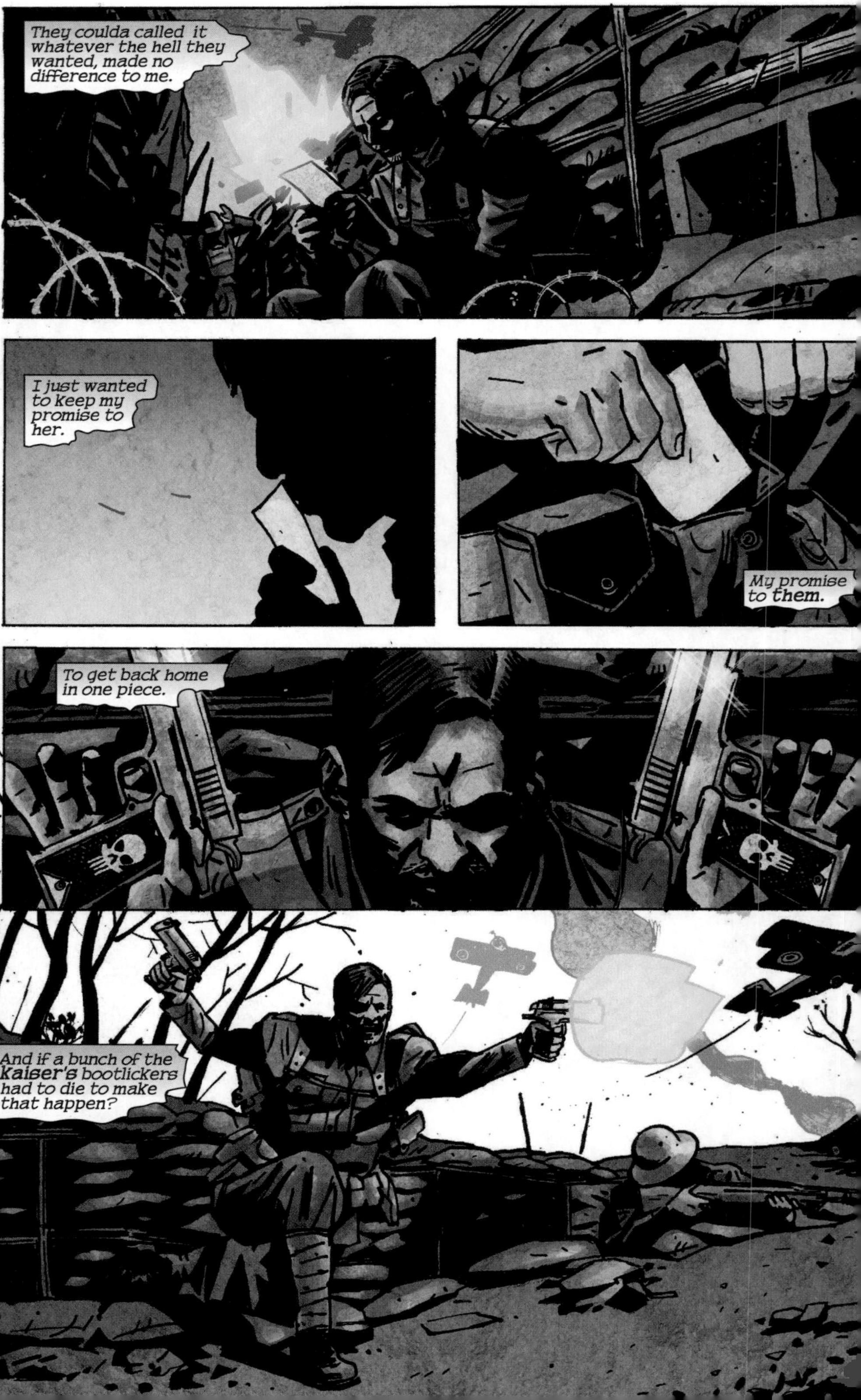
They coulda called it whatever the hell they wanted, made no difference to me.
I just wanted to keep my promise to her.
My promise to them.
To get back home in one piece.
And if a bunch of the Kaiser's bootlickers had to die to make that happen?

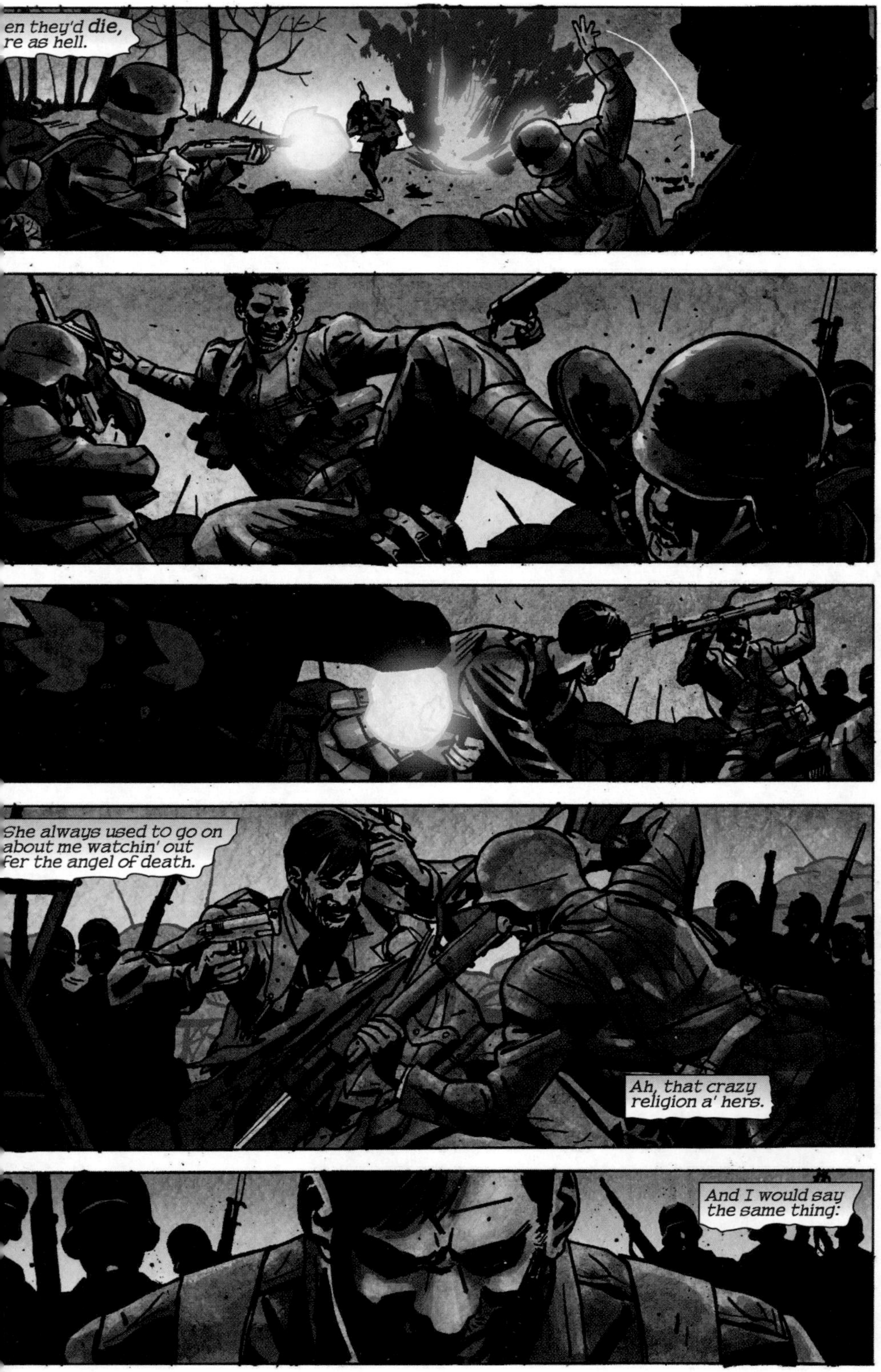
en they'd die,
re as hell.
She always used to go on
about me watchin' out
fer the angel of death.
Ah, that crazy
religion a' hers.
And I would say
the same thing:

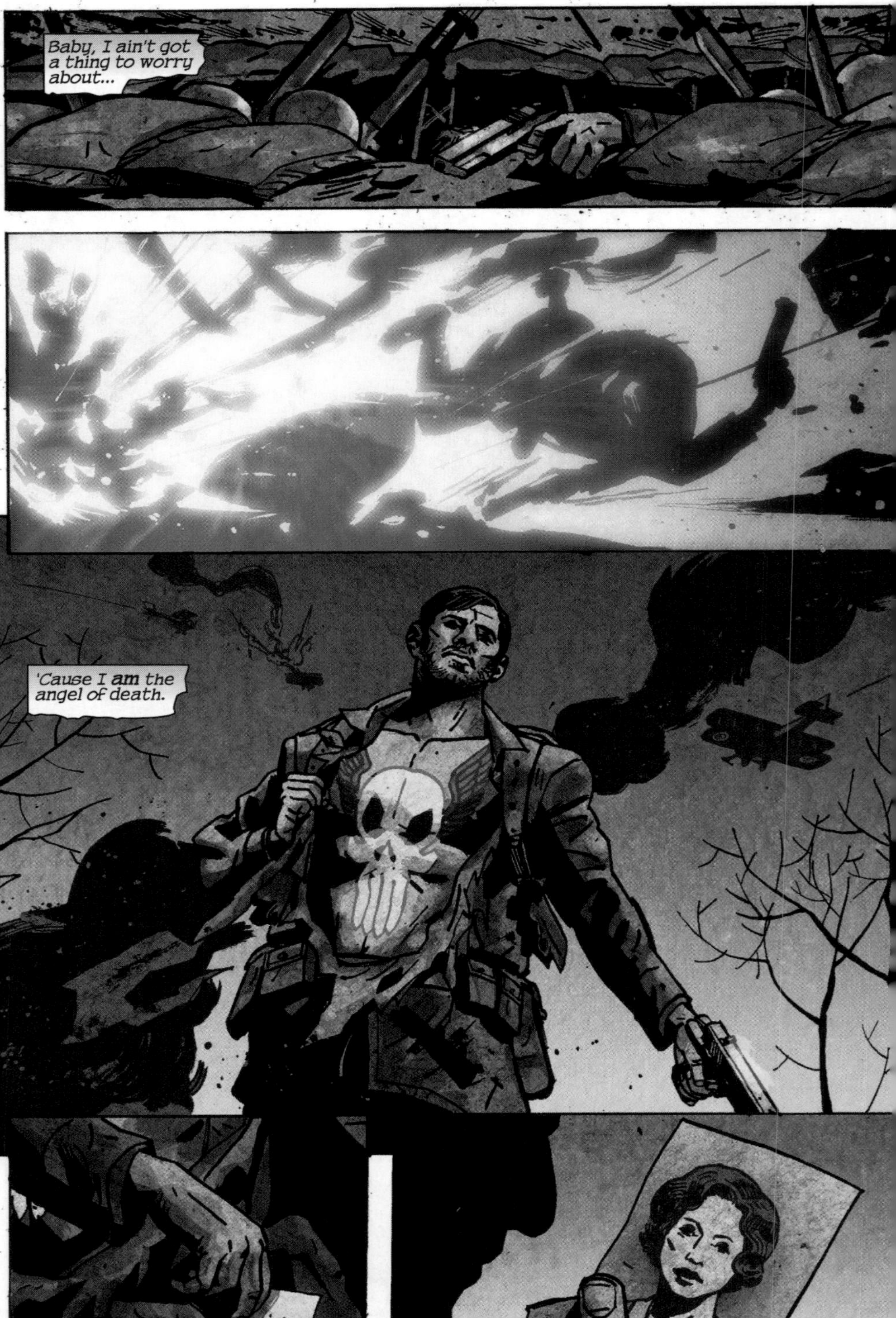
Baby, I ain't got a thing to worry about...
'Cause I am the angel of death.
My belovec Ruth.

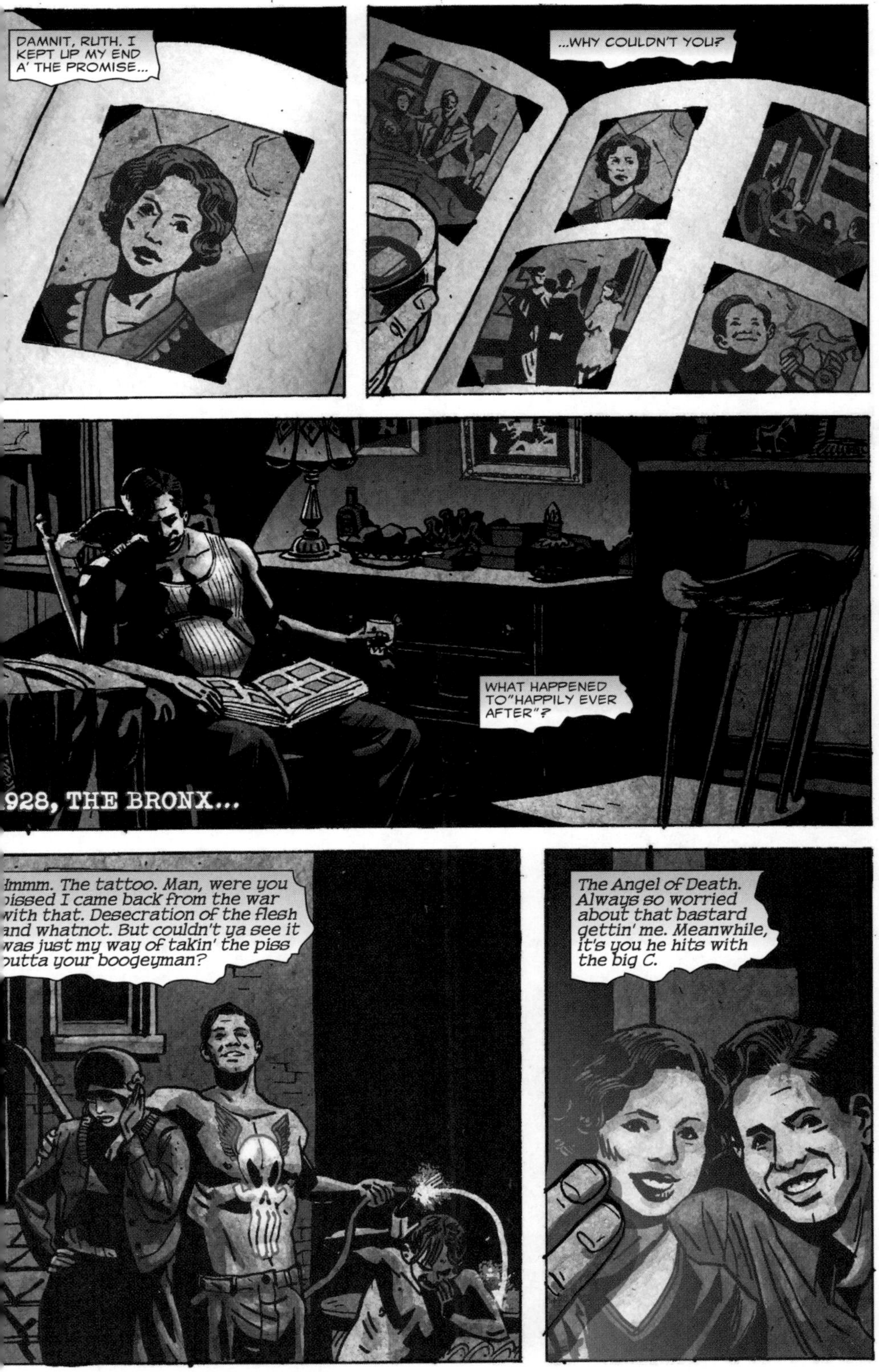

DAMNIT, RUTH. I KEPT UP MY END A' THE PROMISE...
...WHY COULDN'T YOU?
WHAT HAPPENED TO "HAPPILY EVER AFTER"?
928, THE BRONX...
ммм. The tattoo. Man, were you pissed I came back from the war with that. Desecration of the flesh and whatnot. But couldn't ya see it was just my way of takin' the piss outta your boogeyman?
The Angel of Death. Always so worried about that bastard gettin' me. Meanwhile, it's you he hits with the big C.

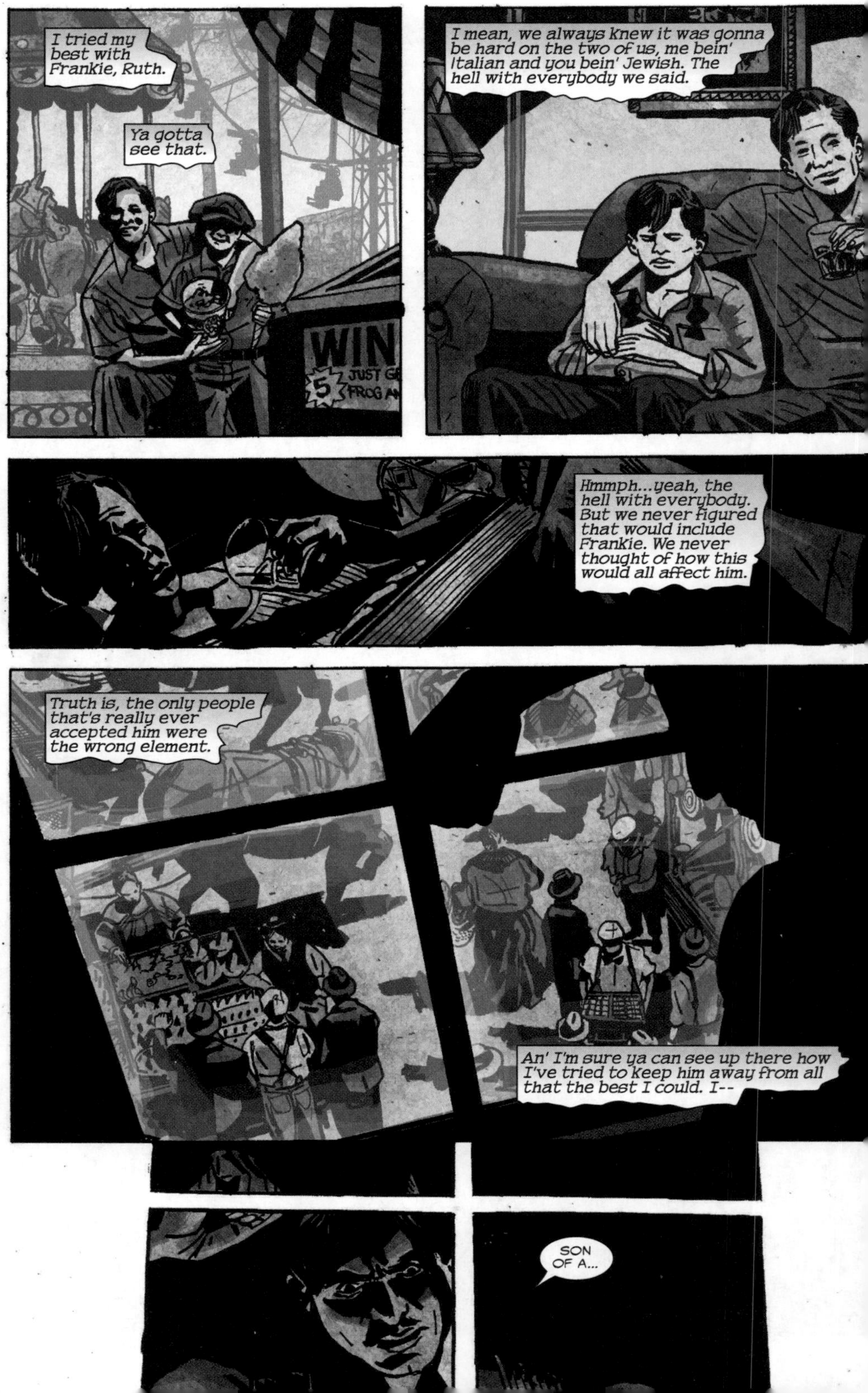

I tried my best with Frankie, Ruth.
Ya gotta see that.
WIN
5
JUST GR
FROG AN
I mean, we always knew it was gonna be hard on the two of us, me bein' Italian and you bein' Jewish. The hell with everybody we said.
Hmmph...yeah, the hell with everybody. But we never figured that would include Frankie. We never thought of how this would all affect him.
Truth is, the only people that's really ever accepted him were the wrong element.
An' I'm sure ya can see up there how I've tried to keep him away from all that the best I could. I--
SON OF A...

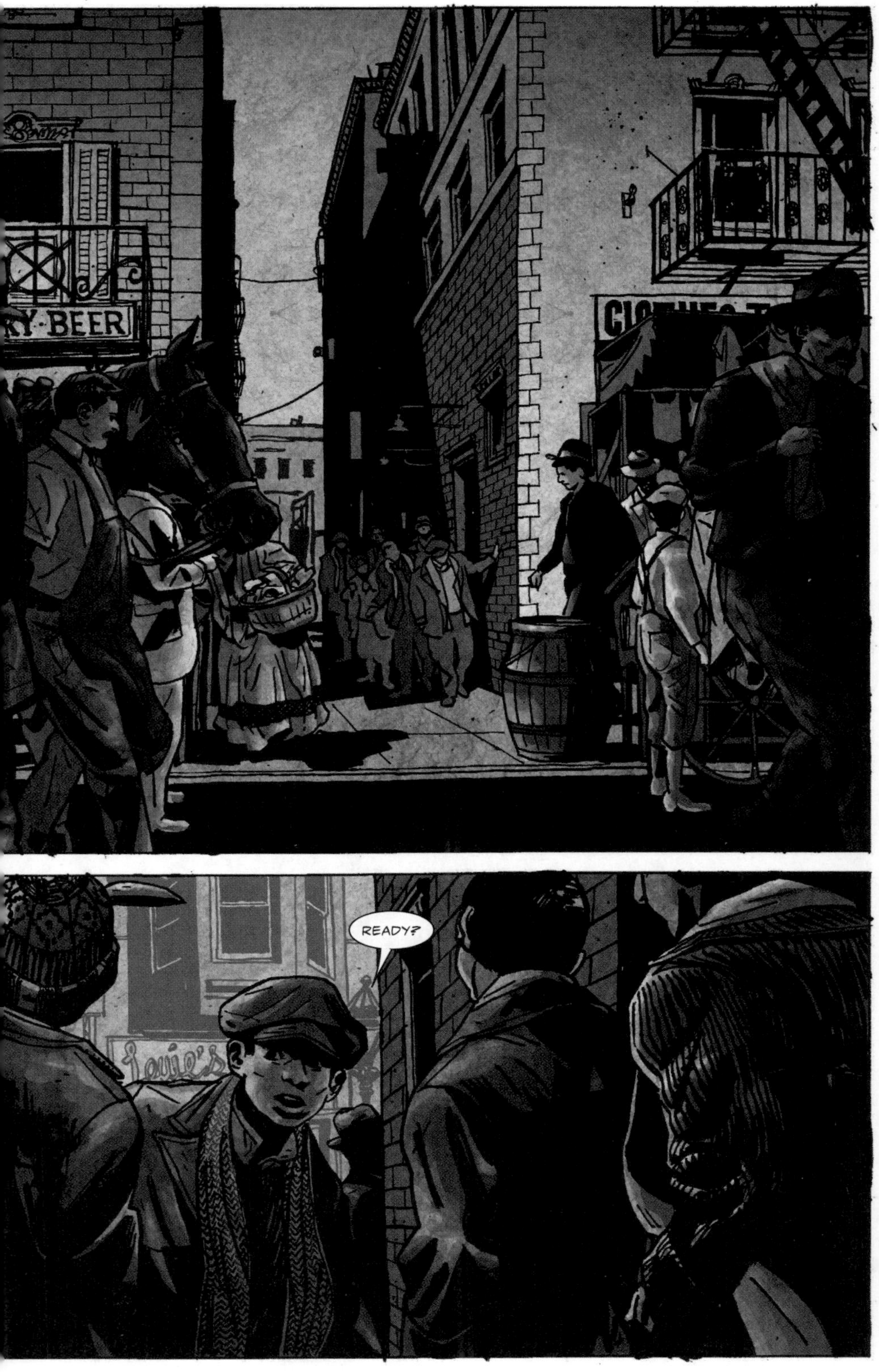
BEER
Louie's
READY?

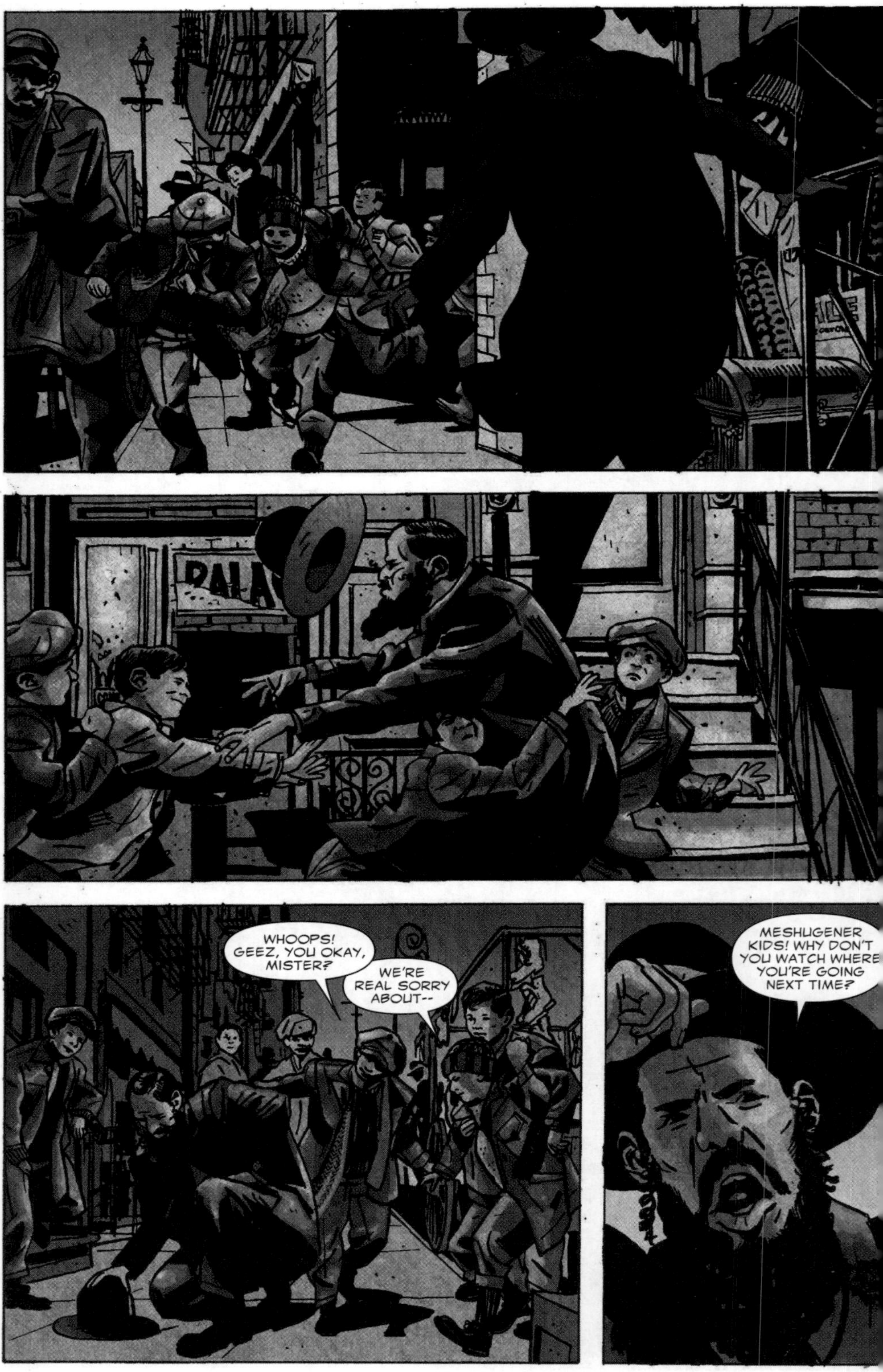
WHOOPS! GEEZ, YOU OKAY, MISTER?
WE'RE REAL SORRY ABOUT--
MESHUGENER KIDS! WHY DON'T YOU WATCH WHERE YOU'RE GOING NEXT TIME?

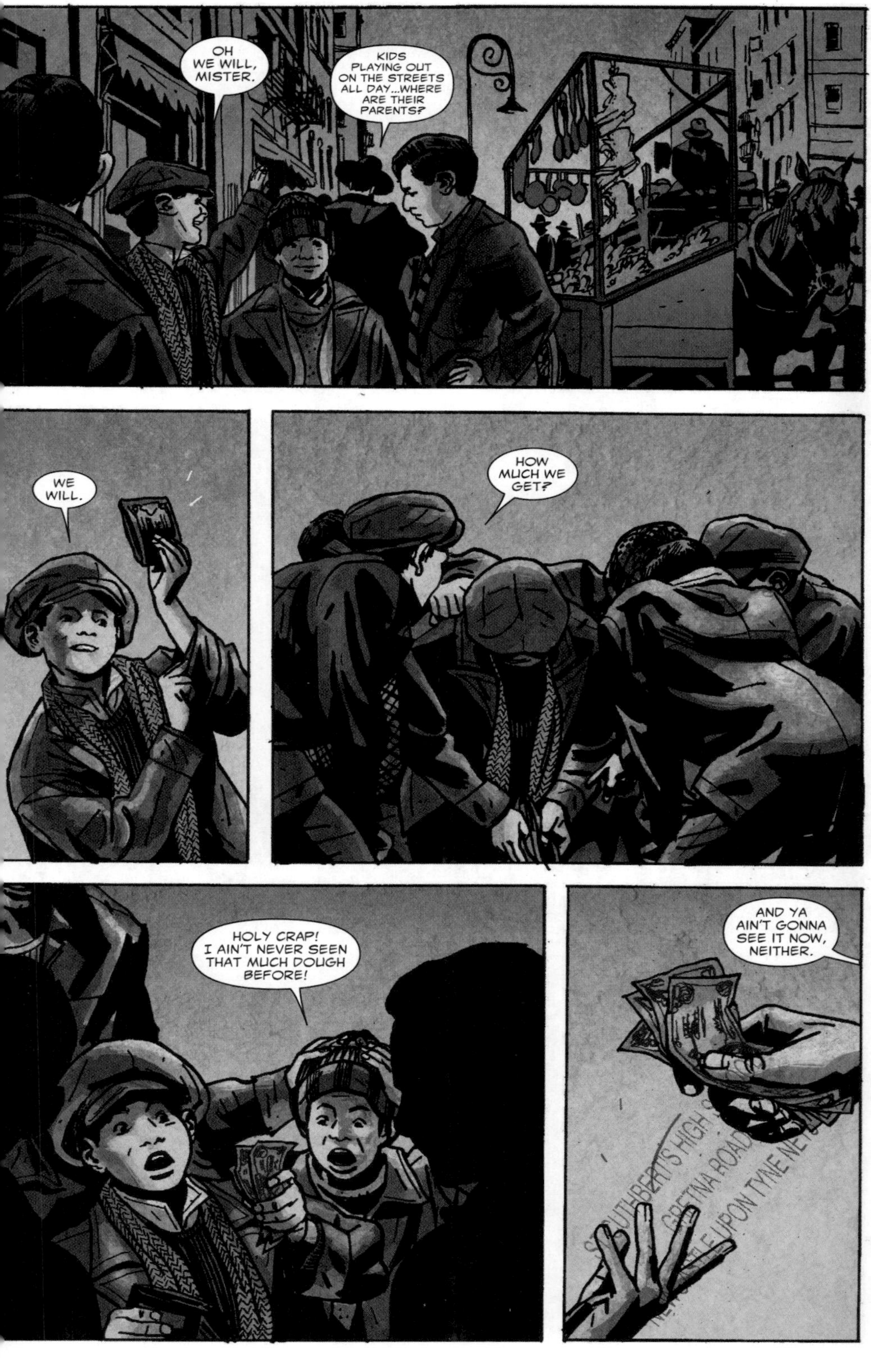
OH WE WILL, MISTER.
KIDS PLAYING OUT ON THE STREETS ALL DAY...WHERE ARE THEIR PARENTS?
WE WILL.
HOW MUCH WE GET?
HOLY CRAP! I AIN'T NEVER SEEN THAT MUCH DOUGH BEFORE!
AND YA AIN'T GONNA SEE IT NOW, NEITHER.

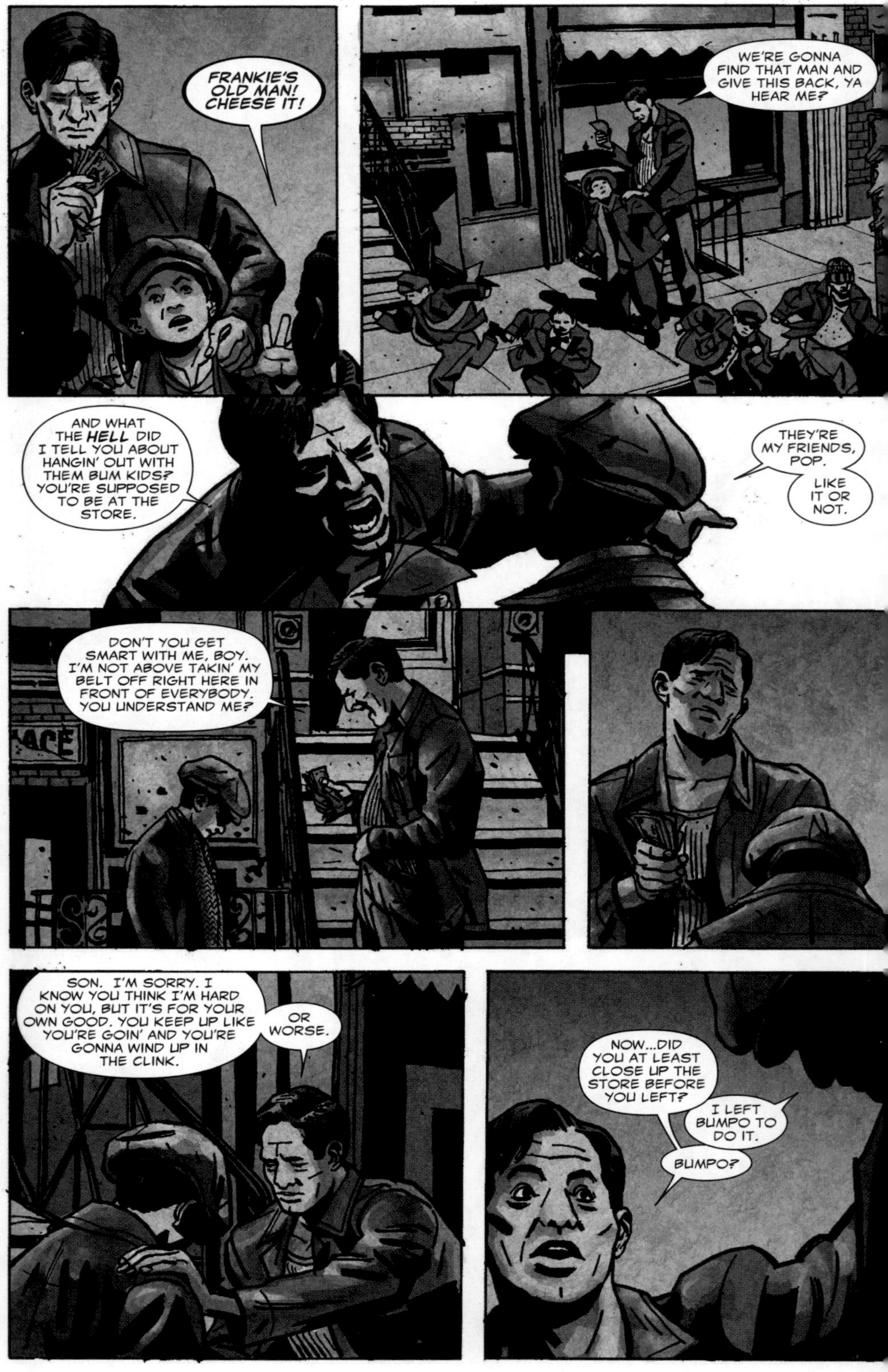

FRANKIE'S OLD MAN! CHEESE IT!
WE'RE GONNA FIND THAT MAN AND GIVE THIS BACK, YA HEAR ME?
AND WHAT THE **HELL** DID I TELL YOU ABOUT HANGIN' OUT WITH THEM BUM KIDS? YOU'RE SUPPOSED TO BE AT THE STORE.
THEY'RE MY FRIENDS, POP.
LIKE IT OR NOT.
DON'T YOU GET SMART WITH ME, BOY. I'M NOT ABOVE TAKIN' MY BELT OFF RIGHT HERE IN FRONT OF EVERYBODY. YOU UNDERSTAND ME?
SON. I'M SORRY. I KNOW YOU THINK I'M HARD ON YOU, BUT IT'S FOR YOUR OWN GOOD. YOU KEEP UP LIKE YOU'RE GOIN' AND YOU'RE GONNA WIND UP IN THE CLINK.
OR WORSE.
NOW...DID YOU AT LEAST CLOSE UP THE STORE BEFORE YOU LEFT?
I LEFT BUMPO TO DO IT.
BUMPO?

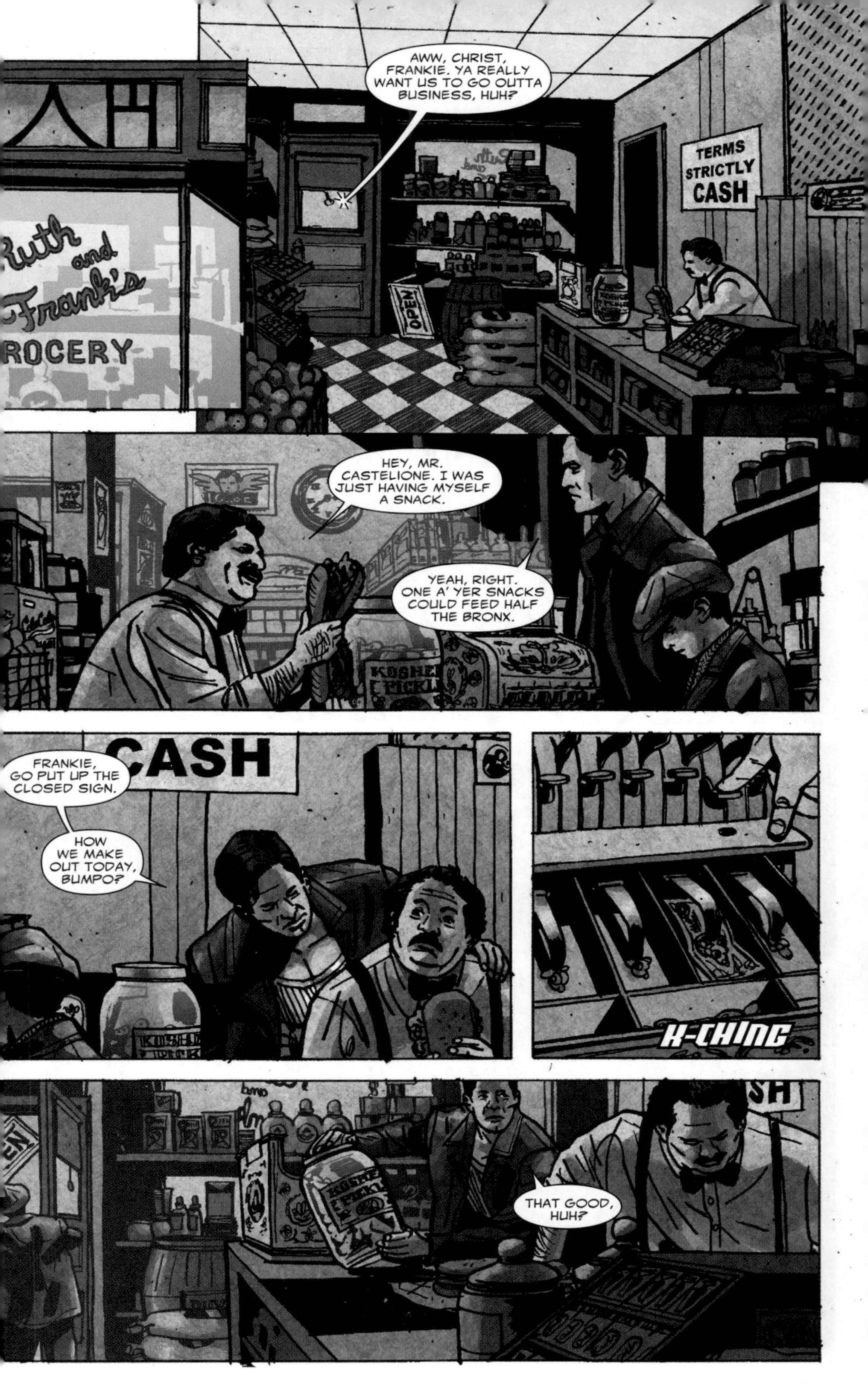
AWW, CHRIST, FRANKIE. YA REALLY WANT US TO GO OUTTA BUSINESS, HUH?
TERMS STRICTLY CASH
Ruth and Frank's GROCERY
OPEN
HEY, MR. CASTELIONE. I WAS JUST HAVING MYSELF A SNACK.
YEAH, RIGHT. ONE A' YER SNACKS COULD FEED HALF THE BRONX.
CASH
FRANKIE, GO PUT UP THE CLOSED SIGN.
HOW WE MAKE OUT TODAY, BUMPO?
K-CHING
THAT GOOD, HUH?

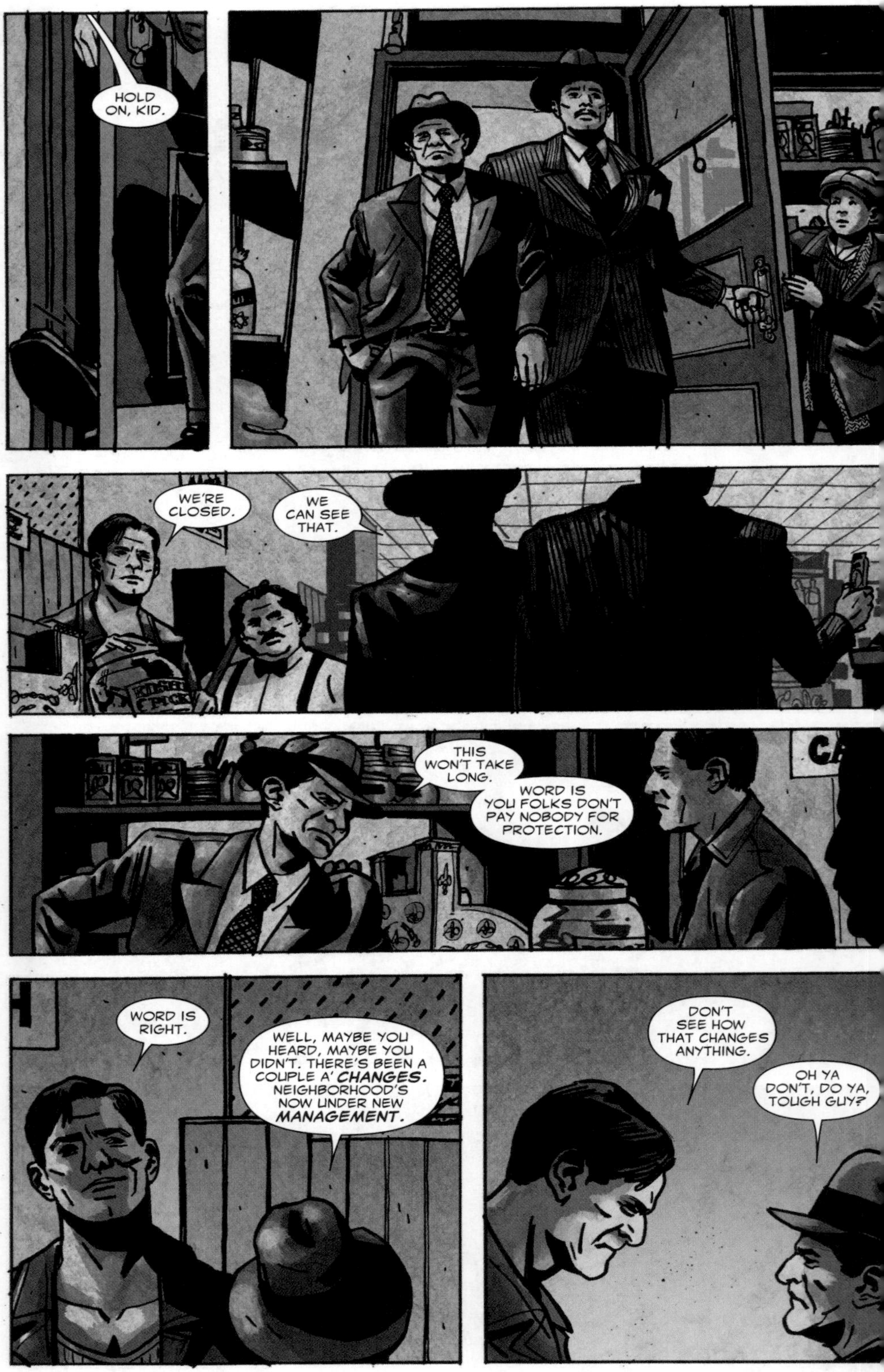

HOLD ON, KID.
WE'RE CLOSED.
WE CAN SEE THAT.
THIS WON'T TAKE LONG.
WORD IS YOU FOLKS DON'T PAY NOBODY FOR PROTECTION.
WORD IS RIGHT.
WELL, MAYBE YOU HEARD, MAYBE YOU DIDN'T. THERE'S BEEN A COUPLE A' CHANGES. NEIGHBORHOOD'S NOW UNDER NEW MANAGEMENT.
DON'T SEE HOW THAT CHANGES ANYTHING.
OH YA DON'T, DO YA, TOUGH GUY?

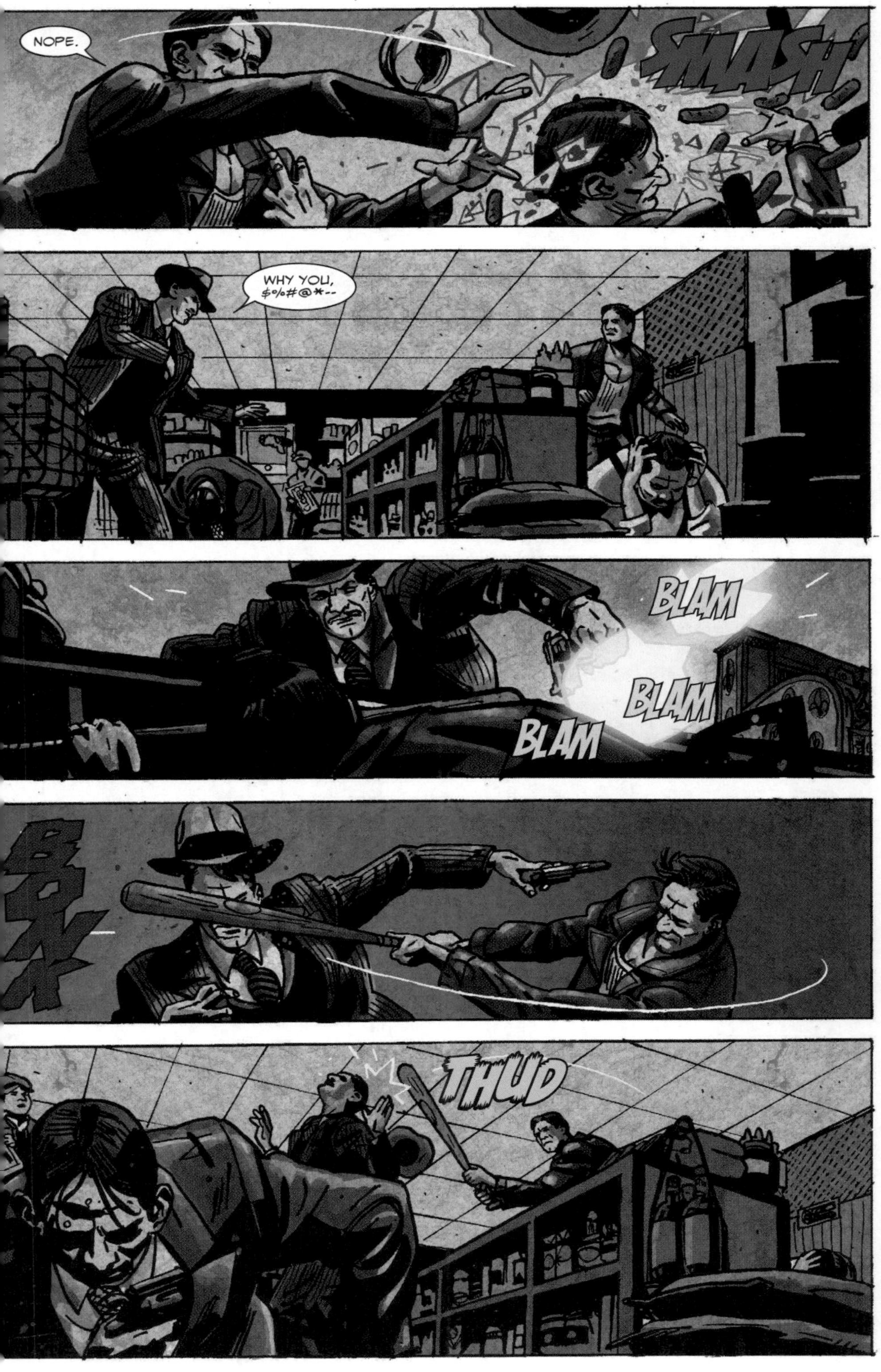
NOPE.
SMASH
WHY YOU, $%#@*--
BLAM
BLAM
BLAM
BONK
THUD

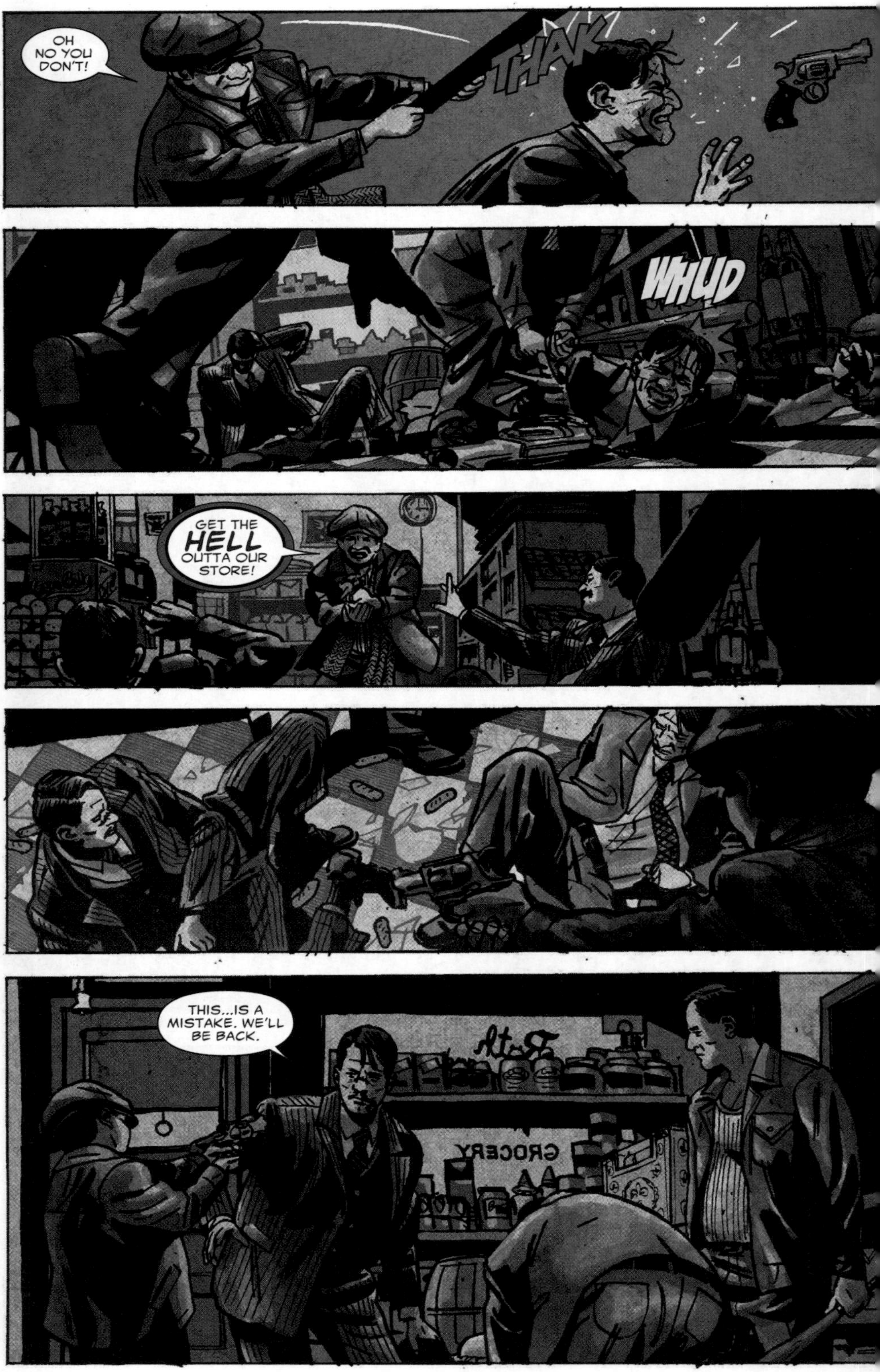
OH NO YOU DON'T!
THAK
WHUD
GET THE HELL OUTTA OUR STORE!
THIS...IS A MISTAKE. WE'LL BE BACK.

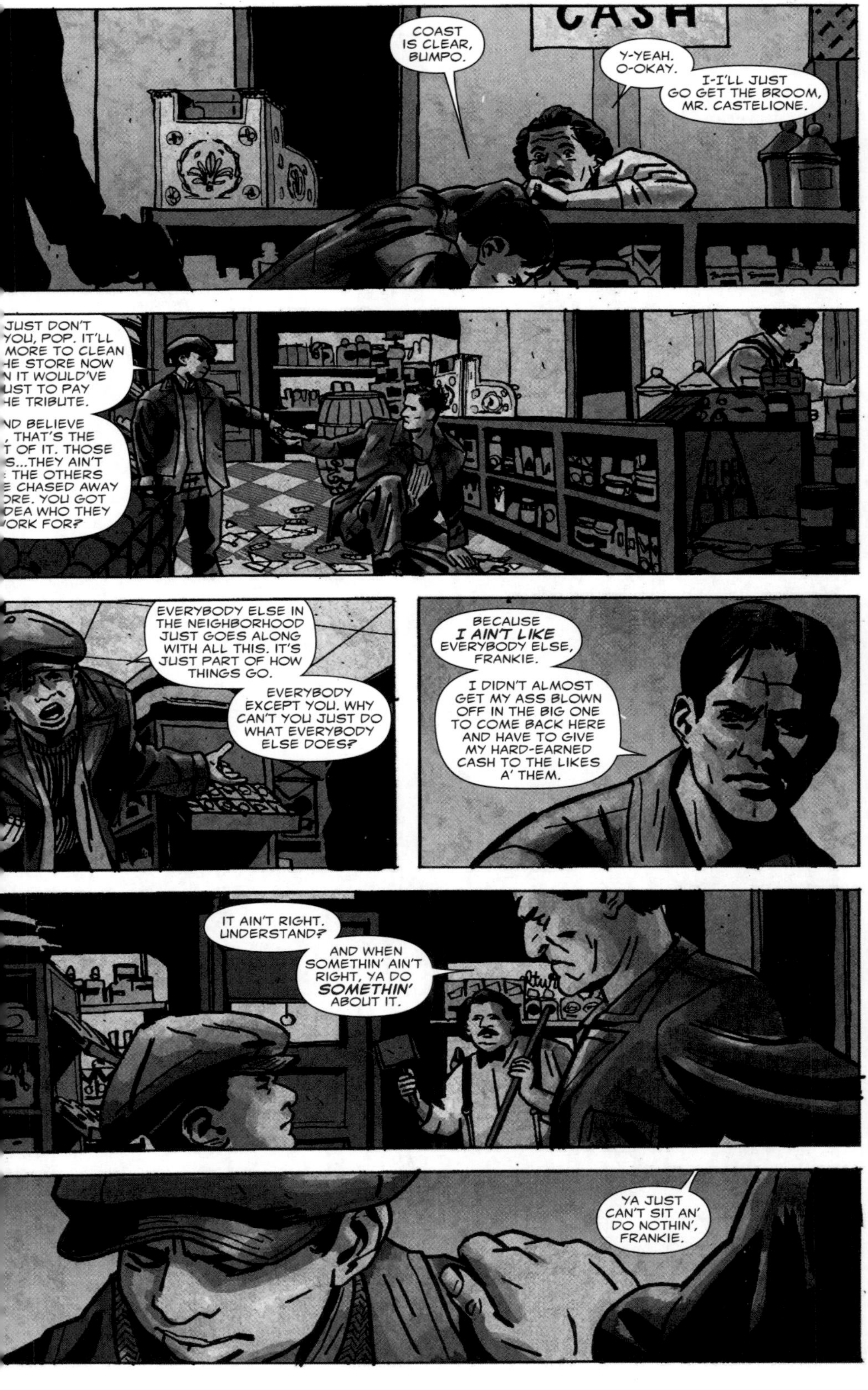
CASH
COAST IS CLEAR, BUMPO.
Y-YEAH. O-OKAY.
I-I'LL JUST GO GET THE BROOM, MR. CASTELIONE.
JUST DON'T YOU, POP. IT'LL MORE TO CLEAN HE STORE NOW N IT WOULD'VE UST TO PAY HE TRIBUTE.
ND BELIEVE , THAT'S THE T OF IT. THOSE S...THEY AIN'T THE OTHERS E CHASED AWAY ORE. YOU GOT DEA WHO THEY WORK FOR?
EVERYBODY ELSE IN THE NEIGHBORHOOD JUST GOES ALONG WITH ALL THIS. IT'S JUST PART OF HOW THINGS GO.
EVERYBODY EXCEPT YOU. WHY CAN'T YOU JUST DO WHAT EVERYBODY ELSE DOES?
BECAUSE ***I AIN'T LIKE*** EVERYBODY ELSE, FRANKIE.
I DIDN'T ALMOST GET MY ASS BLOWN OFF IN THE BIG ONE TO COME BACK HERE AND HAVE TO GIVE MY HARD-EARNED CASH TO THE LIKES A' THEM.
IT AIN'T RIGHT. UNDERSTAND?
AND WHEN SOMETHIN' AIN'T RIGHT, YA DO ***SOMETHIN'*** ABOUT IT.
YA JUST CAN'T SIT AN' DO NOTHIN', FRANKIE.

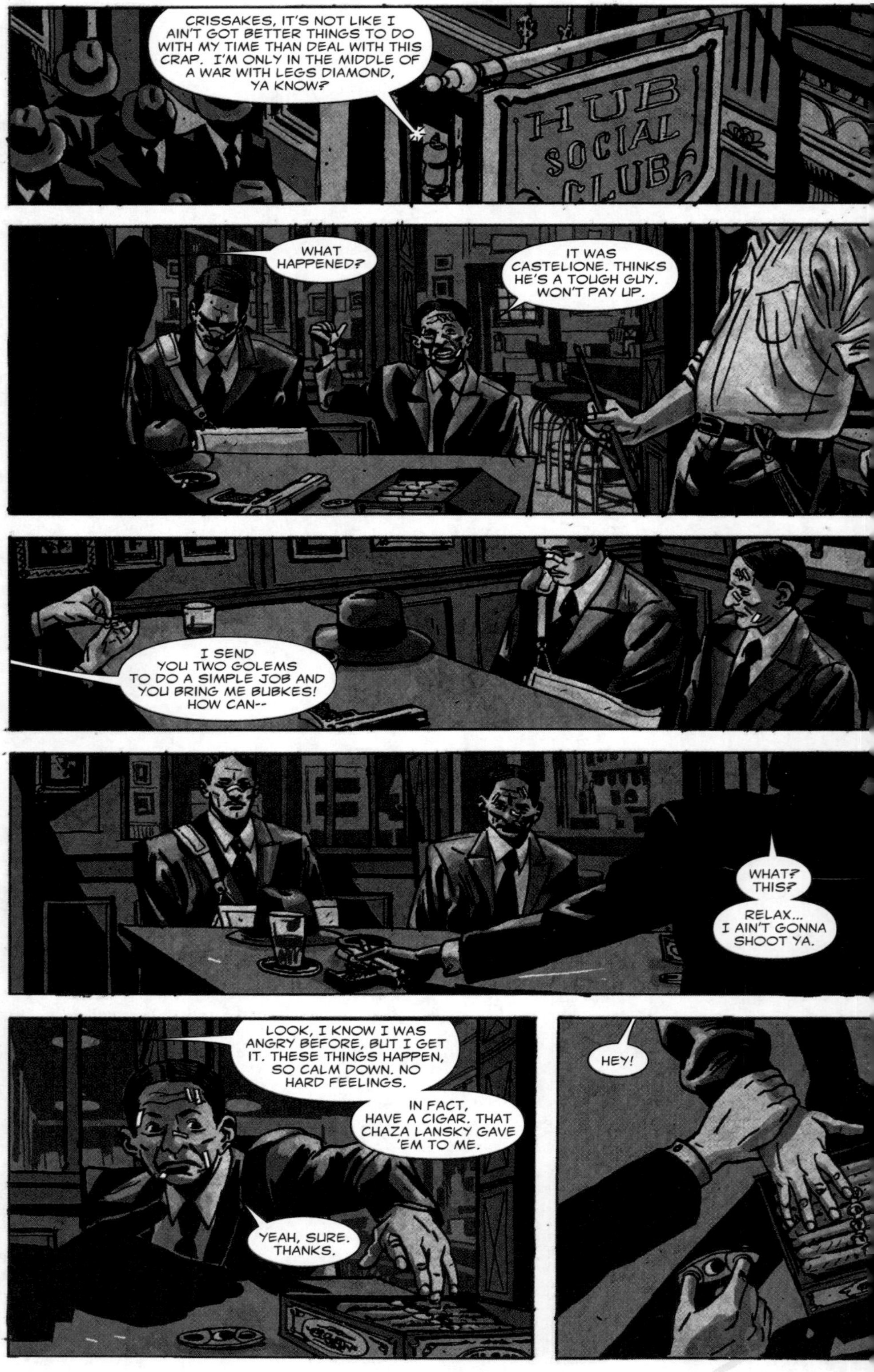
CRISSAKES, IT'S NOT LIKE I AIN'T GOT BETTER THINGS TO DO WITH MY TIME THAN DEAL WITH THIS CRAP. I'M ONLY IN THE MIDDLE OF A WAR WITH LEGS DIAMOND, YA KNOW?
HUB SOCIAL CLUB
WHAT HAPPENED?
IT WAS CASTELIONE. THINKS HE'S A TOUGH GUY. WON'T PAY UP.
I SEND YOU TWO GOLEMS TO DO A SIMPLE JOB AND YOU BRING ME BUBKES! HOW CAN--
WHAT? THIS?
RELAX... I AIN'T GONNA SHOOT YA.
LOOK, I KNOW I WAS ANGRY BEFORE, BUT I GET IT. THESE THINGS HAPPEN, SO CALM DOWN. NO HARD FEELINGS.
IN FACT, HAVE A CIGAR. THAT CHAZA LANSKY GAVE 'EM TO ME.
YEAH, SURE. THANKS.
HEY!

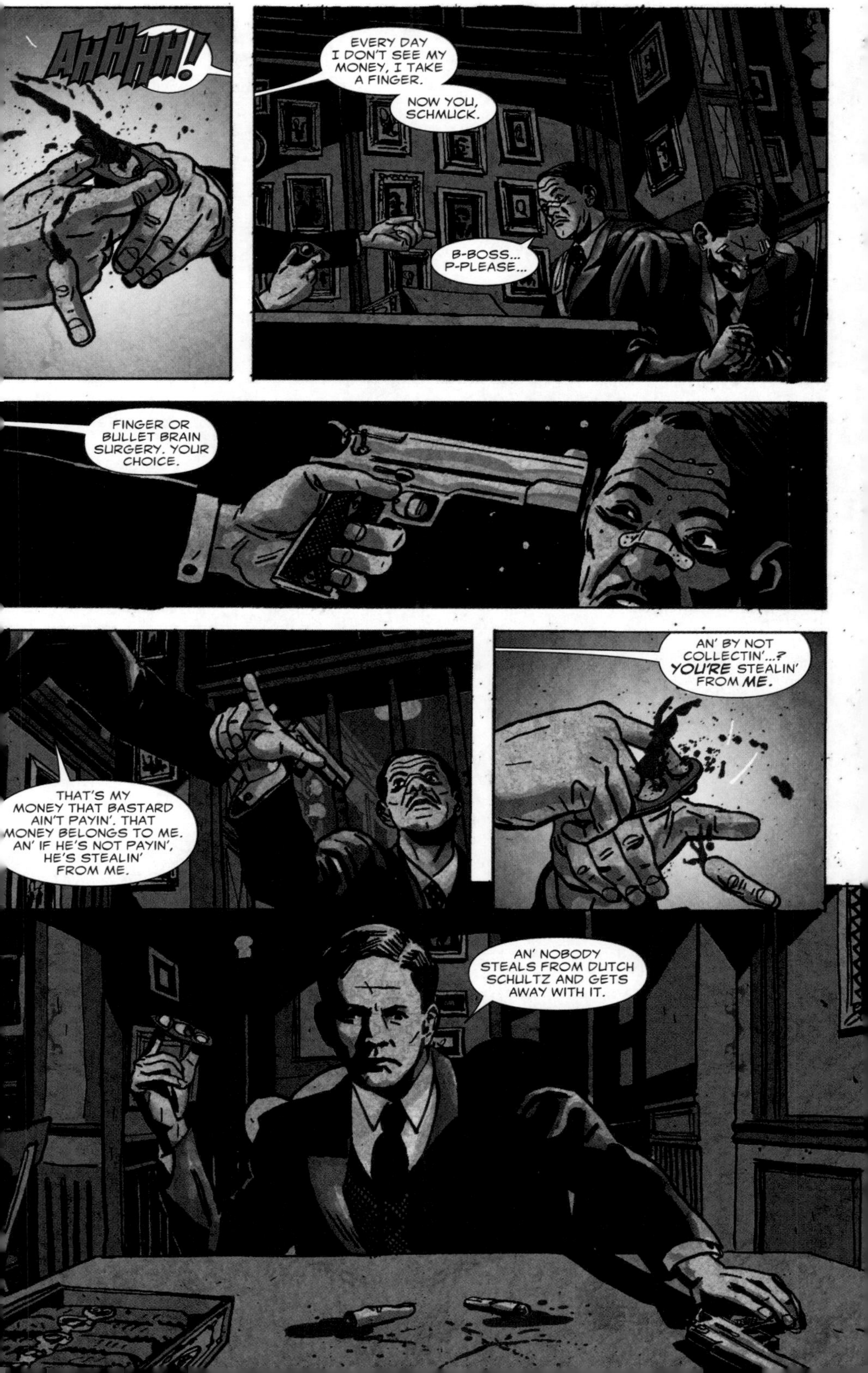
AHHHH!
EVERY DAY I DON'T SEE MY MONEY, I TAKE A FINGER.
NOW YOU, SCHMUCK.
B-BOSS... P-PLEASE...
FINGER OR BULLET BRAIN SURGERY. YOUR CHOICE.
THAT'S MY MONEY THAT BASTARD AIN'T PAYIN'. THAT MONEY BELONGS TO ME. AN' IF HE'S NOT PAYIN', HE'S STEALIN' FROM ME.
AN' BY NOT COLLECTIN'...? YOU'RE STEALIN' FROM ME.
AN' NOBODY STEALS FROM DUTCH SCHULTZ AND GETS AWAY WITH IT.

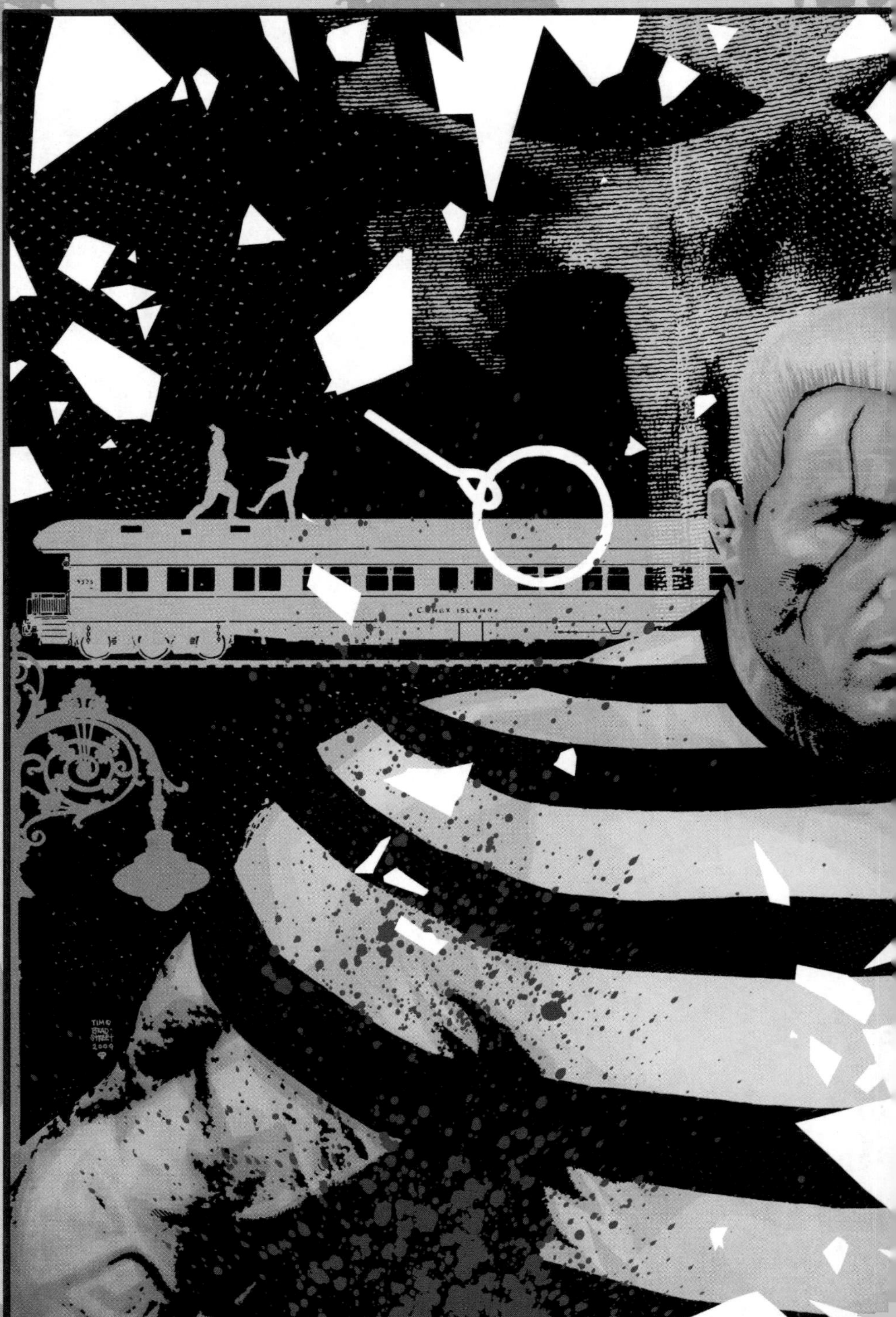
TIMO BRADSTREET 2009

TWO

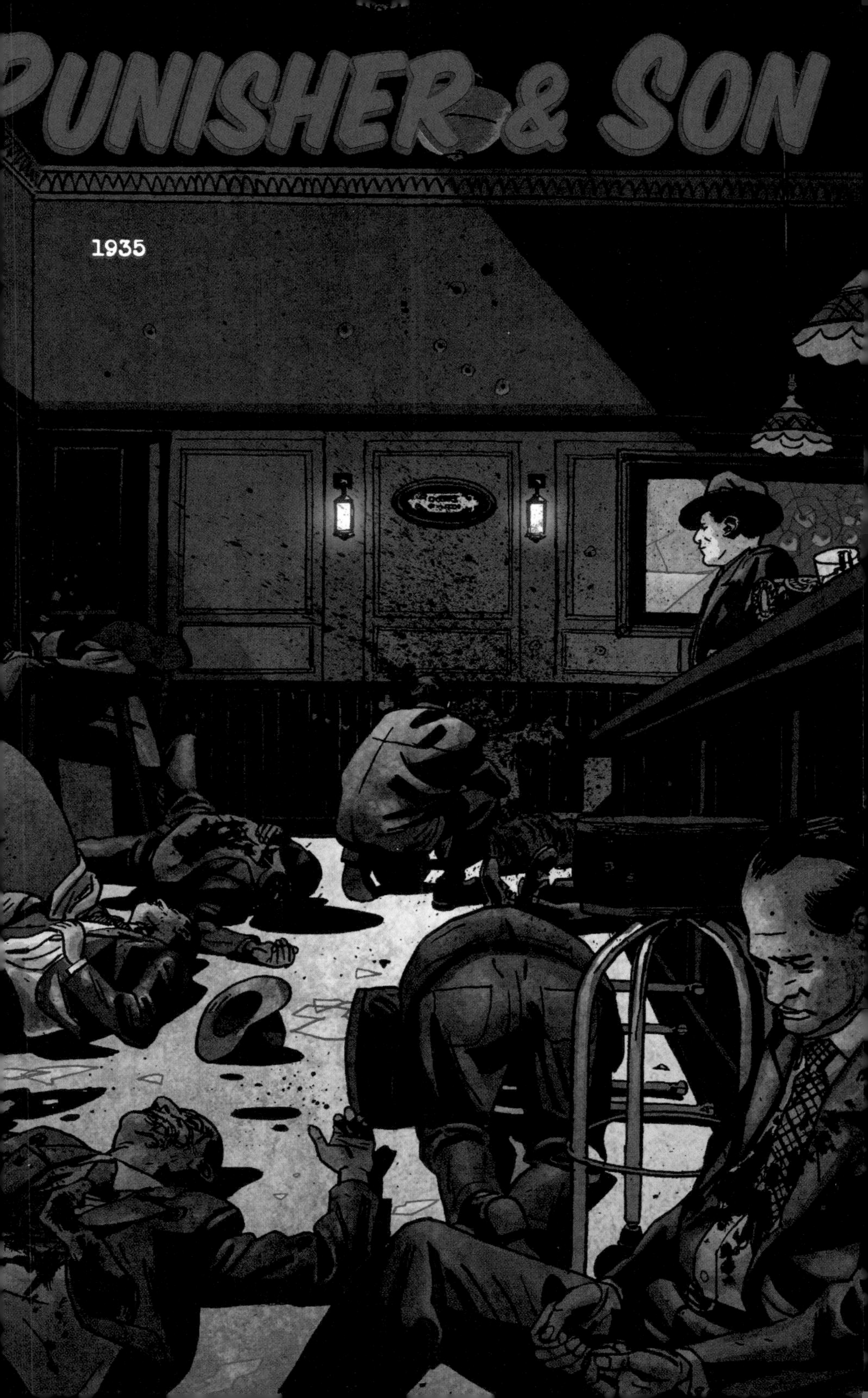
PUNISHER & SON
1935

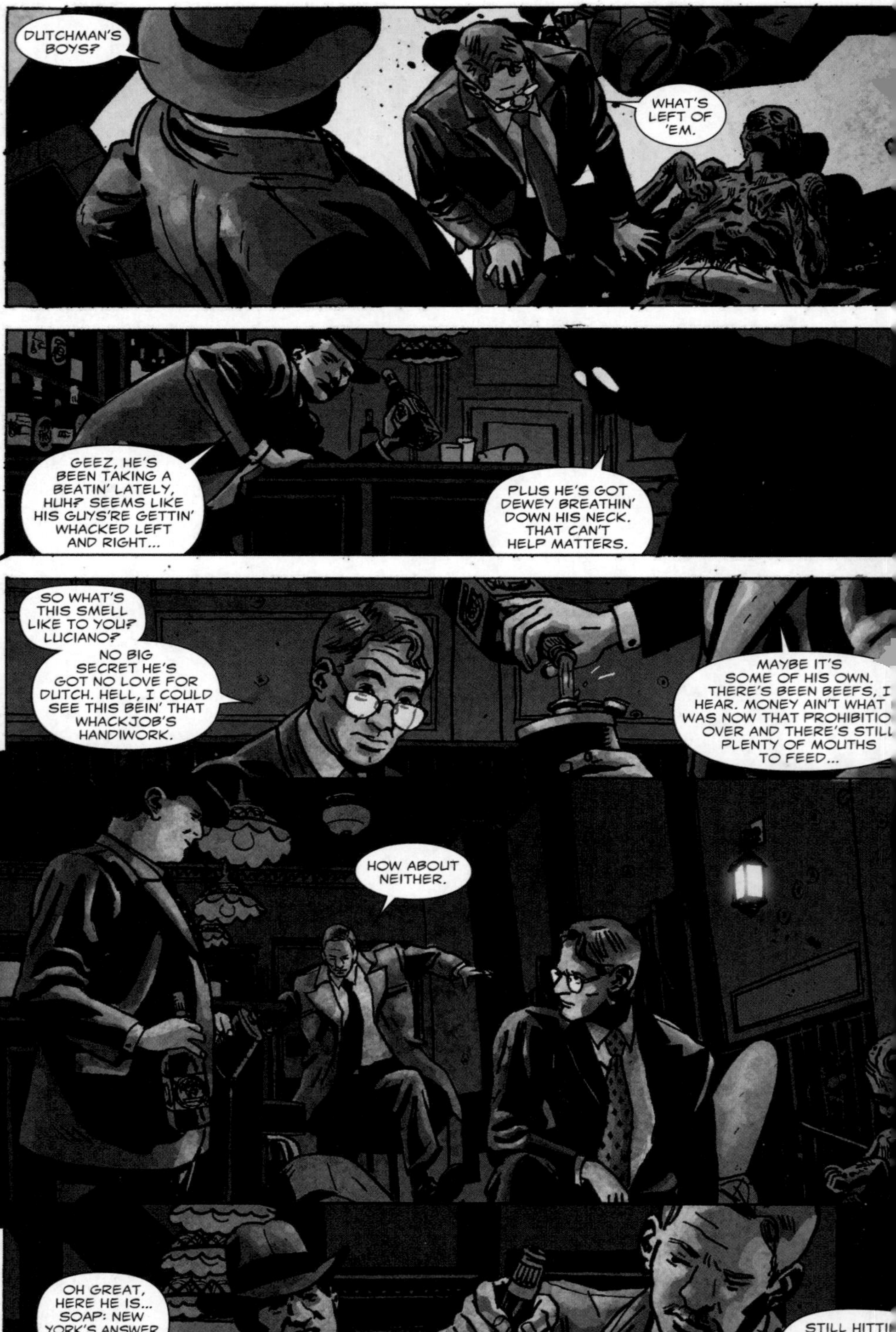
DUTCHMAN'S BOYS?
WHAT'S LEFT OF 'EM.
GEEZ, HE'S BEEN TAKING A BEATIN' LATELY, HUH? SEEMS LIKE HIS GUYS'RE GETTIN' WHACKED LEFT AND RIGHT...
PLUS HE'S GOT DEWEY BREATHIN' DOWN HIS NECK. THAT CAN'T HELP MATTERS.
SO WHAT'S THIS SMELL LIKE TO YOU? LUCIANO?
NO BIG SECRET HE'S GOT NO LOVE FOR DUTCH. HELL, I COULD SEE THIS BEIN' THAT WHACKJOB'S HANDIWORK.
MAYBE IT'S SOME OF HIS OWN. THERE'S BEEN BEEFS, I HEAR. MONEY AIN'T WHAT I WAS NOW THAT PROHIBITIO OVER AND THERE'S STILL PLENTY OF MOUTHS TO FEED...
HOW ABOUT NEITHER.
OH GREAT, HERE HE IS... SOAP: NEW YORK'S ANSWER TO ELLIOT NESS.
STILL HITTI THE SAUCE I MIKE. PROBA ACCOUNTS F YOUR STELL DETECTIVE W

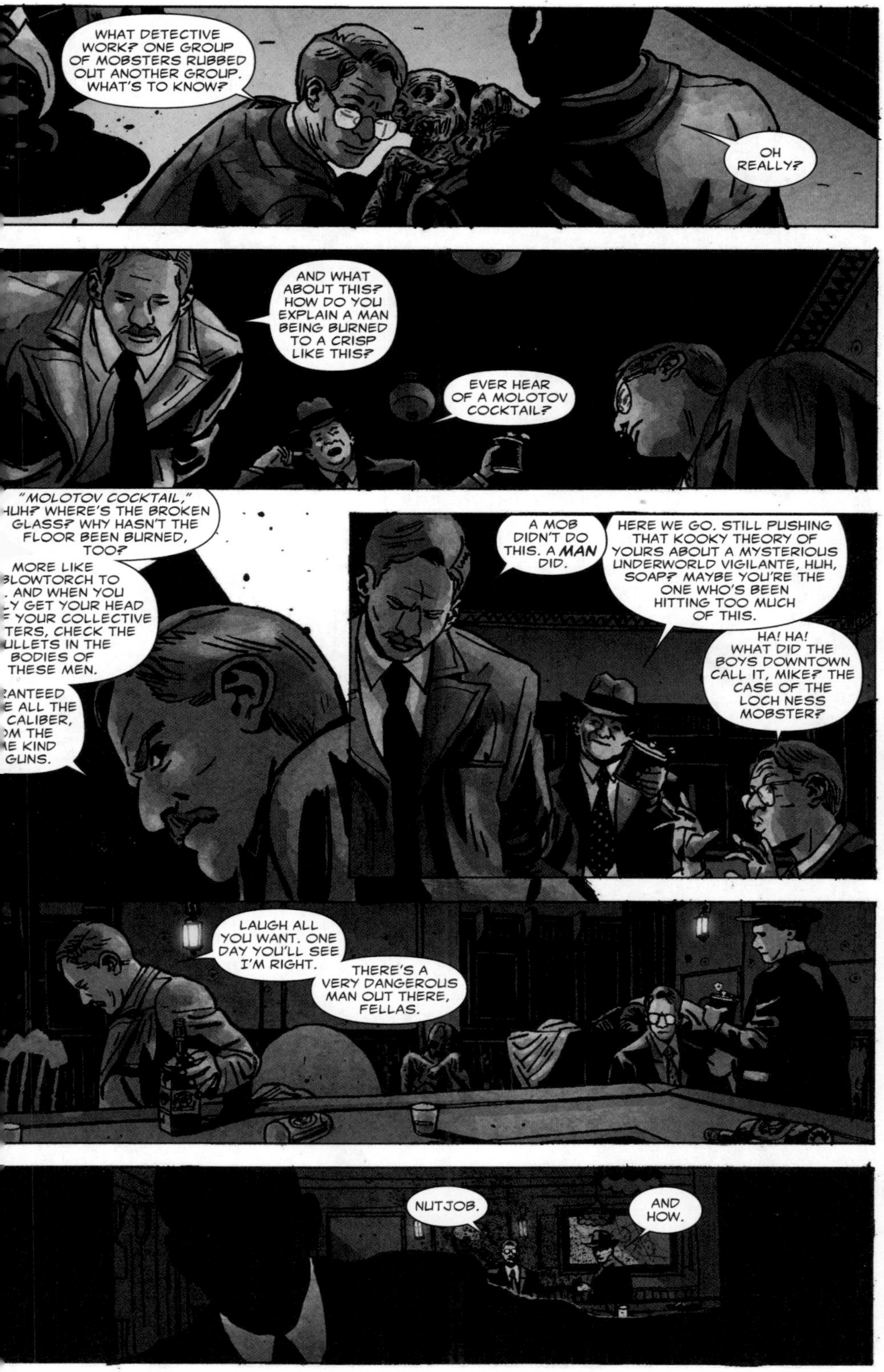

WHAT DETECTIVE WORK? ONE GROUP OF MOBSTERS RUBBED OUT ANOTHER GROUP. WHAT'S TO KNOW?
OH REALLY?
AND WHAT ABOUT THIS? HOW DO YOU EXPLAIN A MAN BEING BURNED TO A CRISP LIKE THIS?
EVER HEAR OF A MOLOTOV COCKTAIL?
"MOLOTOV COCKTAIL," HUH? WHERE'S THE BROKEN GLASS? WHY HASN'T THE FLOOR BEEN BURNED, TOO?
MORE LIKE BLOWTORCH TO . AND WHEN YOU LY GET YOUR HEAD F YOUR COLLECTIVE TERS, CHECK THE ULLETS IN THE BODIES OF THESE MEN.
RANTEED E ALL THE CALIBER, OM THE E KIND GUNS.
A MOB DIDN'T DO THIS. A **MAN** DID.
HERE WE GO. STILL PUSHING THAT KOOKY THEORY OF YOURS ABOUT A MYSTERIOUS UNDERWORLD VIGILANTE, HUH, SOAP? MAYBE YOU'RE THE ONE WHO'S BEEN HITTING TOO MUCH OF THIS.
HA! HA! WHAT DID THE BOYS DOWNTOWN CALL IT, MIKE? THE CASE OF THE LOCH NESS MOBSTER?
LAUGH ALL YOU WANT. ONE DAY YOU'LL SEE I'M RIGHT.
THERE'S A VERY DANGEROUS MAN OUT THERE, FELLAS.
NUTJOB.
AND HOW.

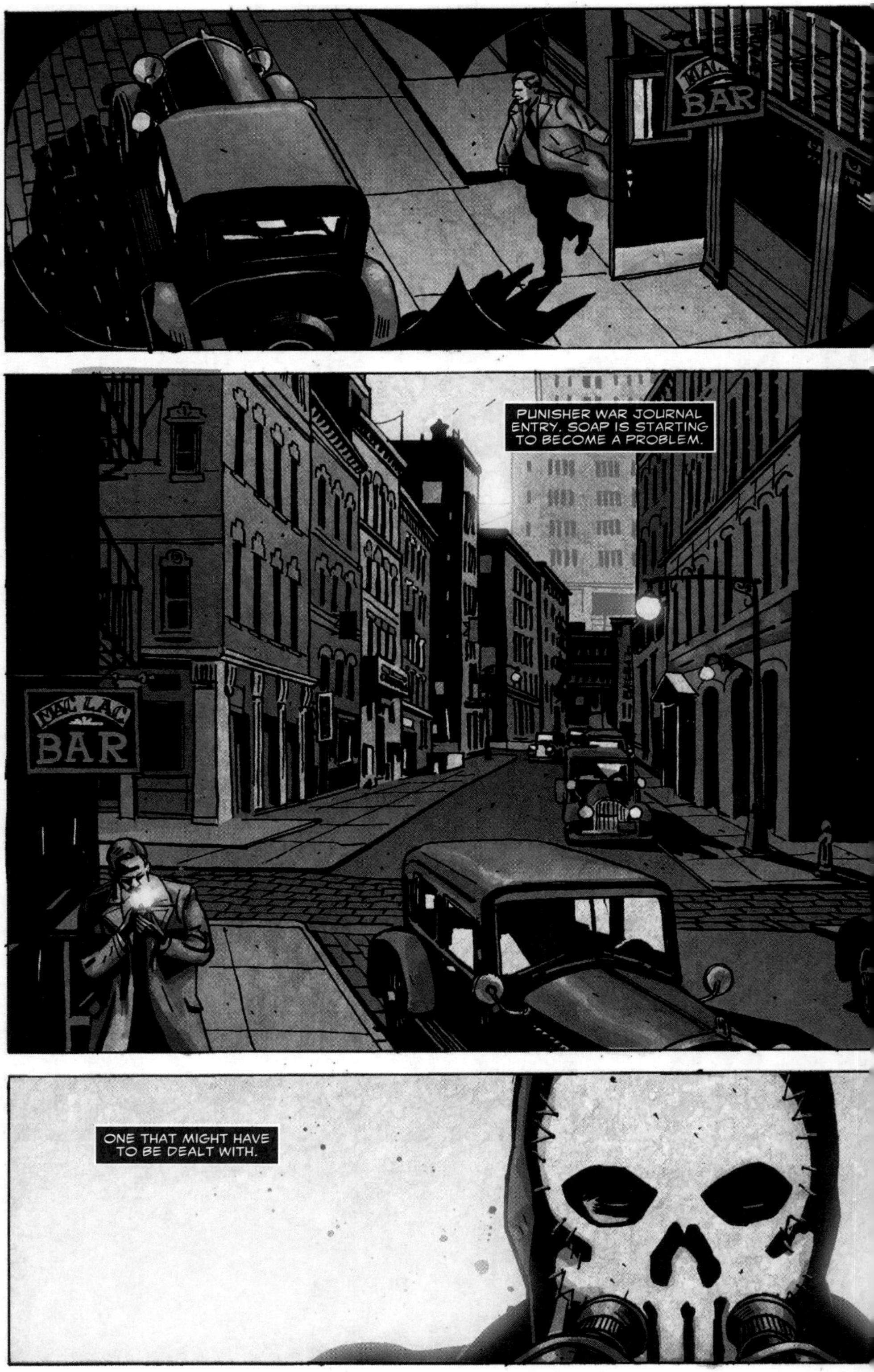
BAR
PUNISHER WAR JOURNAL ENTRY. SOAP IS STARTING TO BECOME A PROBLEM.
MAC LAC
BAR
ONE THAT MIGHT HAVE TO BE DEALT WITH.

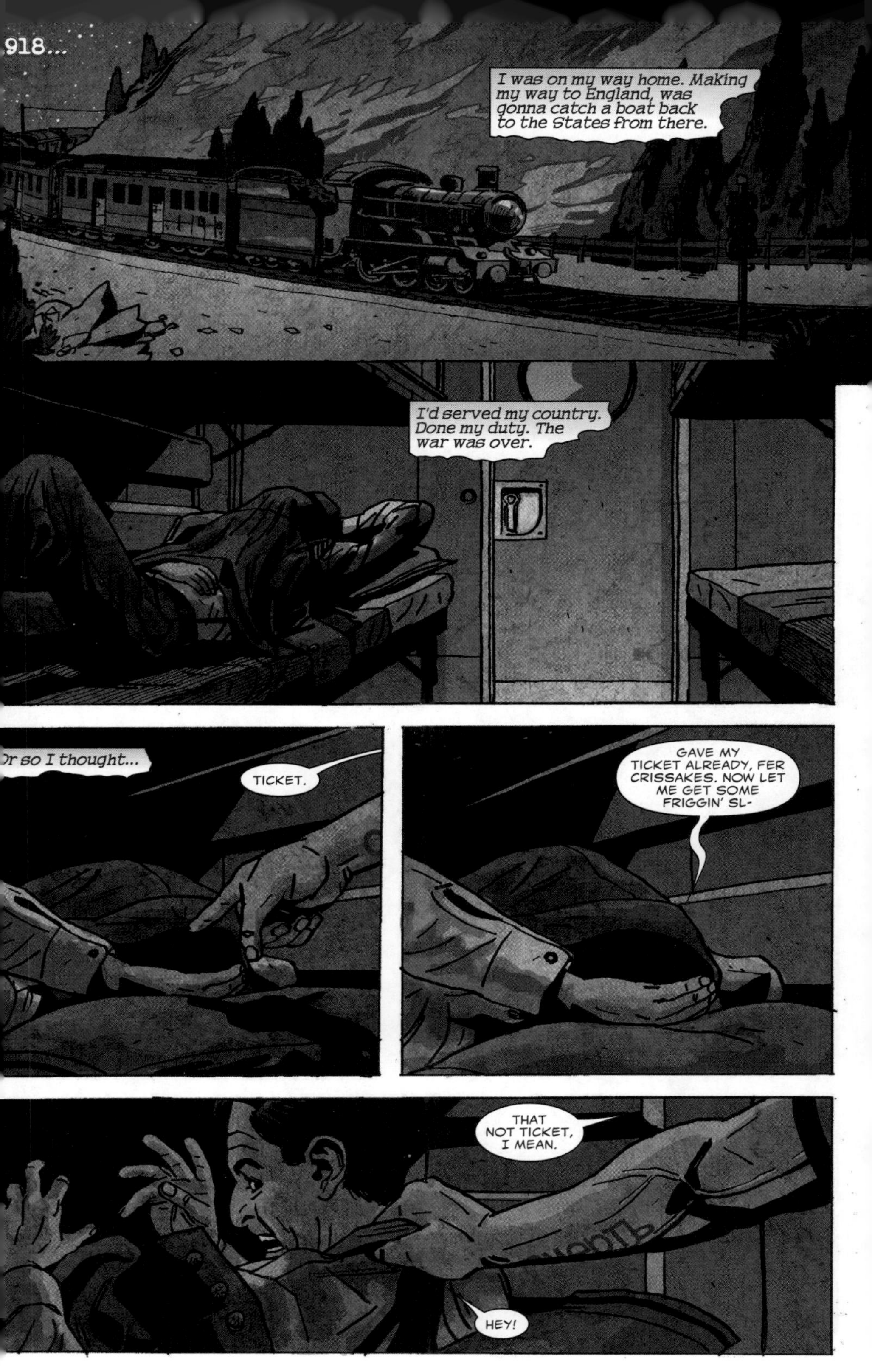
918...
I was on my way home. Making my way to England, was gonna catch a boat back to the States from there.
I'd served my country. Done my duty. The war was over.
Or so I thought...
TICKET.
GAVE MY TICKET ALREADY, FER CRISSAKES. NOW LET ME GET SOME FRIGGIN' SL-
THAT NOT TICKET, I MEAN.
HEY!

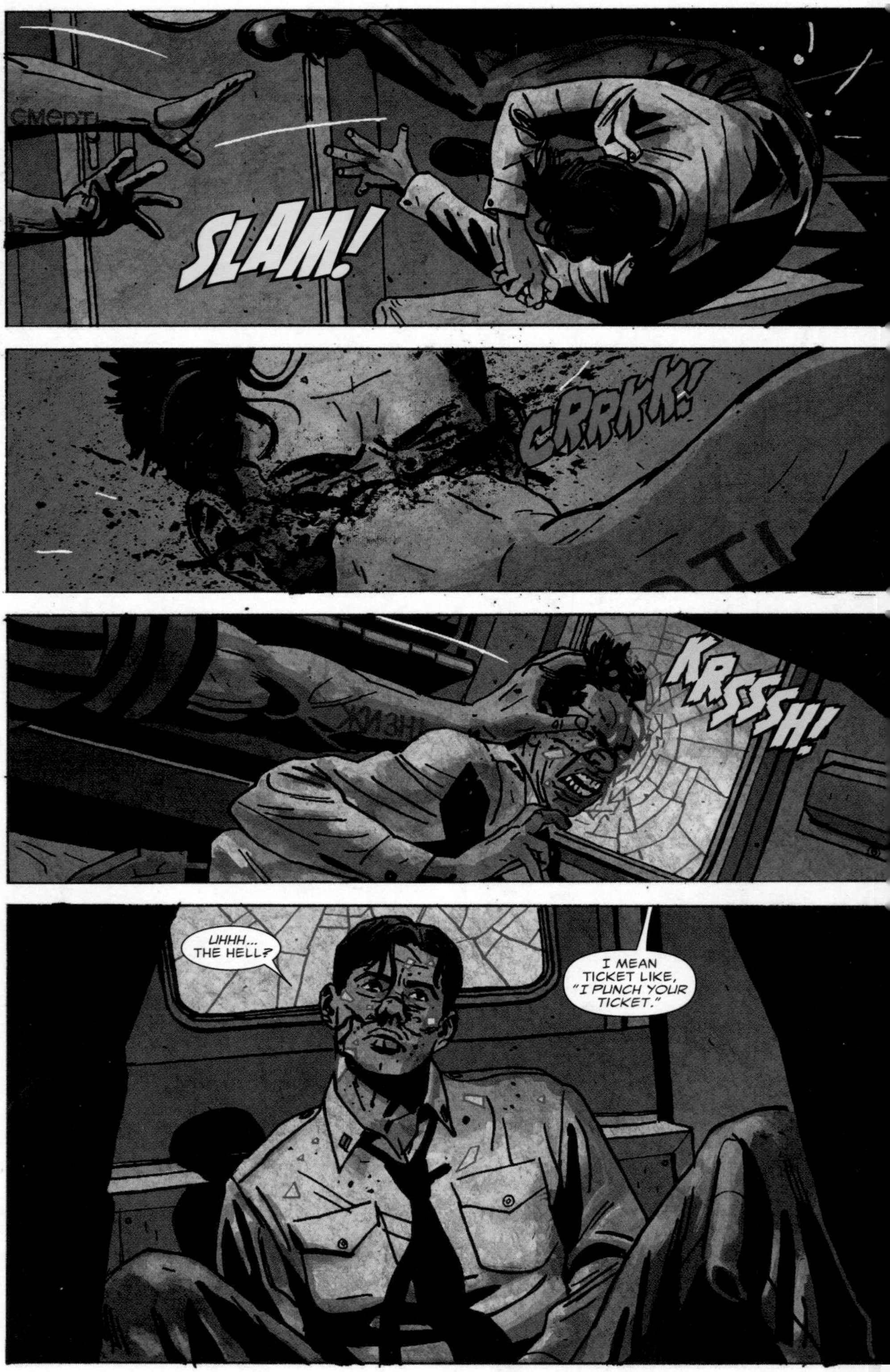
SLAM!
CRRKK!
KRSSSH!
UHHH... THE HELL?
I MEAN TICKET LIKE, "I PUNCH YOUR TICKET."

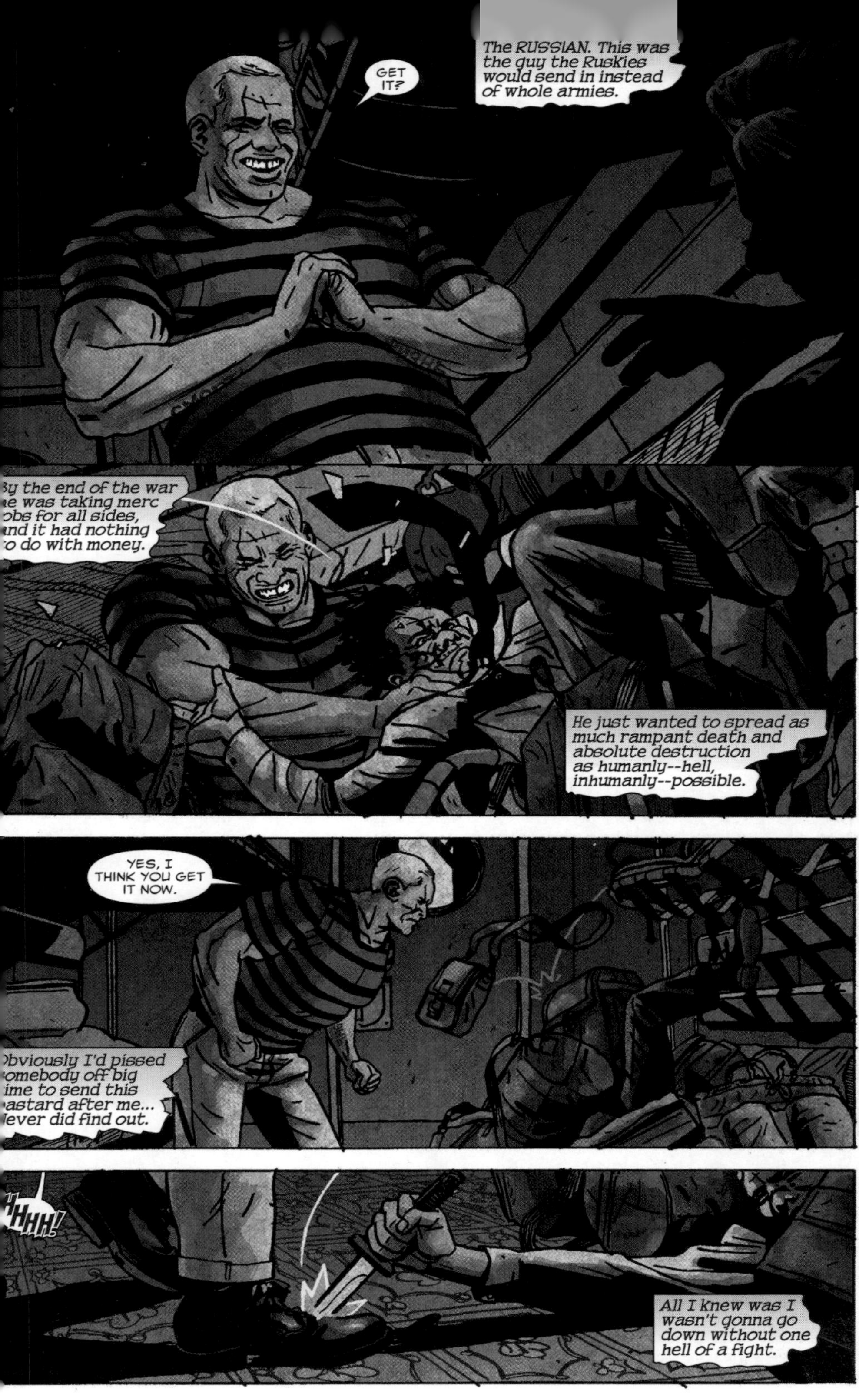
GET IT?
The RUSSIAN. This was the guy the Ruskies would send in instead of whole armies.
y the end of the war e was taking merc obs for all sides, nd it had nothing o do with money.
He just wanted to spread as much rampant death and absolute destruction as humanly--hell, inhumanly--possible.
YES, I THINK YOU GET IT NOW.
bviously I'd pissed omebody off big ime to send this astard after me... ever did find out.
All I knew was I wasn't gonna go down without one hell of a fight.

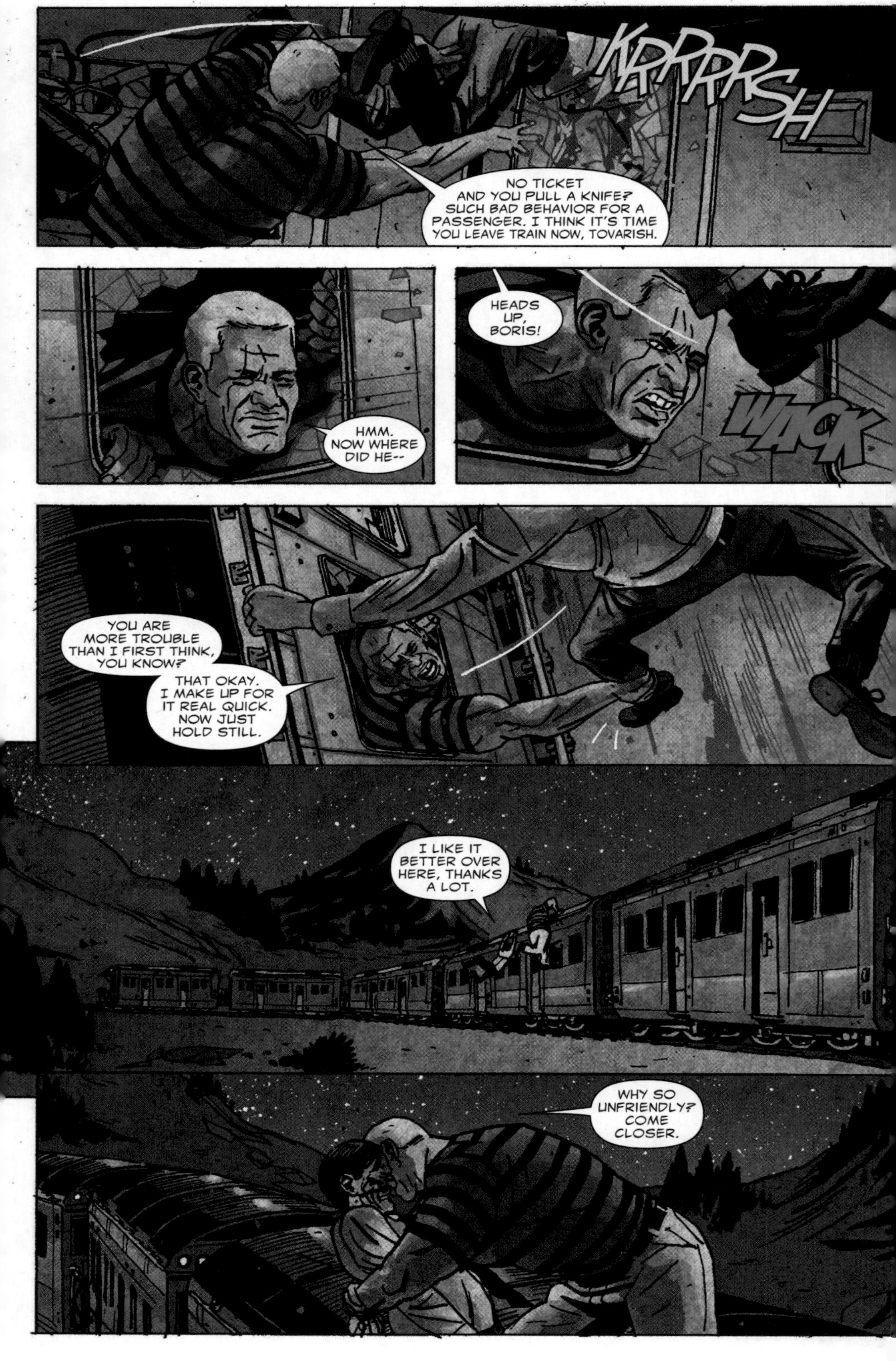
KRRRRSH
NO TICKET AND YOU PULL A KNIFE? SUCH BAD BEHAVIOR FOR A PASSENGER. I THINK IT'S TIME YOU LEAVE TRAIN NOW, TOVARISH.
HMM. NOW WHERE DID HE--
HEADS UP, BORIS!
WACK
YOU ARE MORE TROUBLE THAN I FIRST THINK, YOU KNOW?
THAT OKAY. I MAKE UP FOR IT REAL QUICK. NOW JUST HOLD STILL.
I LIKE IT BETTER OVER HERE, THANKS A LOT.
WHY SO UNFRIENDLY? COME CLOSER.

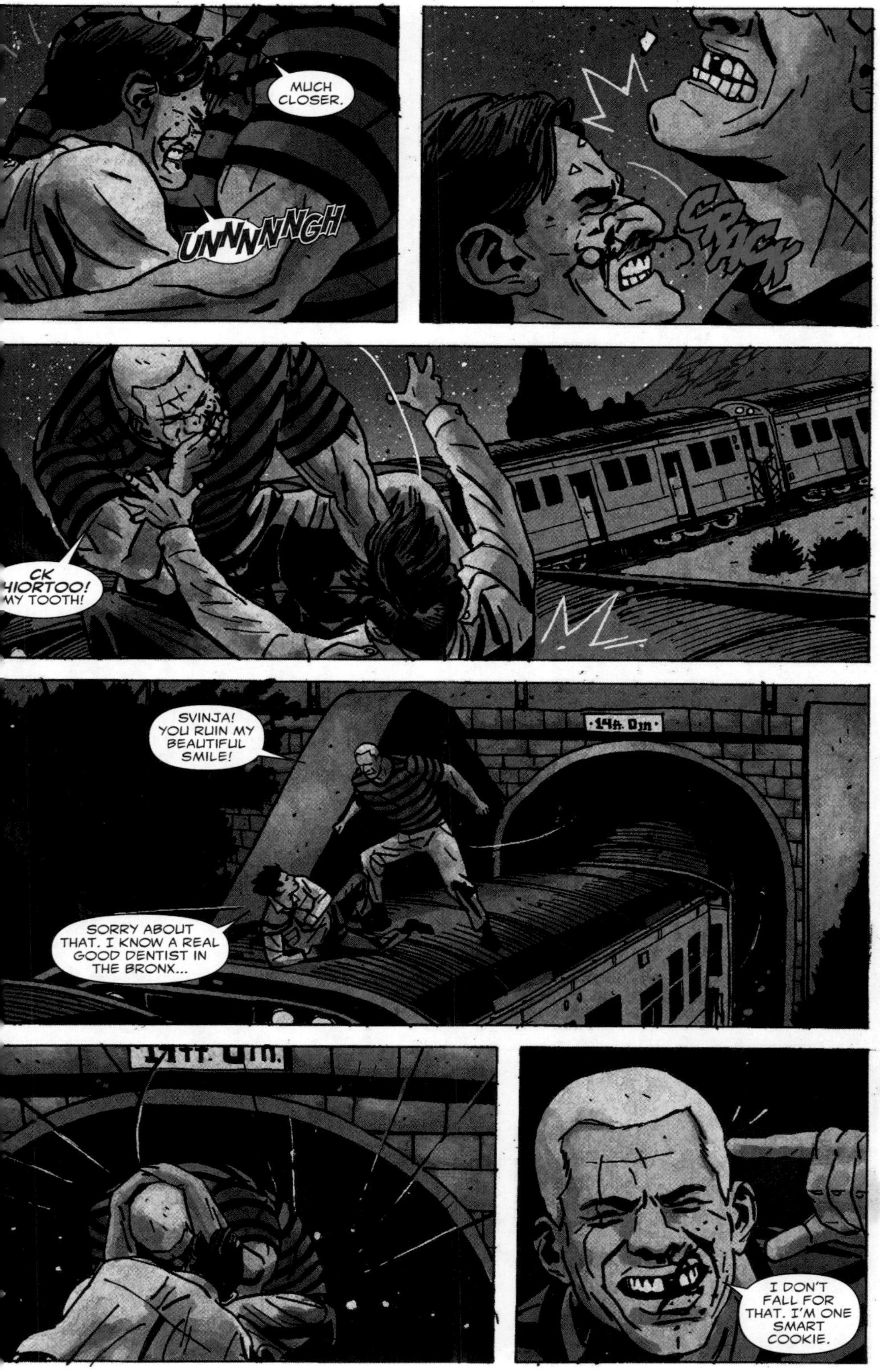
MUCH CLOSER.
UNNNNNGH
CRACK
CK HIORTOO! MY TOOTH!
SVINJA! YOU RUIN MY BEAUTIFUL SMILE!
SORRY ABOUT THAT. I KNOW A REAL GOOD DENTIST IN THE BRONX...
I DON'T FALL FOR THAT. I'M ONE SMART COOKIE.

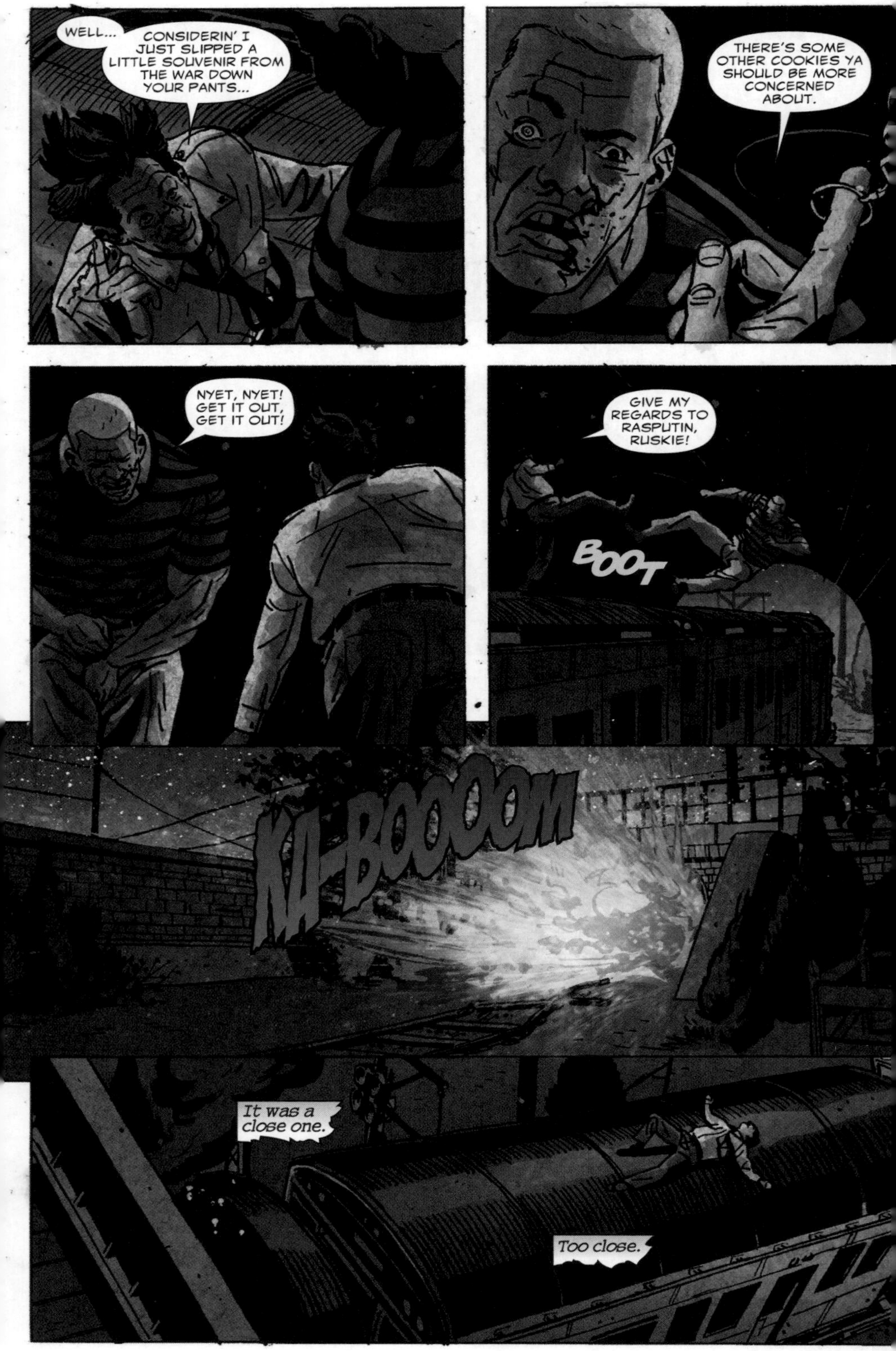
WELL...
CONSIDERIN' I JUST SLIPPED A LITTLE SOUVENIR FROM THE WAR DOWN YOUR PANTS...
THERE'S SOME OTHER COOKIES YA SHOULD BE MORE CONCERNED ABOUT.
NYET, NYET! GET IT OUT, GET IT OUT!
GIVE MY REGARDS TO RASPUTIN, RUSKIE!
BOOT
KA-BOOOOM
It was a close one.
Too close.

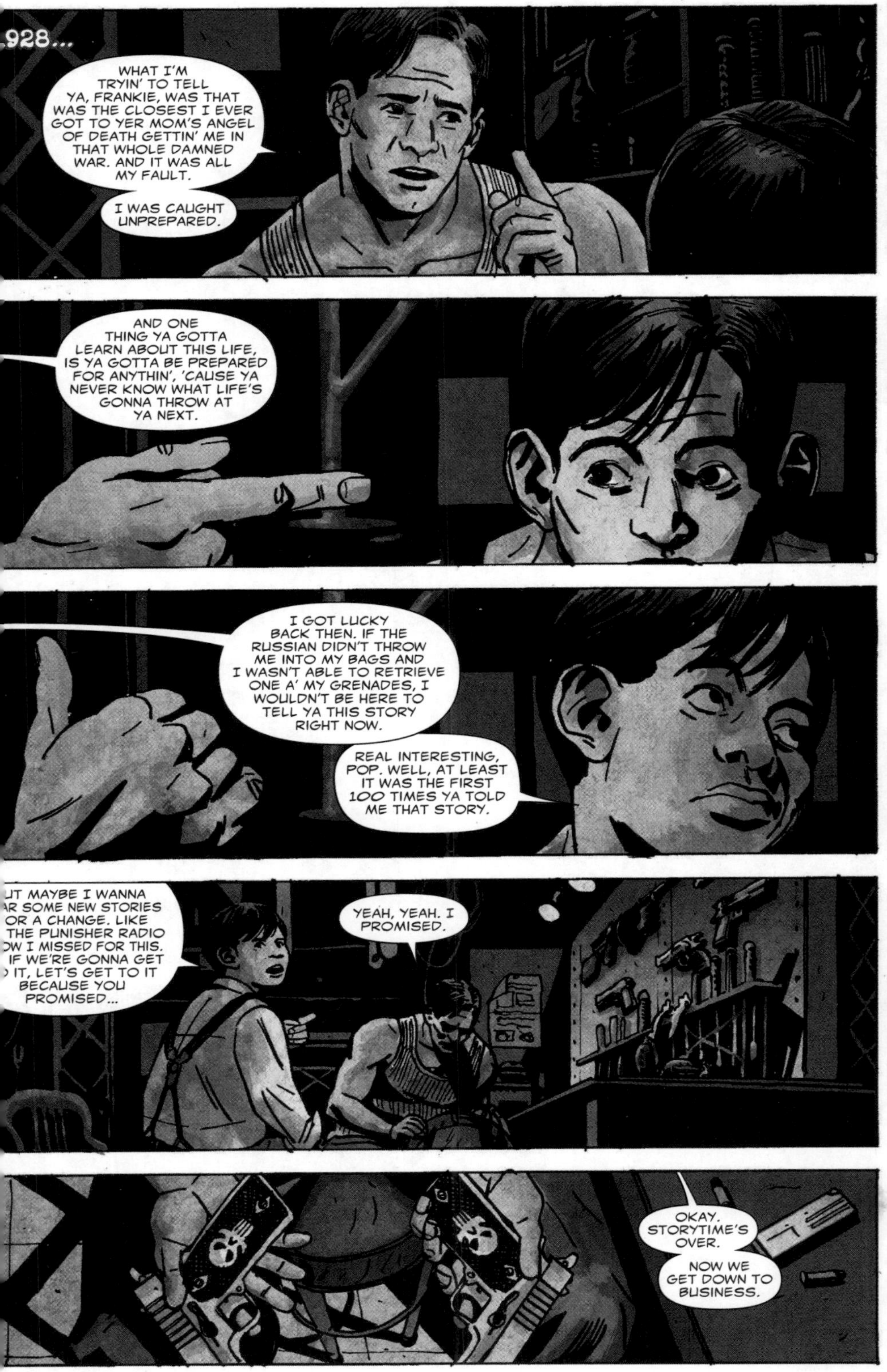

928...
WHAT I'M TRYIN' TO TELL YA, FRANKIE, WAS THAT WAS THE CLOSEST I EVER GOT TO YER MOM'S ANGEL OF DEATH GETTIN' ME IN THAT WHOLE DAMNED WAR. AND IT WAS ALL MY FAULT.
I WAS CAUGHT UNPREPARED.
AND ONE THING YA GOTTA LEARN ABOUT THIS LIFE, IS YA GOTTA BE PREPARED FOR ANYTHIN', 'CAUSE YA NEVER KNOW WHAT LIFE'S GONNA THROW AT YA NEXT.
I GOT LUCKY BACK THEN. IF THE RUSSIAN DIDN'T THROW ME INTO MY BAGS AND I WASN'T ABLE TO RETRIEVE ONE A' MY GRENADES, I WOULDN'T BE HERE TO TELL YA THIS STORY RIGHT NOW.
REAL INTERESTING, POP. WELL, AT LEAST IT WAS THE FIRST 100 TIMES YA TOLD ME THAT STORY.
UT MAYBE I WANNA AR SOME NEW STORIES OR A CHANGE. LIKE THE PUNISHER RADIO OW I MISSED FOR THIS. IF WE'RE GONNA GET IT, LET'S GET TO IT BECAUSE YOU PROMISED...
YEAH, YEAH. I PROMISED.
OKAY. STORYTIME'S OVER.
NOW WE GET DOWN TO BUSINESS.

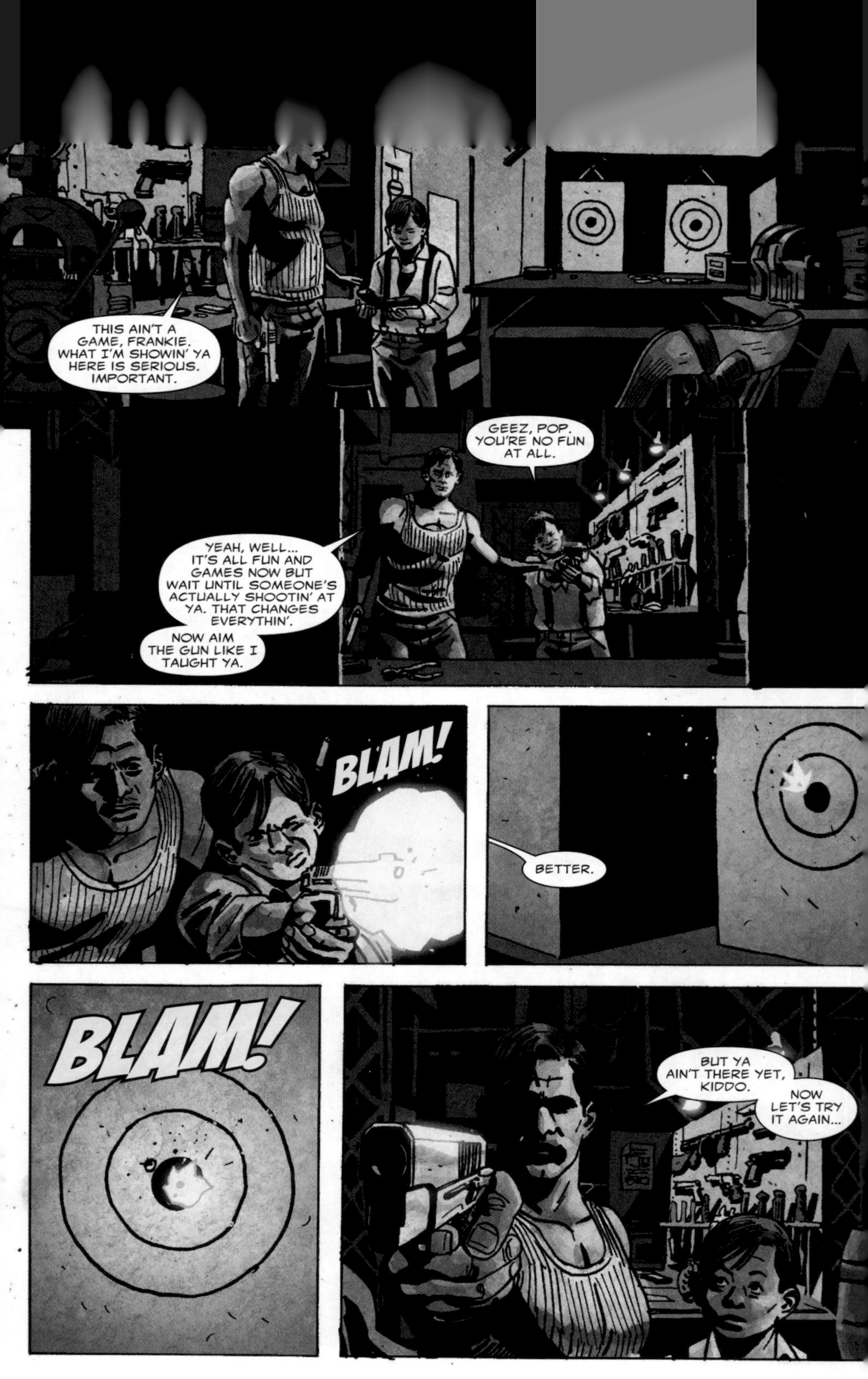
THIS AIN'T A GAME, FRANKIE. WHAT I'M SHOWIN' YA HERE IS SERIOUS. IMPORTANT.
GEEZ, POP. YOU'RE NO FUN AT ALL.
YEAH, WELL... IT'S ALL FUN AND GAMES NOW BUT WAIT UNTIL SOMEONE'S ACTUALLY SHOOTIN' AT YA. THAT CHANGES EVERYTHIN'.
NOW AIM THE GUN LIKE I TAUGHT YA.
BLAM!
BETTER.
BLAM!
BUT YA AIN'T THERE YET, KIDDO.
NOW LET'S TRY IT AGAIN...

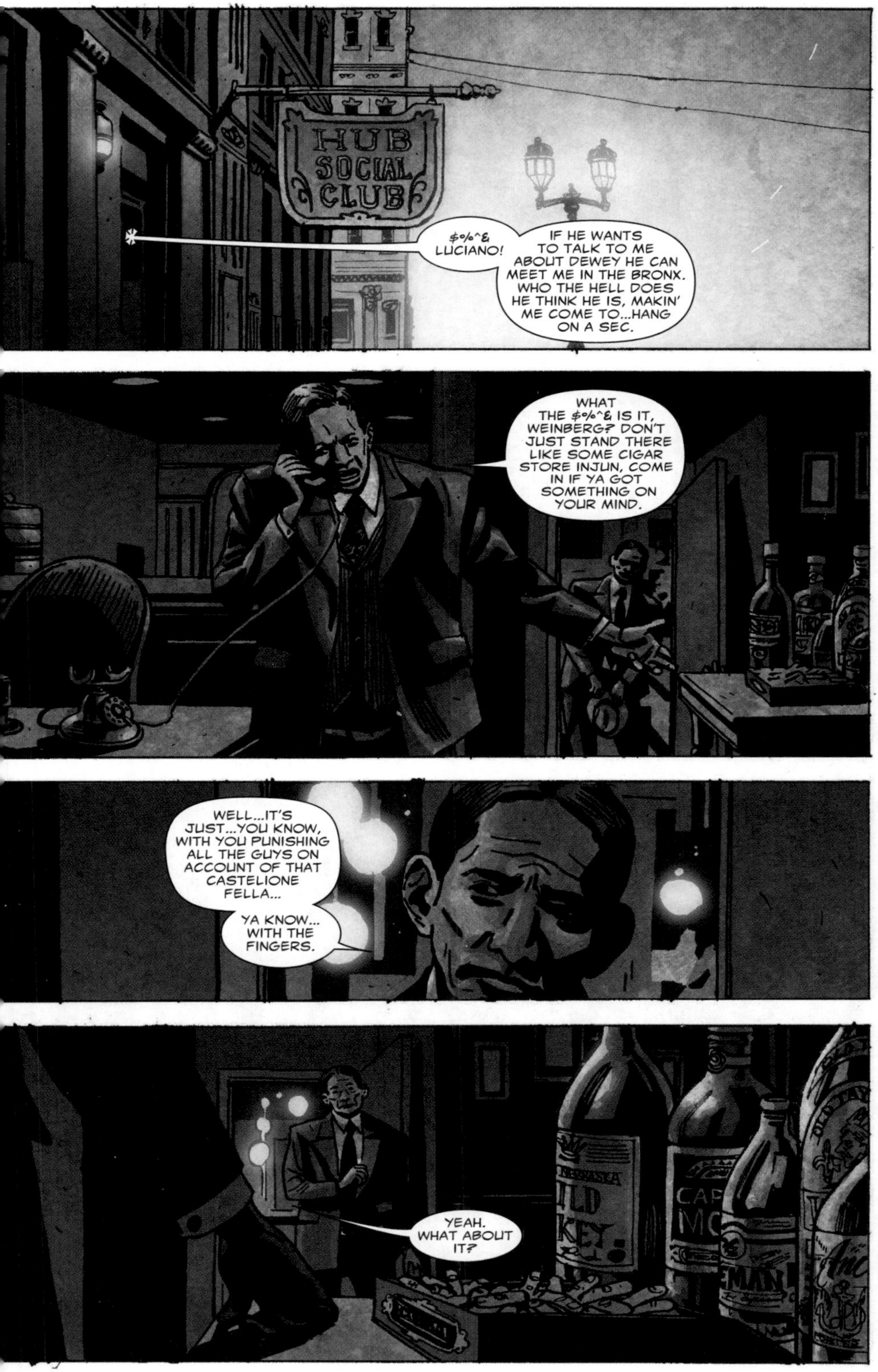
HUB SOCIAL CLUB
$%^& LUCIANO!
IF HE WANTS TO TALK TO ME ABOUT DEWEY HE CAN MEET ME IN THE BRONX. WHO THE HELL DOES HE THINK HE IS, MAKIN' ME COME TO...HANG ON A SEC.
WHAT THE $%^& IS IT, WEINBERG? DON'T JUST STAND THERE LIKE SOME CIGAR STORE INJUN, COME IN IF YA GOT SOMETHING ON YOUR MIND.
WELL...IT'S JUST...YOU KNOW, WITH YOU PUNISHING ALL THE GUYS ON ACCOUNT OF THAT CASTELIONE FELLA...
YA KNOW... WITH THE FINGERS.
YEAH. WHAT ABOUT IT?

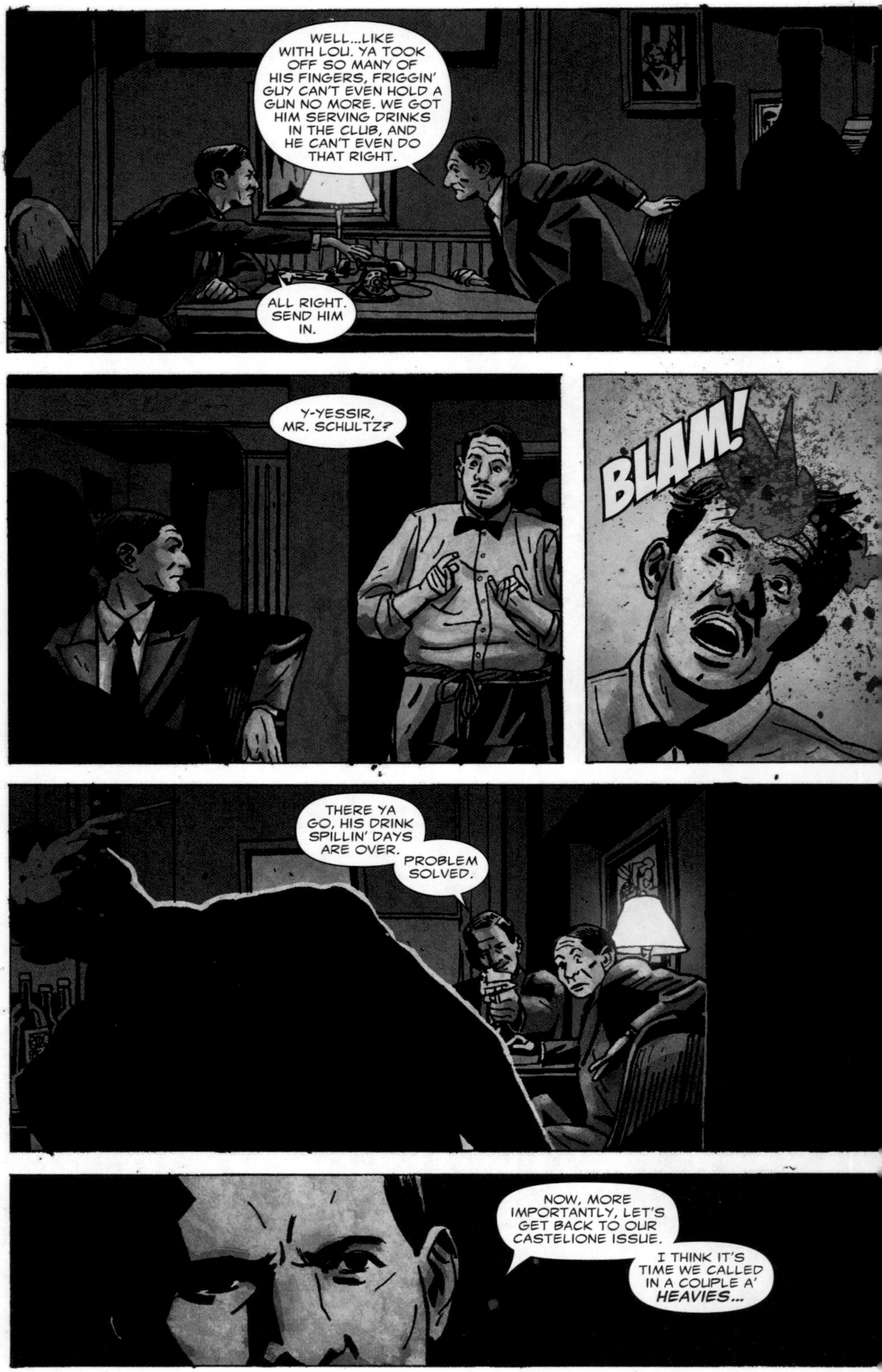
WELL...LIKE WITH LOU. YA TOOK OFF SO MANY OF HIS FINGERS, FRIGGIN' GUY CAN'T EVEN HOLD A GUN NO MORE. WE GOT HIM SERVING DRINKS IN THE CLUB, AND HE CAN'T EVEN DO THAT RIGHT.
ALL RIGHT. SEND HIM IN.
Y-YESSIR, MR. SCHULTZ?
BLAM!
THERE YA GO, HIS DRINK SPILLIN' DAYS ARE OVER.
PROBLEM SOLVED.
NOW, MORE IMPORTANTLY, LET'S GET BACK TO OUR CASTELIONE ISSUE.
I THINK IT'S TIME WE CALLED IN A COUPLE A' HEAVIES...

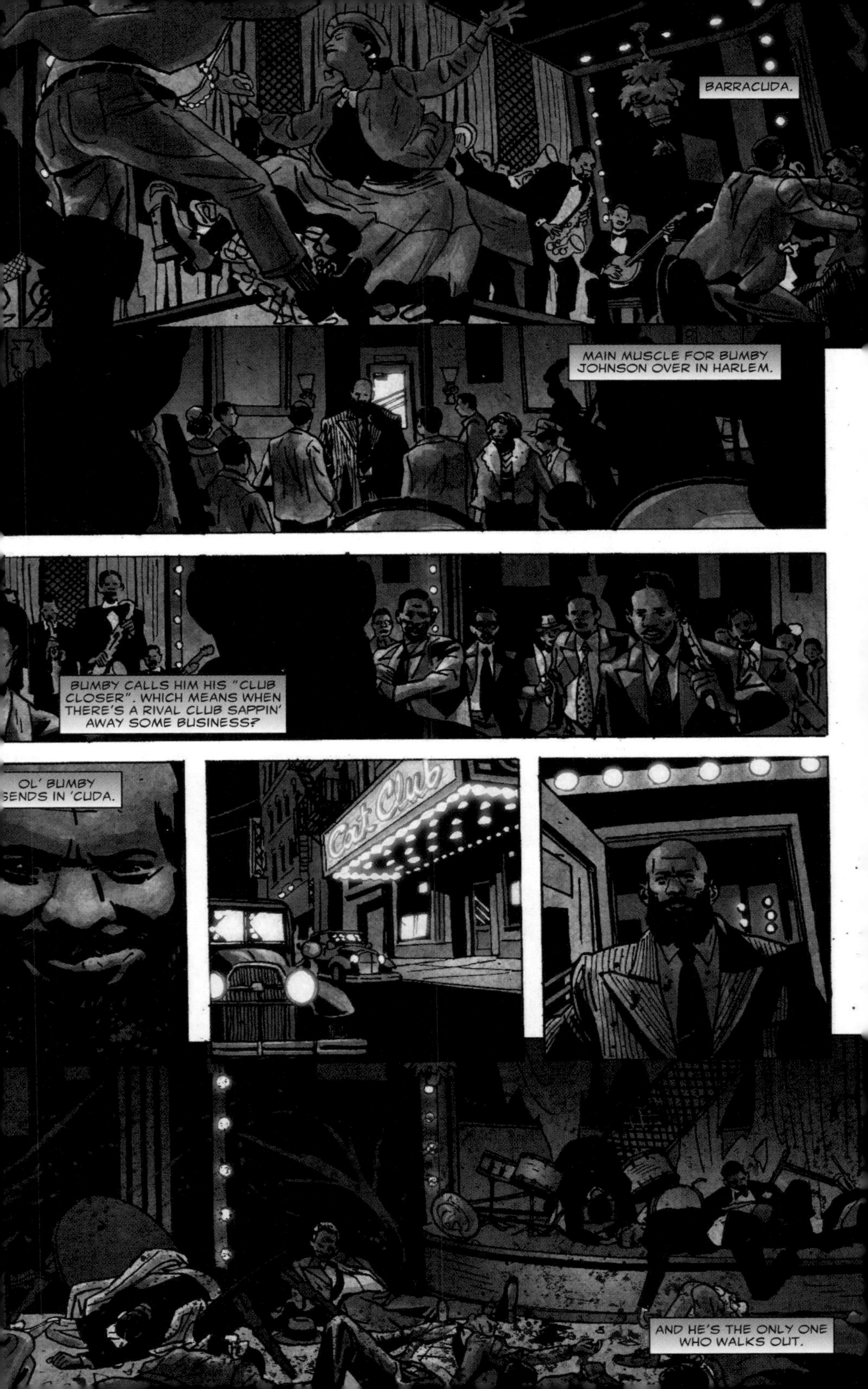
BARRACUDA.
MAIN MUSCLE FOR BUMBY JOHNSON OVER IN HARLEM.
BUMBY CALLS HIM HIS "CLUB CLOSER". WHICH MEANS WHEN THERE'S A RIVAL CLUB SAPPIN' AWAY SOME BUSINESS?
OL' BUMBY SENDS IN 'CUDA.
AND HE'S THE ONLY ONE WHO WALKS OUT.

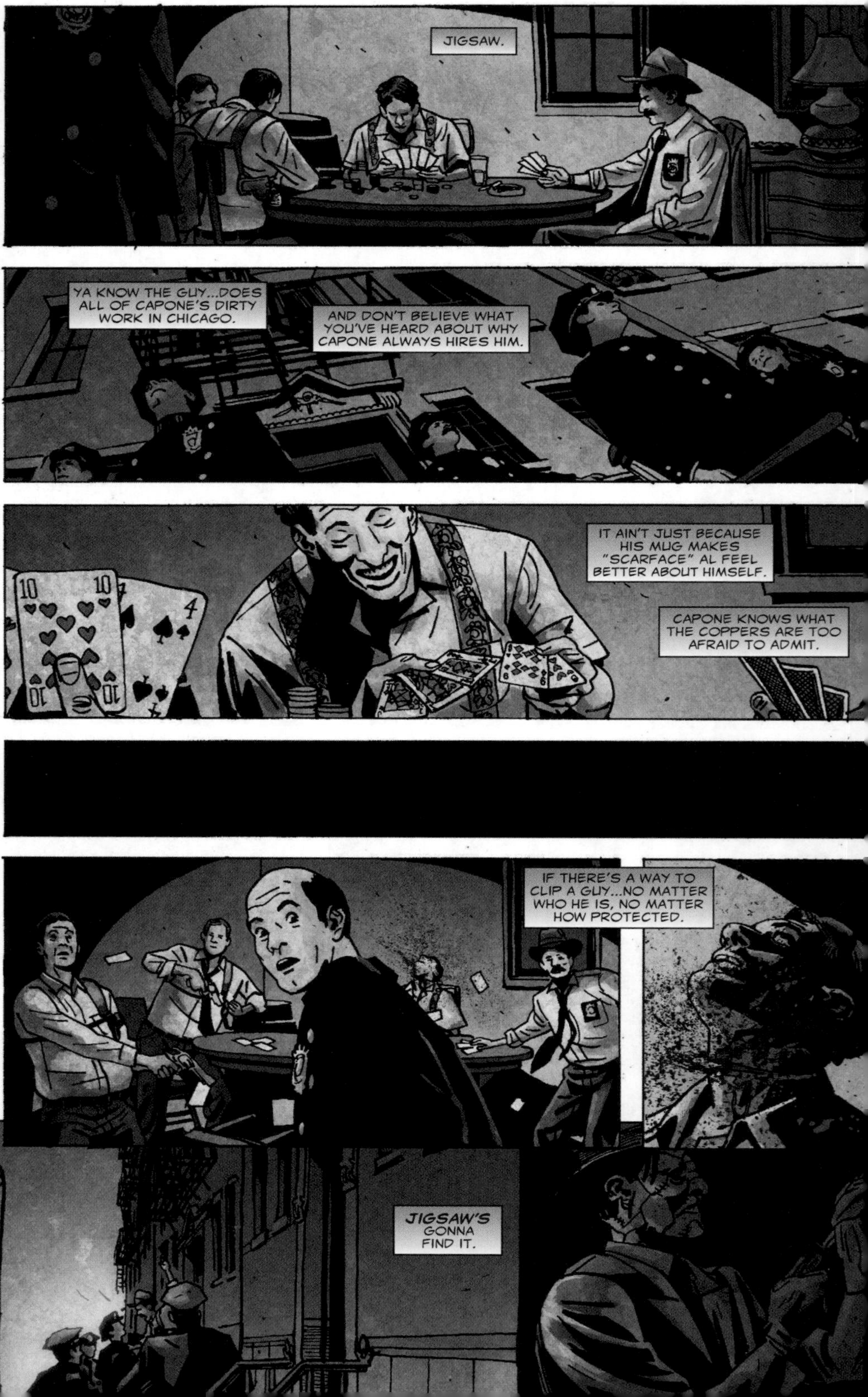
JIGSAW.
YA KNOW THE GUY...DOES ALL OF CAPONE'S DIRTY WORK IN CHICAGO.
AND DON'T BELIEVE WHAT YOU'VE HEARD ABOUT WHY CAPONE ALWAYS HIRES HIM.
IT AIN'T JUST BECAUSE HIS MUG MAKES "SCARFACE" AL FEEL BETTER ABOUT HIMSELF.
CAPONE KNOWS WHAT THE COPPERS ARE TOO AFRAID TO ADMIT.
IF THERE'S A WAY TO CLIP A GUY...NO MATTER WHO HE IS, NO MATTER HOW PROTECTED.
JIGSAW'S GONNA FIND IT.

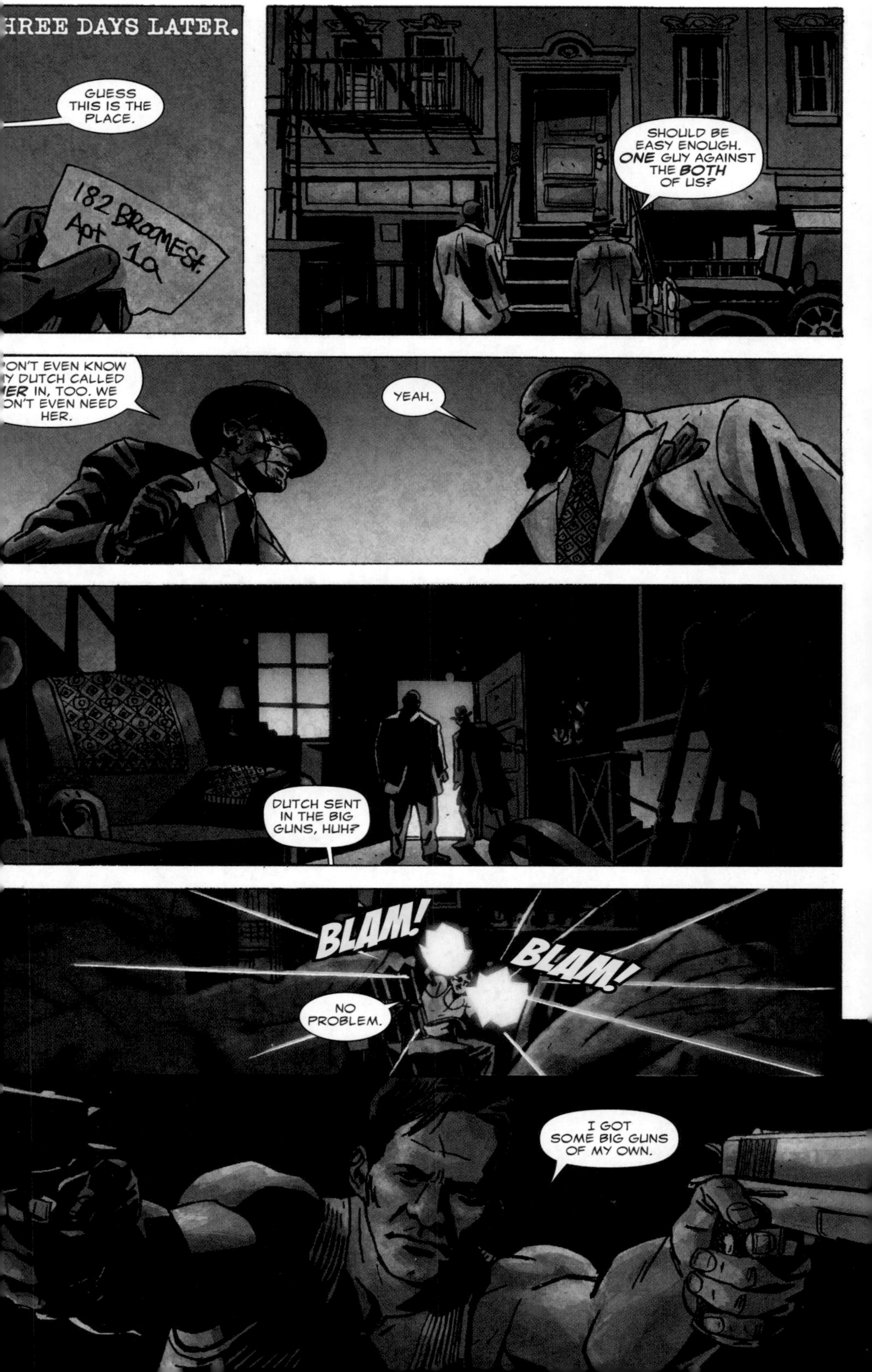
HREE DAYS LATER.
GUESS THIS IS THE PLACE.
182 BROOMEST. Apt 1a
SHOULD BE EASY ENOUGH. ONE GUY AGAINST THE BOTH OF US?
ON'T EVEN KNOW Y DUTCH CALLED ER IN, TOO. WE ON'T EVEN NEED HER.
YEAH.
DUTCH SENT IN THE BIG GUNS, HUH?
BLAM!
BLAM!
NO PROBLEM.
I GOT SOME BIG GUNS OF MY OWN.

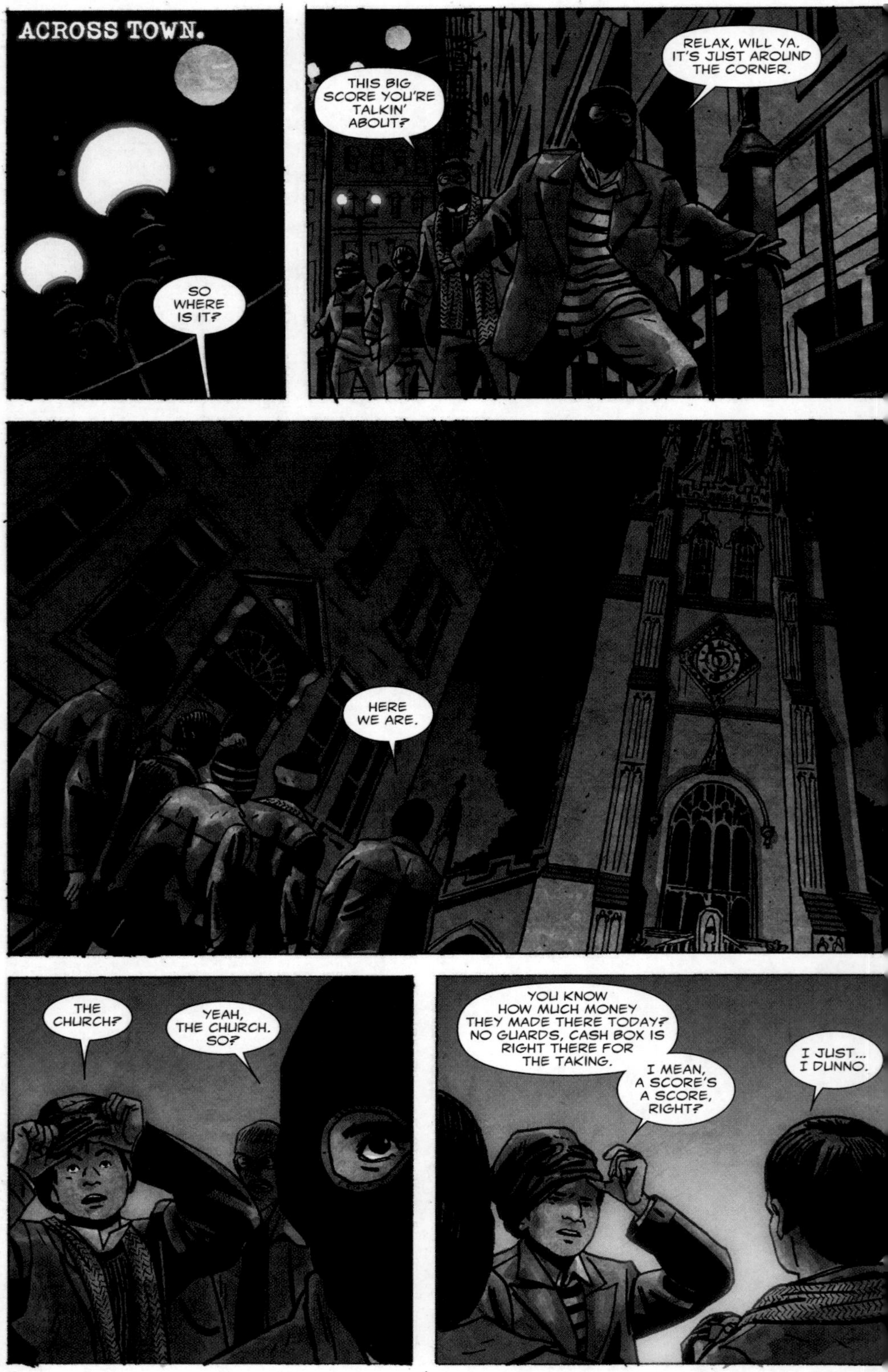
ACROSS TOWN.
SO WHERE IS IT?
THIS BIG SCORE YOU'RE TALKIN' ABOUT?
RELAX, WILL YA. IT'S JUST AROUND THE CORNER.
HERE WE ARE.
THE CHURCH?
YEAH, THE CHURCH. SO?
YOU KNOW HOW MUCH MONEY THEY MADE THERE TODAY? NO GUARDS, CASH BOX IS RIGHT THERE FOR THE TAKING.
I MEAN, A SCORE'S A SCORE, RIGHT?
I JUST... I DUNNO.

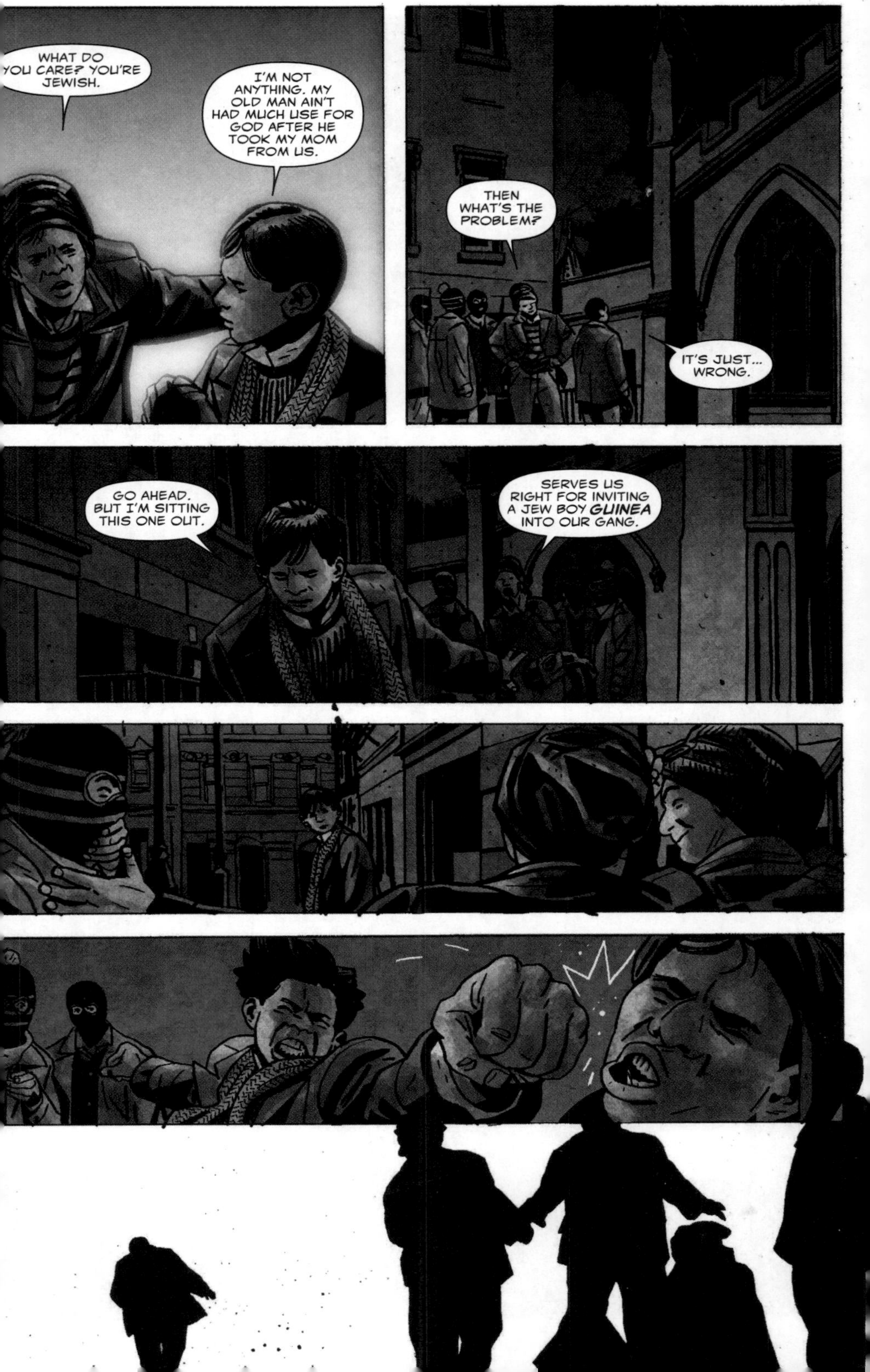
WHAT DO YOU CARE? YOU'RE JEWISH.
I'M NOT ANYTHING. MY OLD MAN AIN'T HAD MUCH USE FOR GOD AFTER HE TOOK MY MOM FROM US.
THEN WHAT'S THE PROBLEM?
IT'S JUST... WRONG.
GO AHEAD. BUT I'M SITTING THIS ONE OUT.
SERVES US RIGHT FOR INVITING A JEW BOY GUINEA INTO OUR GANG.

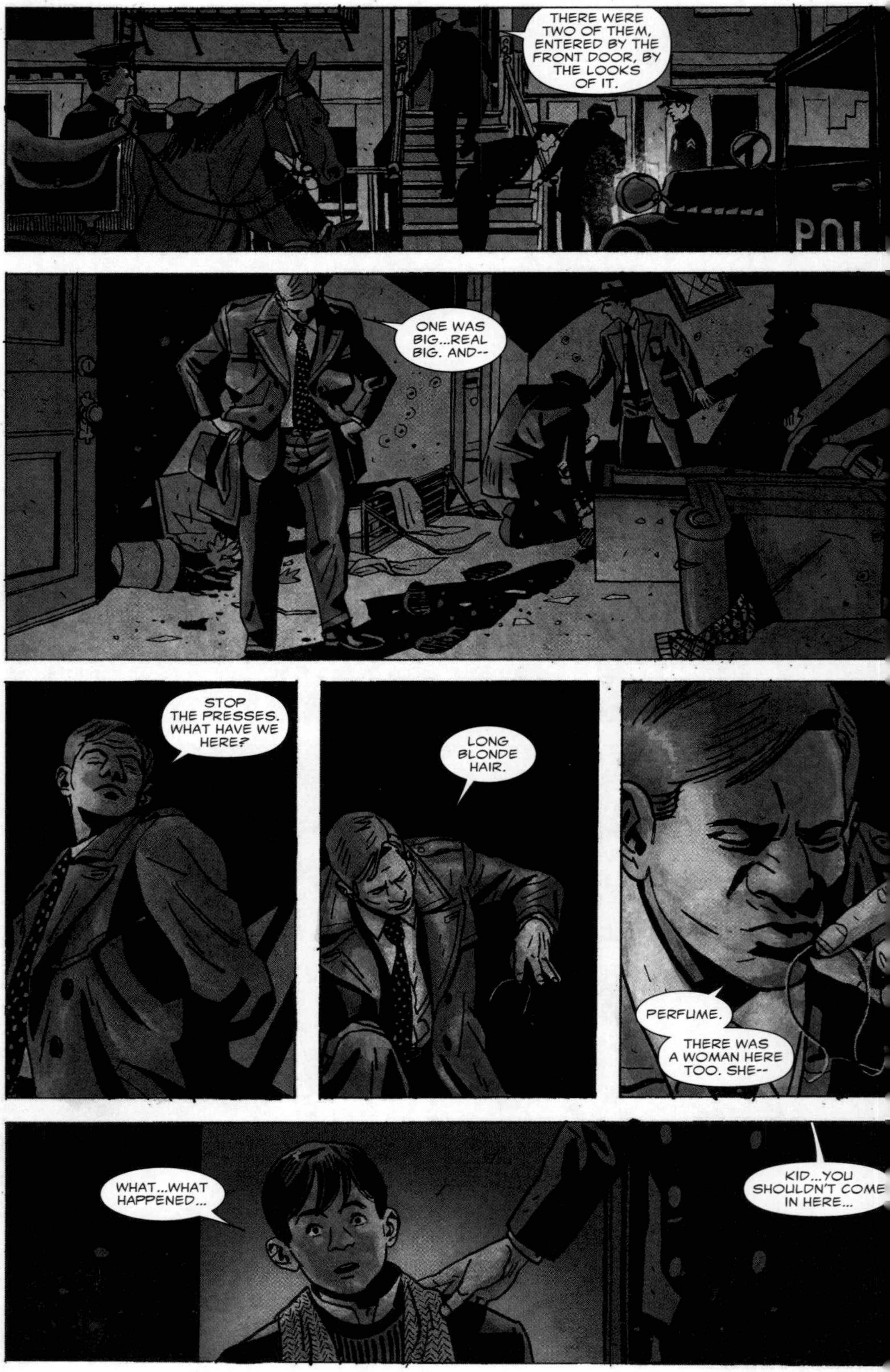
THERE WERE TWO OF THEM, ENTERED BY THE FRONT DOOR, BY THE LOOKS OF IT.
PO
ONE WAS BIG...REAL BIG. AND--
STOP THE PRESSES. WHAT HAVE WE HERE?
LONG BLONDE HAIR.
PERFUME.
THERE WAS A WOMAN HERE TOO. SHE--
WHAT...WHAT HAPPENED...
KID...YOU SHOULDN'T COME IN HERE...

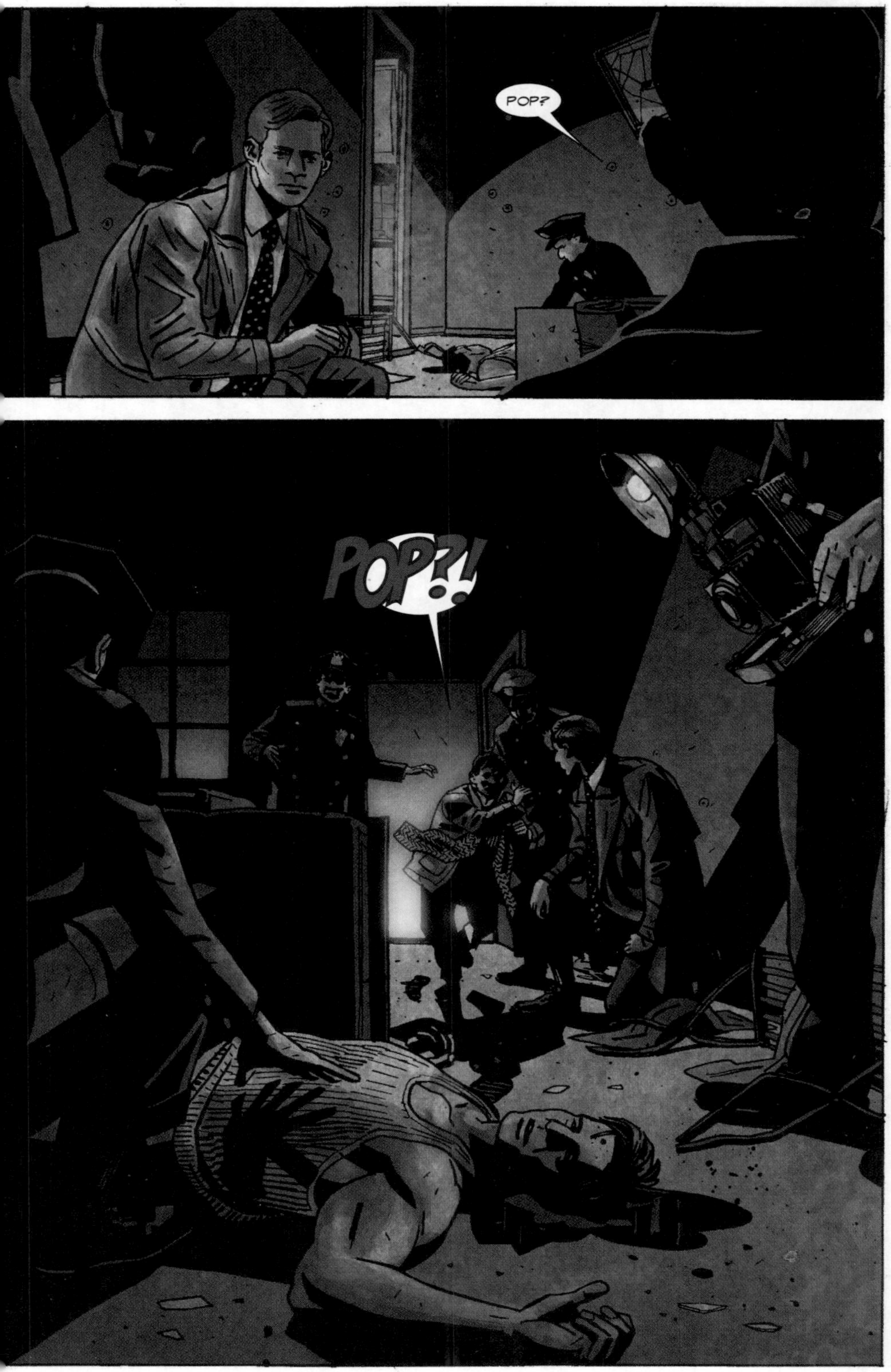
POP?
POP?!

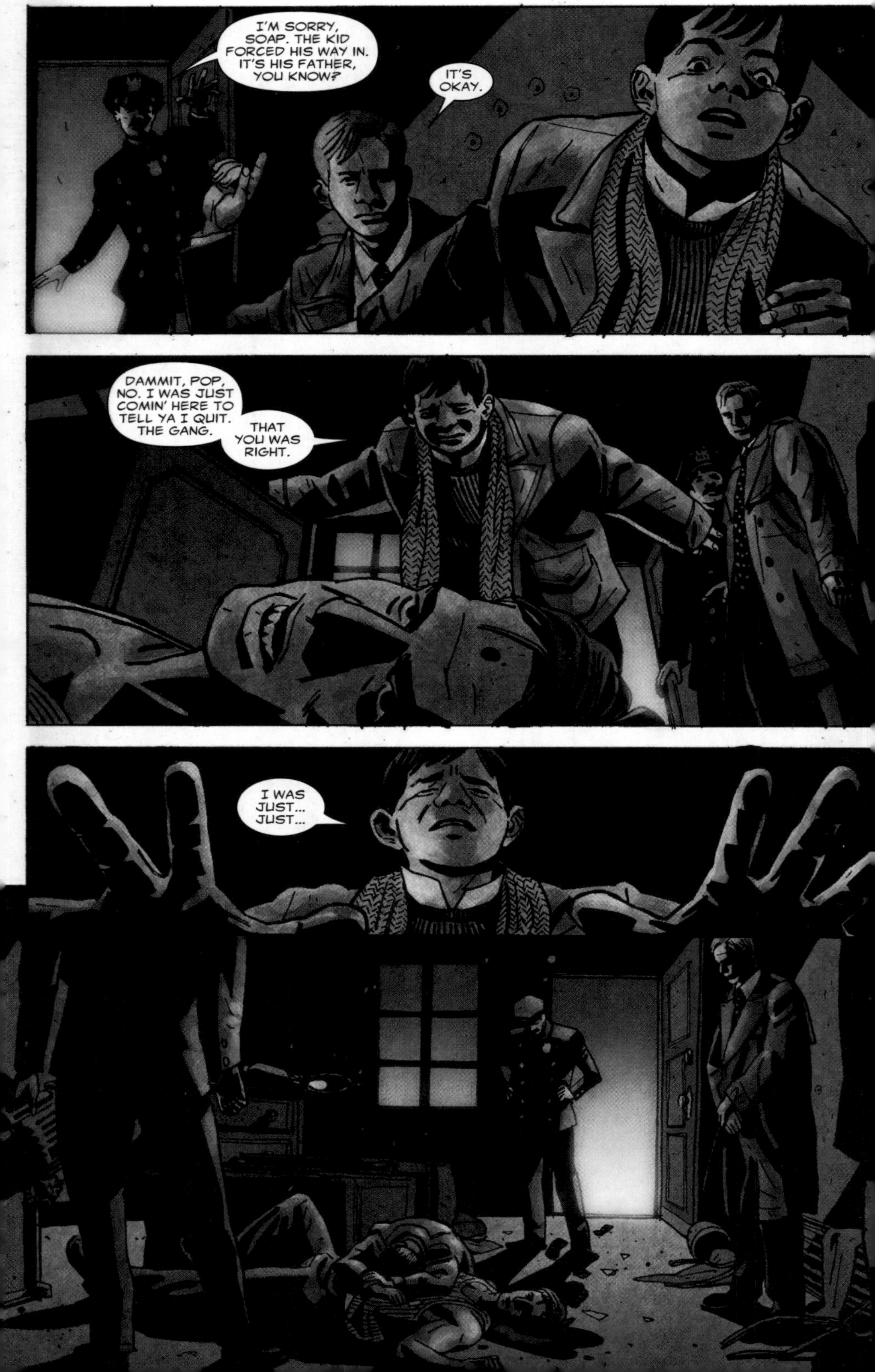
I'M SORRY, SOAP. THE KID FORCED HIS WAY IN. IT'S HIS FATHER, YOU KNOW?
IT'S OKAY.
DAMMIT, POP, NO. I WAS JUST COMIN' HERE TO TELL YA I QUIT. THE GANG.
THAT YOU WAS RIGHT.
I WAS JUST... JUST...

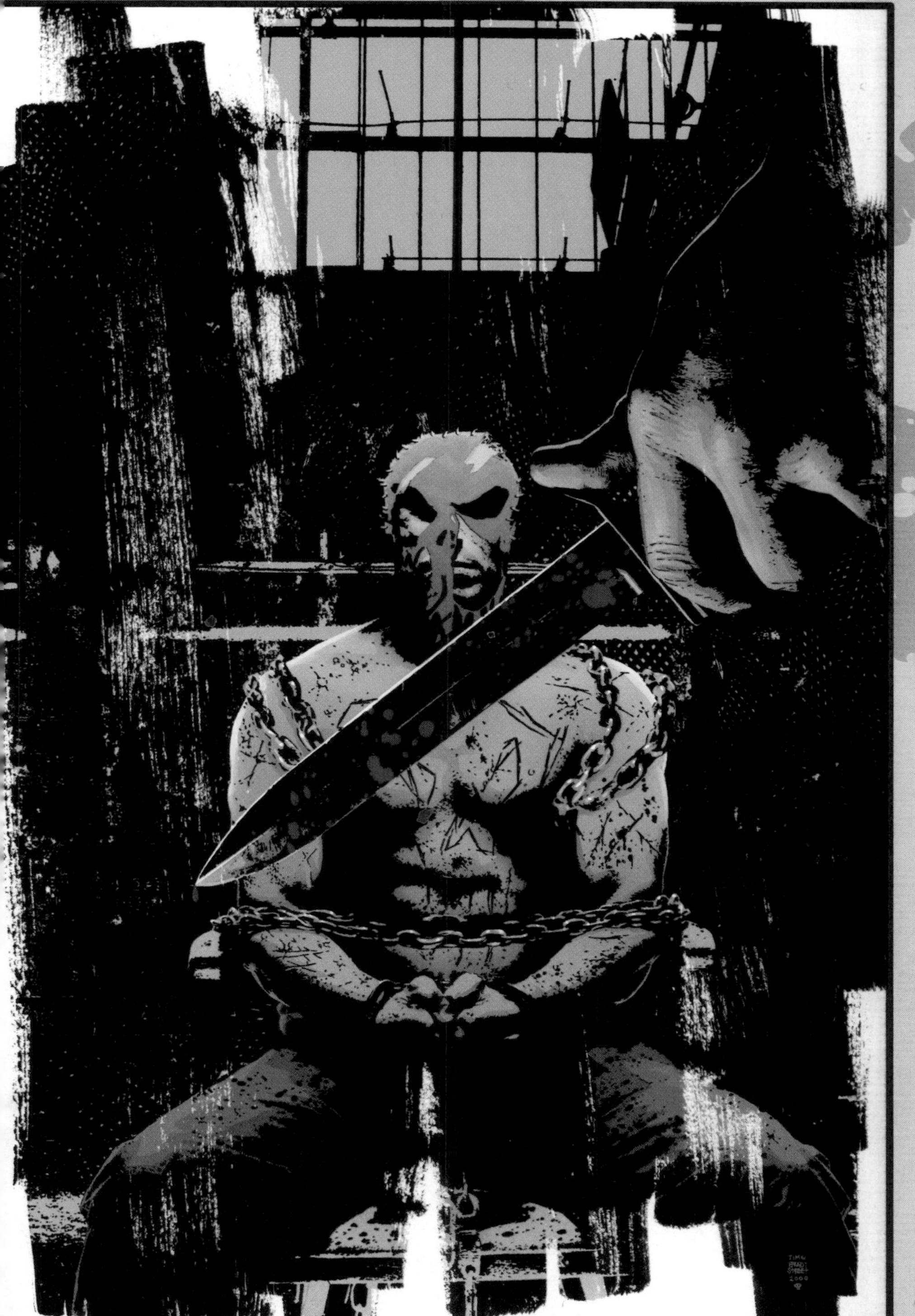

THREE

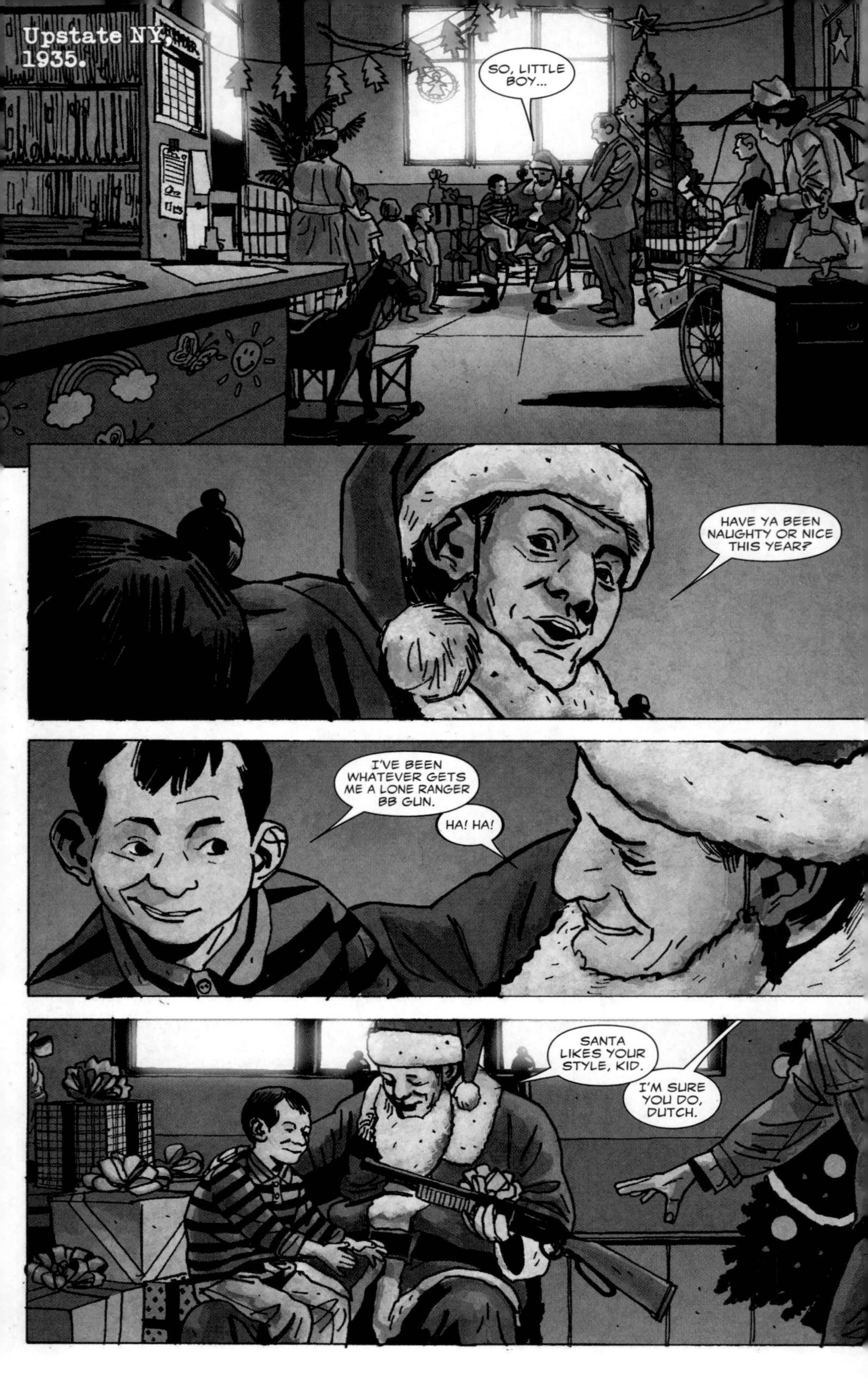
Upstate NY, 1935.
SO, LITTLE BOY...
HAVE YA BEEN NAUGHTY OR NICE THIS YEAR?
I'VE BEEN WHATEVER GETS ME A LONE RANGER BB GUN.
HA! HA!
SANTA LIKES YOUR STYLE, KID.
I'M SURE YOU DO, DUTCH.

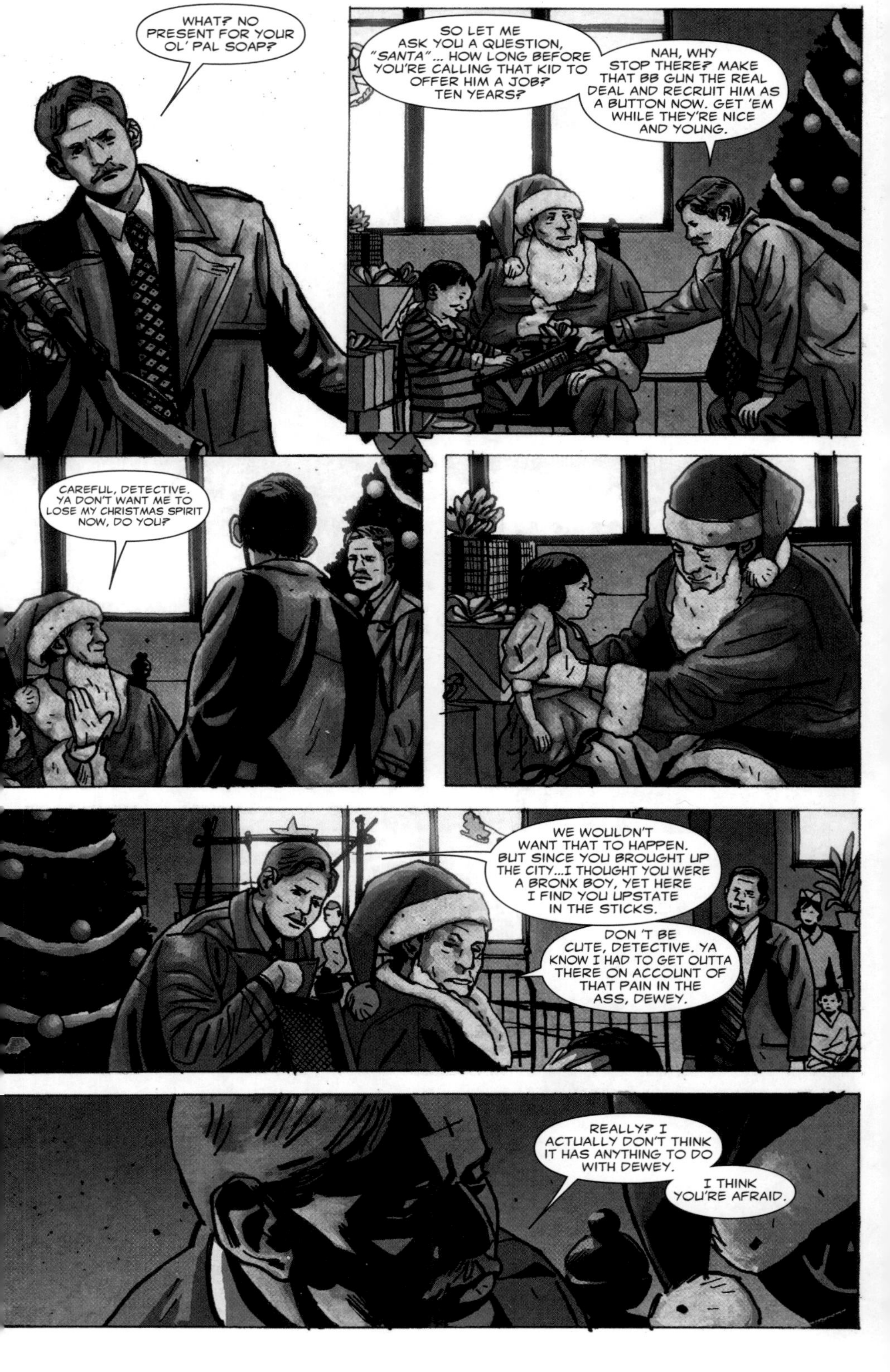
WHAT? NO PRESENT FOR YOUR OL' PAL SOAP?
SO LET ME ASK YOU A QUESTION, "SANTA"... HOW LONG BEFORE YOU'RE CALLING THAT KID TO OFFER HIM A JOB? TEN YEARS?
NAH, WHY STOP THERE? MAKE THAT BB GUN THE REAL DEAL AND RECRUIT HIM AS A BUTTON NOW. GET 'EM WHILE THEY'RE NICE AND YOUNG.
CAREFUL, DETECTIVE. YA DON'T WANT ME TO LOSE MY CHRISTMAS SPIRIT NOW, DO YOU?
WE WOULDN'T WANT THAT TO HAPPEN. BUT SINCE YOU BROUGHT UP THE CITY...I THOUGHT YOU WERE A BRONX BOY, YET HERE I FIND YOU UPSTATE IN THE STICKS.
DON 'T BE CUTE, DETECTIVE. YA KNOW I HAD TO GET OUTTA THERE ON ACCOUNT OF THAT PAIN IN THE ASS, DEWEY.
REALLY? I ACTUALLY DON'T THINK IT HAS ANYTHING TO DO WITH DEWEY.
I THINK YOU'RE AFRAID.

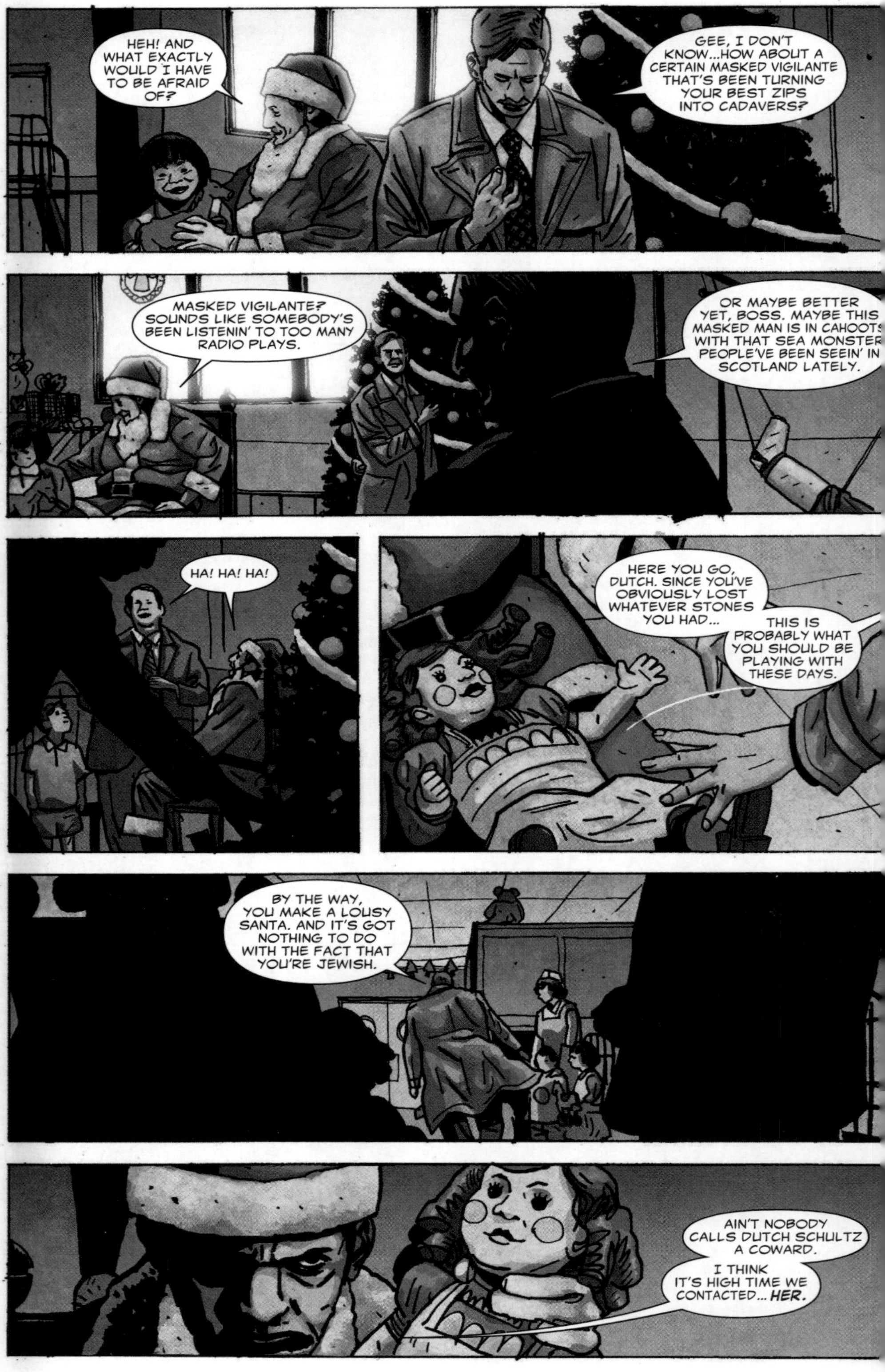
HEH! AND WHAT EXACTLY WOULD I HAVE TO BE AFRAID OF?
GEE, I DON'T KNOW...HOW ABOUT A CERTAIN MASKED VIGILANTE THAT'S BEEN TURNING YOUR BEST ZIPS INTO CADAVERS?
MASKED VIGILANTE? SOUNDS LIKE SOMEBODY'S BEEN LISTENIN' TO TOO MANY RADIO PLAYS.
OR MAYBE BETTER YET, BOSS. MAYBE THIS MASKED MAN IS IN CAHOOTS WITH THAT SEA MONSTER PEOPLE'VE BEEN SEEIN' IN SCOTLAND LATELY.
HA! HA! HA!
HERE YOU GO, DUTCH. SINCE YOU'VE OBVIOUSLY LOST WHATEVER STONES YOU HAD...
THIS IS PROBABLY WHAT YOU SHOULD BE PLAYING WITH THESE DAYS.
BY THE WAY, YOU MAKE A LOUSY SANTA. AND IT'S GOT NOTHING TO DO WITH THE FACT THAT YOU'RE JEWISH.
AIN'T NOBODY CALLS DUTCH SCHULTZ A COWARD.
I THINK IT'S HIGH TIME WE CONTACTED... *HER.*

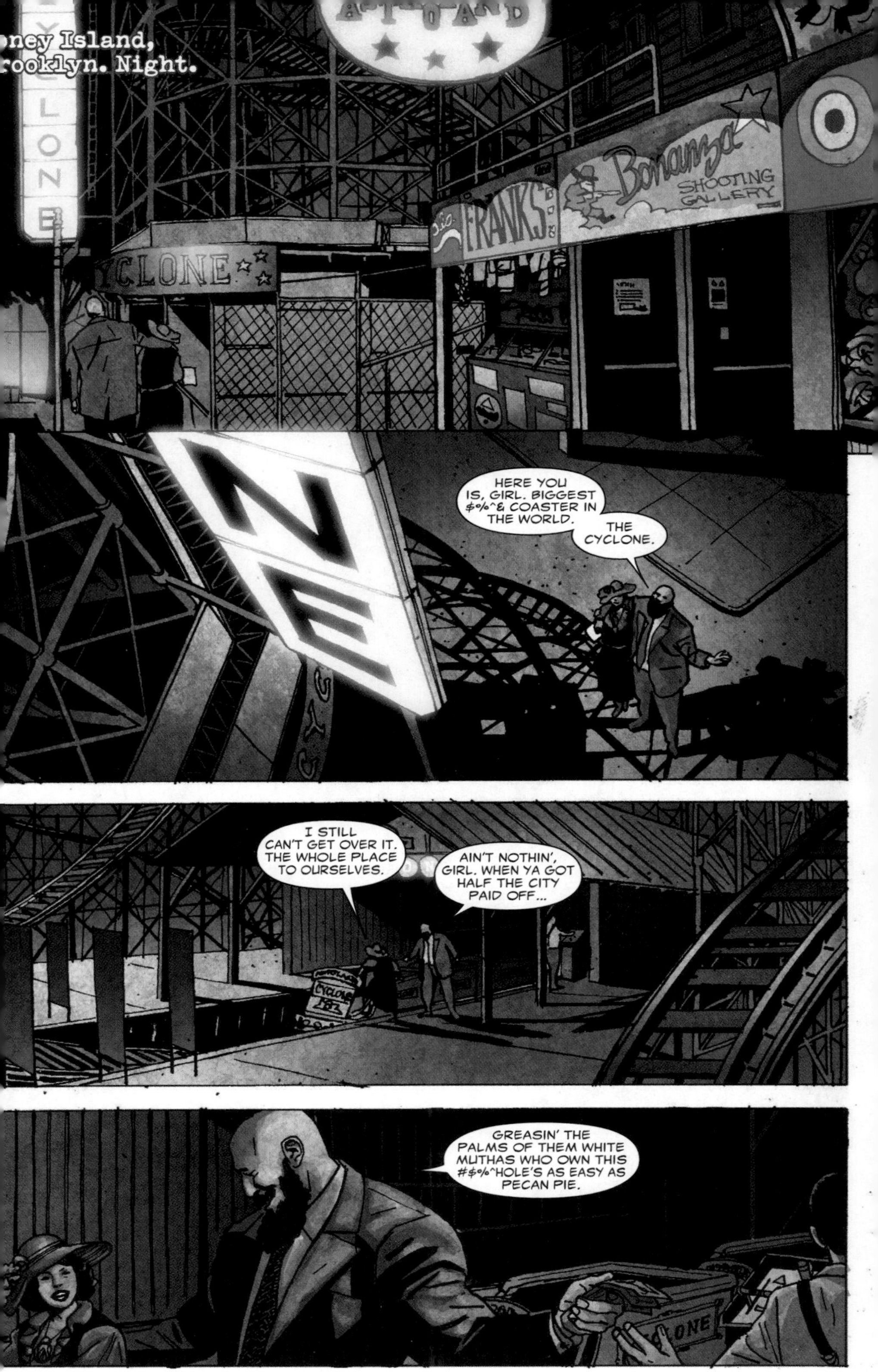
ney Island,
rooklyn. Night.
CYCLONE
FRANKS
Bonanza
SHOOTING GALLERY
HERE YOU IS, GIRL. BIGGEST $%^& COASTER IN THE WORLD.
THE CYCLONE.
I STILL CAN'T GET OVER IT. THE WHOLE PLACE TO OURSELVES.
AIN'T NOTHIN', GIRL. WHEN YA GOT HALF THE CITY PAID OFF...
GREASIN' THE PALMS OF THEM WHITE MUTHAS WHO OWN THIS #$%^HOLE'S AS EASY AS PECAN PIE.

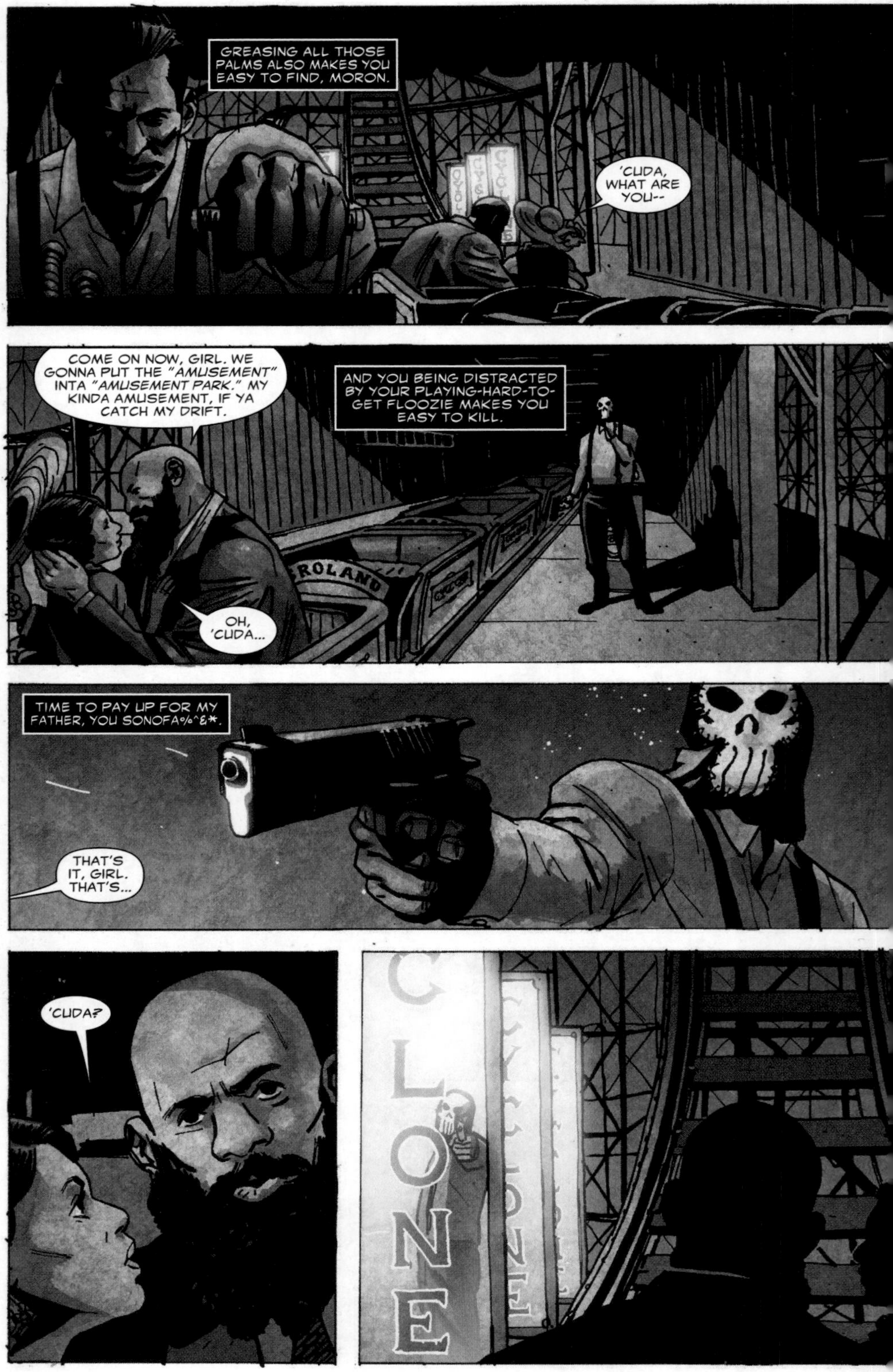
GREASING ALL THOSE PALMS ALSO MAKES YOU EASY TO FIND, MORON.
'CUDA, WHAT ARE YOU--
COME ON NOW, GIRL. WE GONNA PUT THE "AMUSEMENT" INTA "AMUSEMENT PARK." MY KINDA AMUSEMENT, IF YA CATCH MY DRIFT.
AND YOU BEING DISTRACTED BY YOUR PLAYING-HARD-TO-GET FLOOZIE MAKES YOU EASY TO KILL.
OH, 'CUDA...
TIME TO PAY UP FOR MY FATHER, YOU SONOFA%^&*.
THAT'S IT, GIRL. THAT'S...
'CUDA?
CLONE

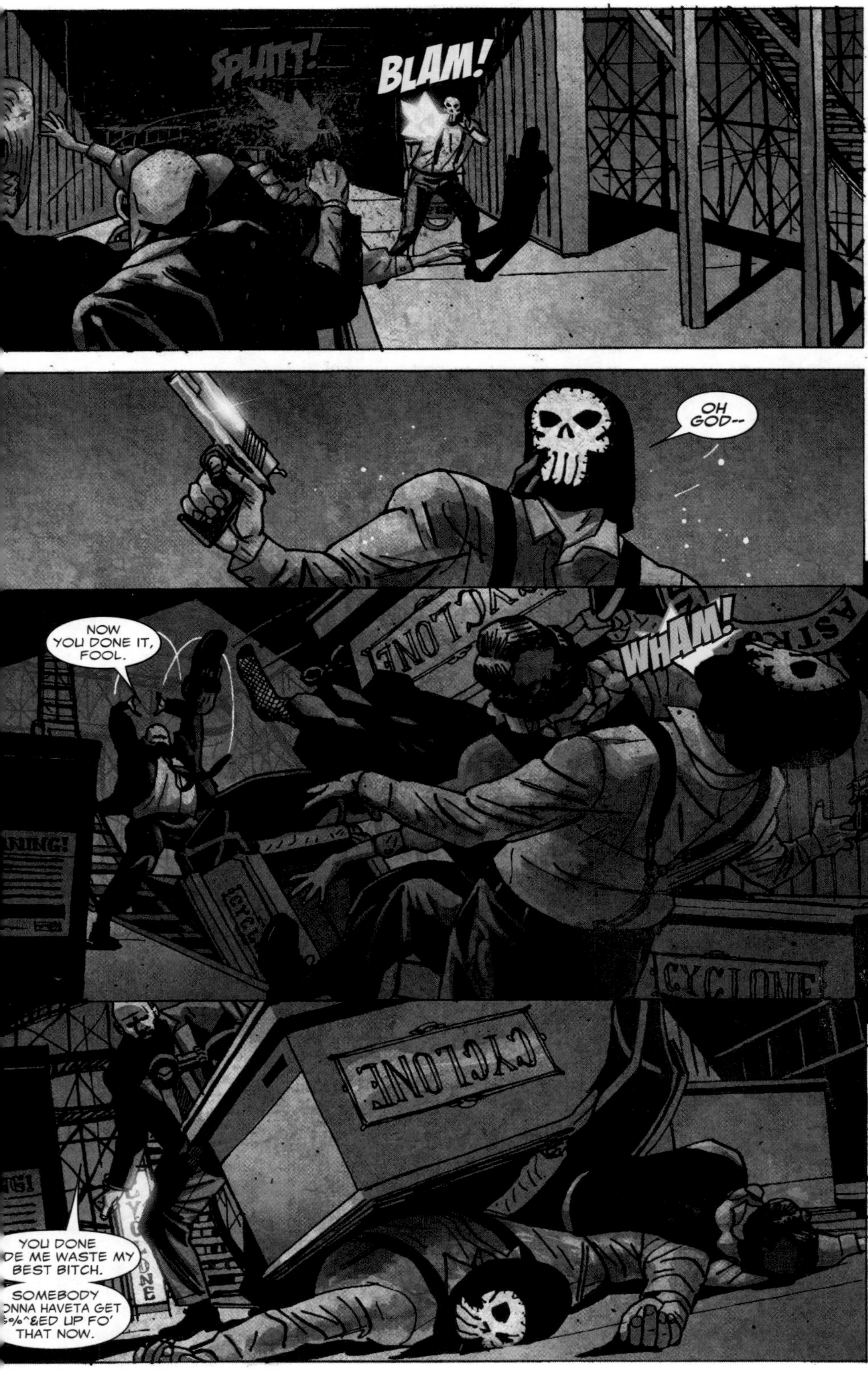
SPLATT!
BLAM!
OH GOD--
NOW YOU DONE IT, FOOL.
CYCLONE
WHAM!
YOU DONE
DE ME WASTE MY
BEST BITCH.
SOMEBODY
ONNA HAVETA GET
%^&ED UP FO'
THAT NOW.

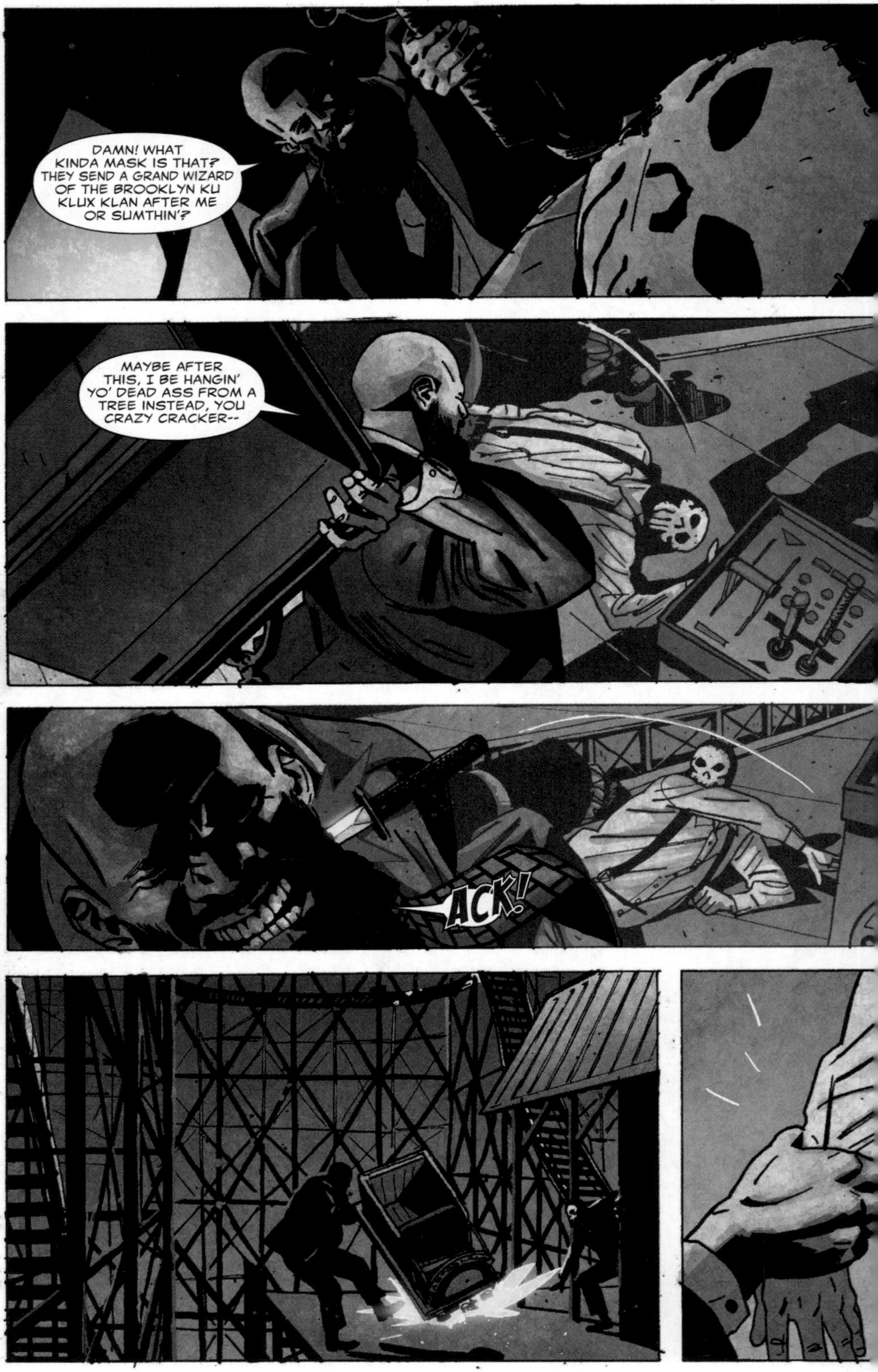
DAMN! WHAT KINDA MASK IS THAT? THEY SEND A GRAND WIZARD OF THE BROOKLYN KU KLUX KLAN AFTER ME OR SUMTHIN'?
MAYBE AFTER THIS, I BE HANGIN' YO' DEAD ASS FROM A TREE INSTEAD, YOU CRAZY CRACKER--
ACK!

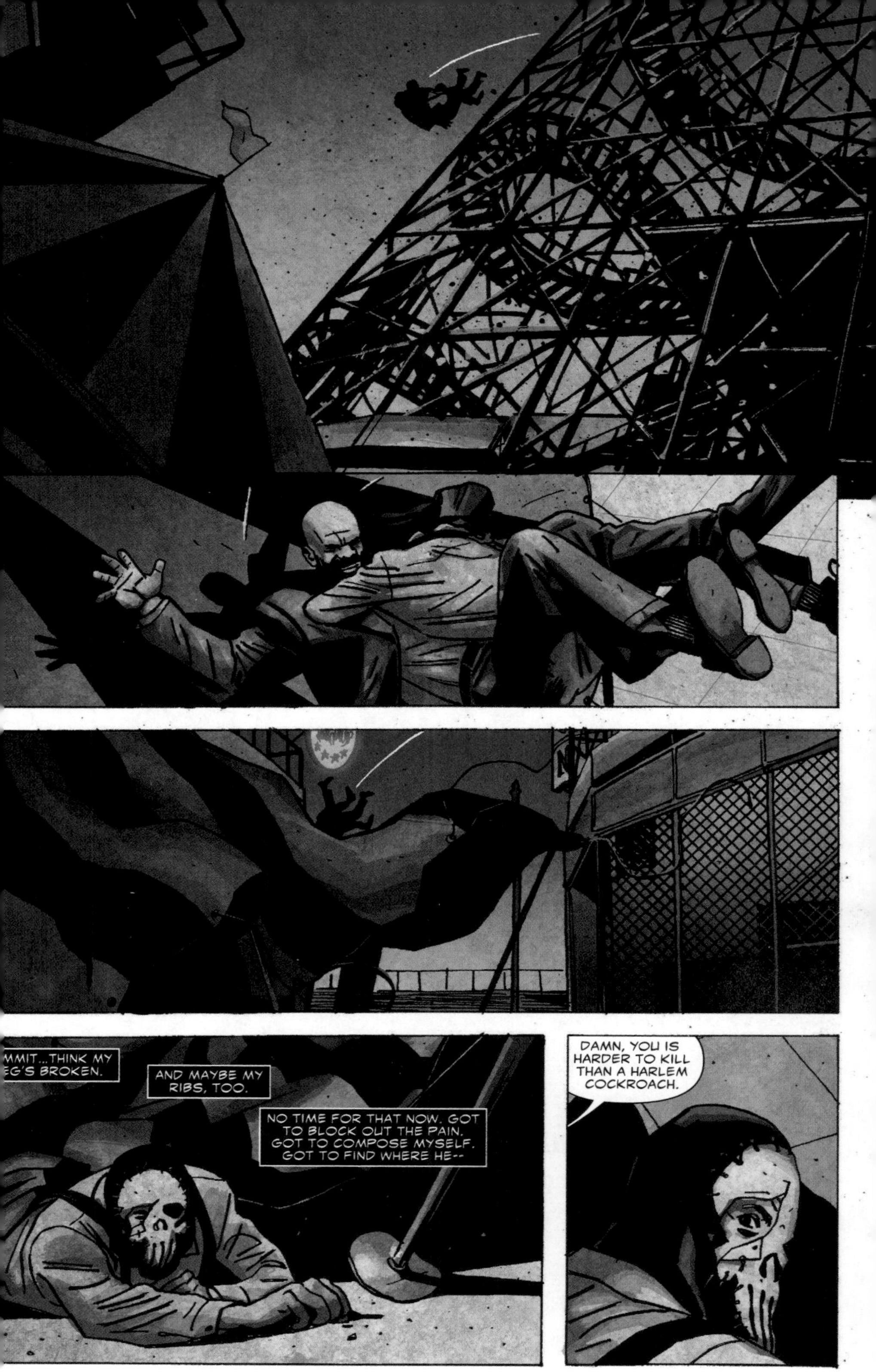
MMIT...THINK MY
EG'S BROKEN.
AND MAYBE MY RIBS, TOO.
NO TIME FOR THAT NOW. GOT TO BLOCK OUT THE PAIN. GOT TO COMPOSE MYSELF. GOT TO FIND WHERE HE--
DAMN, YOU IS HARDER TO KILL THAN A HARLEM COCKROACH.

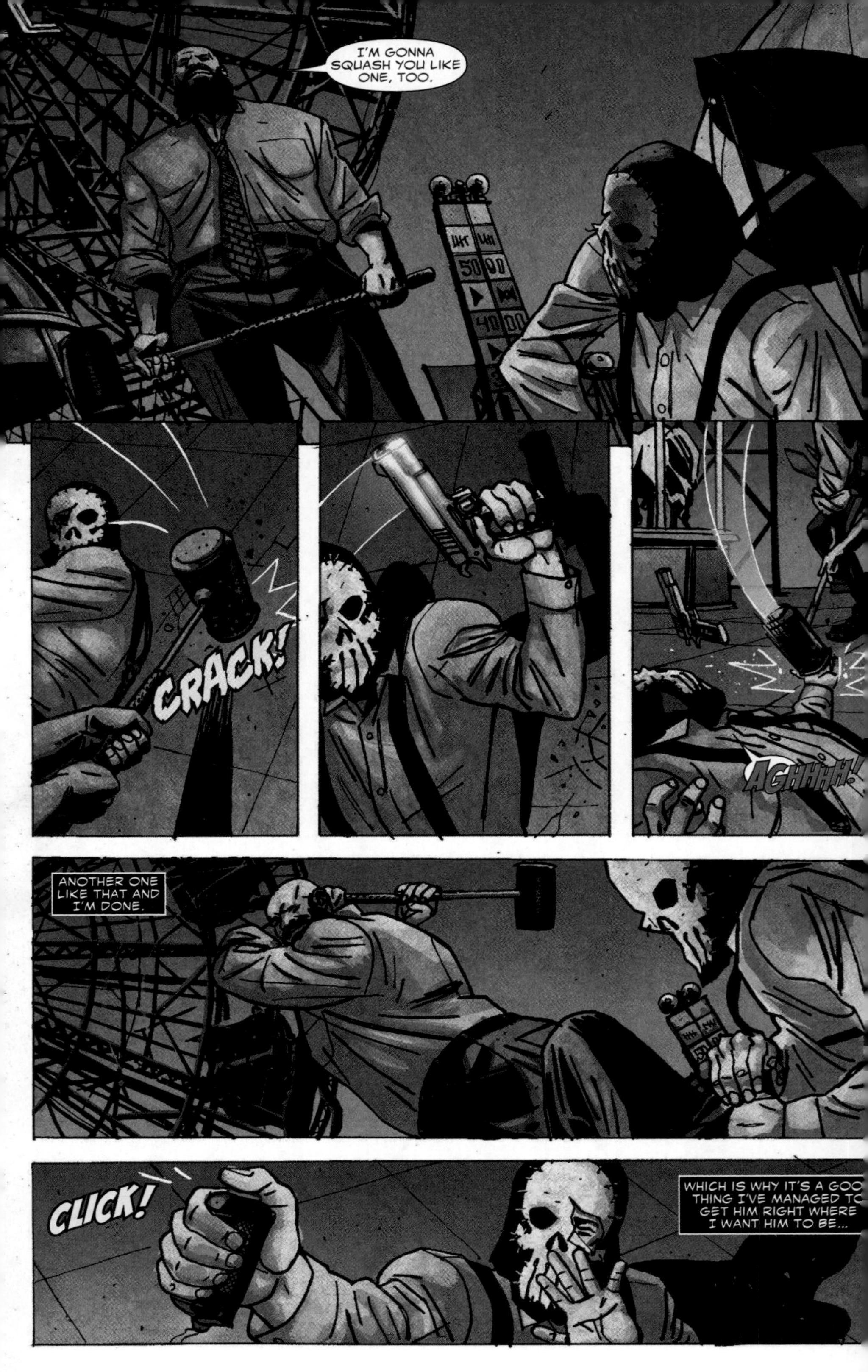
I'M GONNA SQUASH YOU LIKE ONE, TOO.
CRACK!
AGHHHH!
ANOTHER ONE LIKE THAT AND I'M DONE.
CLICK!
WHICH IS WHY IT'S A GOO
THING I'VE MANAGED TO
GET HIM RIGHT WHERE
I WANT HIM TO BE...

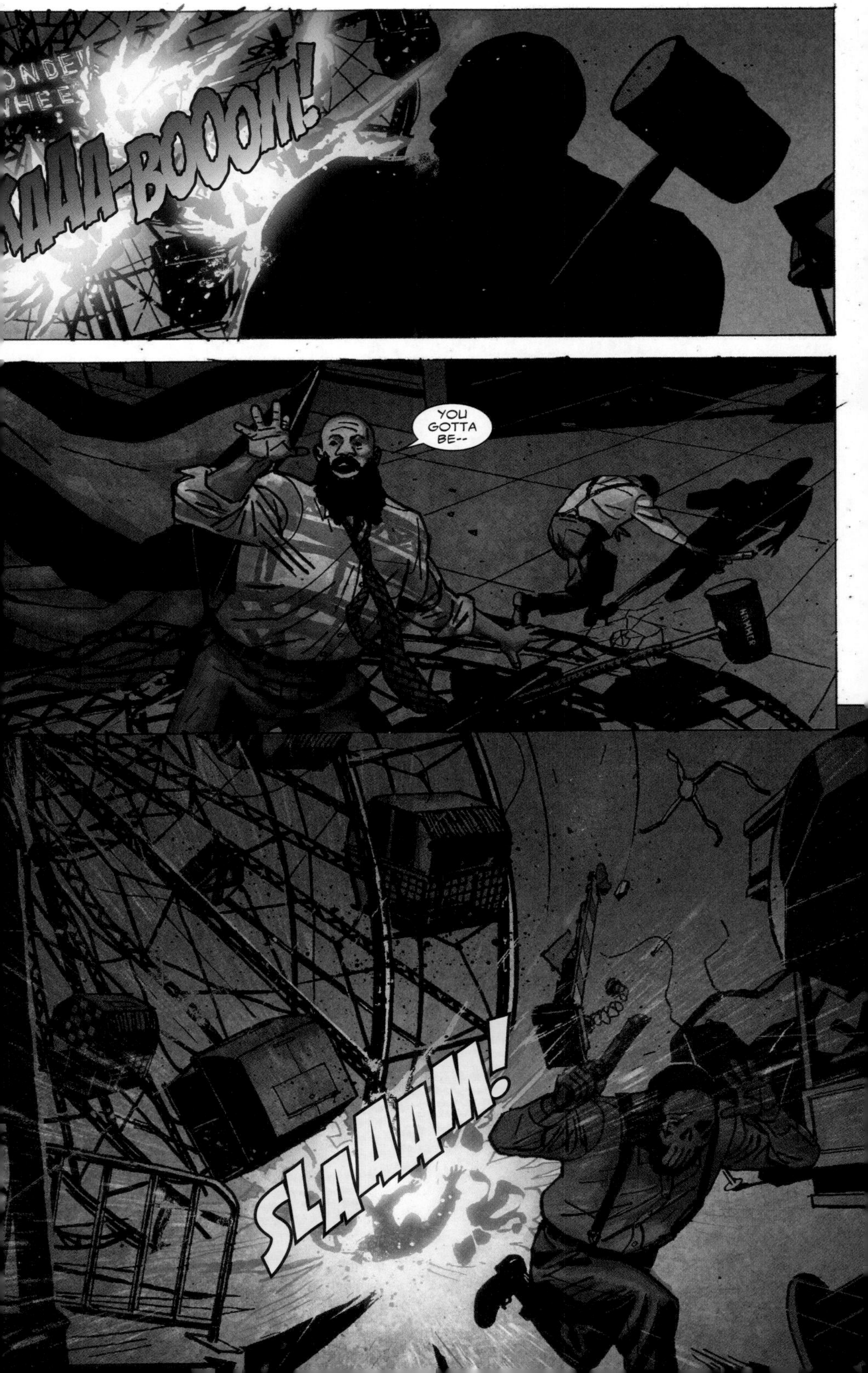
AAA-BOOOM!
YOU GOTTA BE--
SLAAAM!

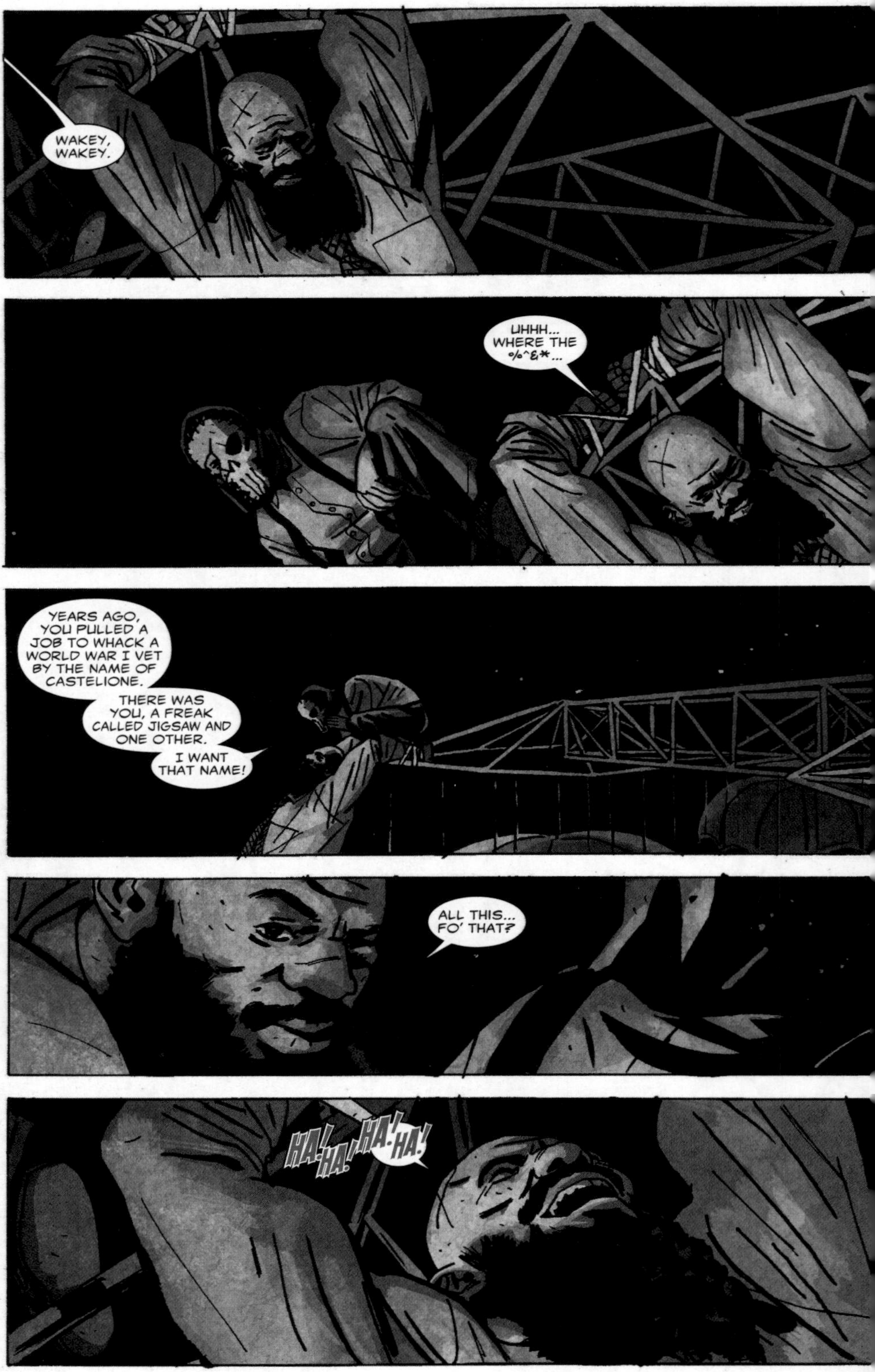
WAKEY, WAKEY.
UHHH... WHERE THE %^&*...
YEARS AGO, YOU PULLED A JOB TO WHACK A WORLD WAR I VET BY THE NAME OF CASTELIONE.
THERE WAS YOU, A FREAK CALLED JIGSAW AND ONE OTHER.
I WANT THAT NAME!
ALL THIS... FO' THAT?
HA! HA! HA! HA!

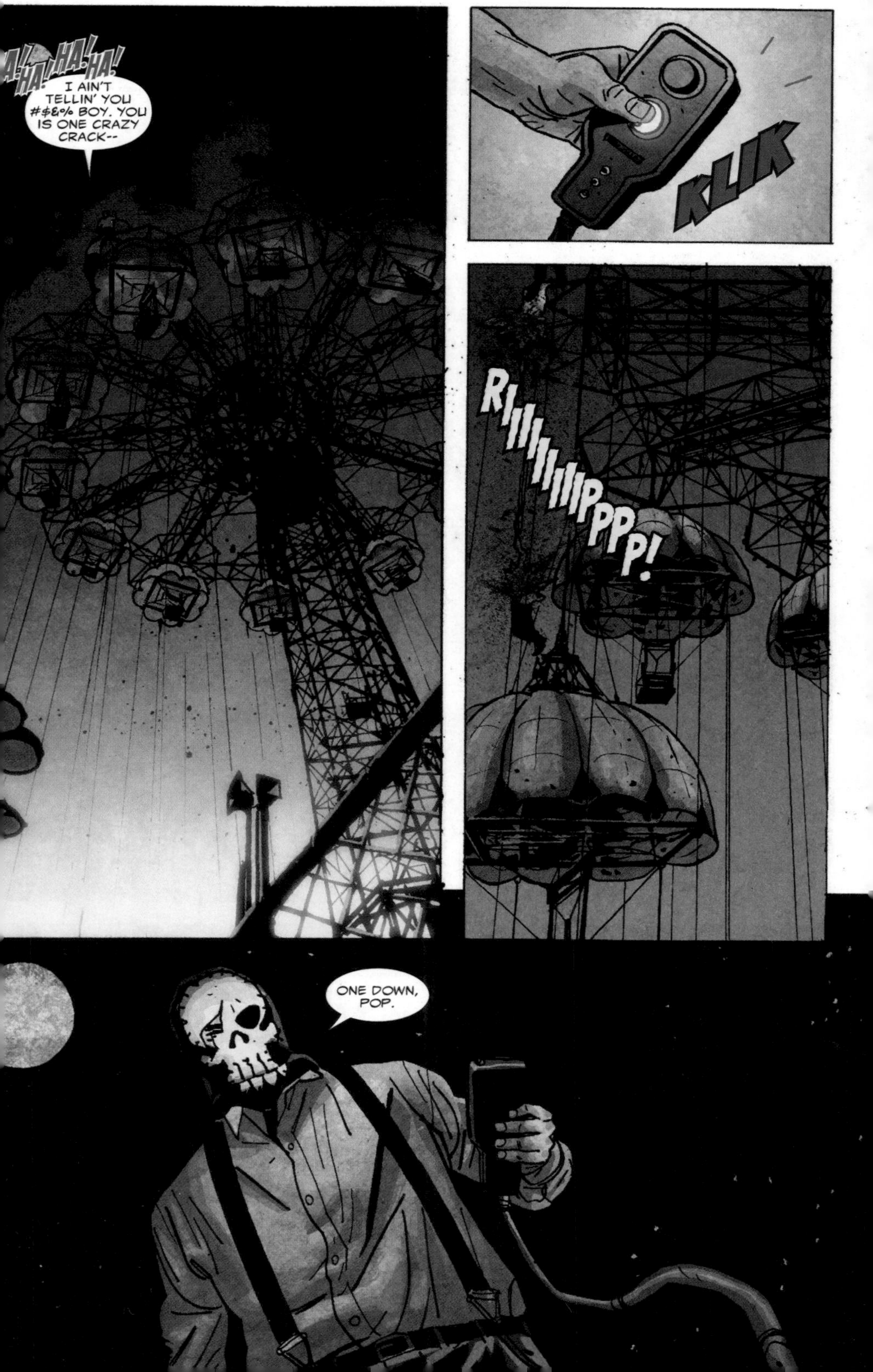
HA! HA! HA! HA!
I AIN'T TELLIN' YOU #$&% BOY. YOU IS ONE CRAZY CRACK--
KLIK
RIIIIIIIIPPPP!
ONE DOWN, POP.

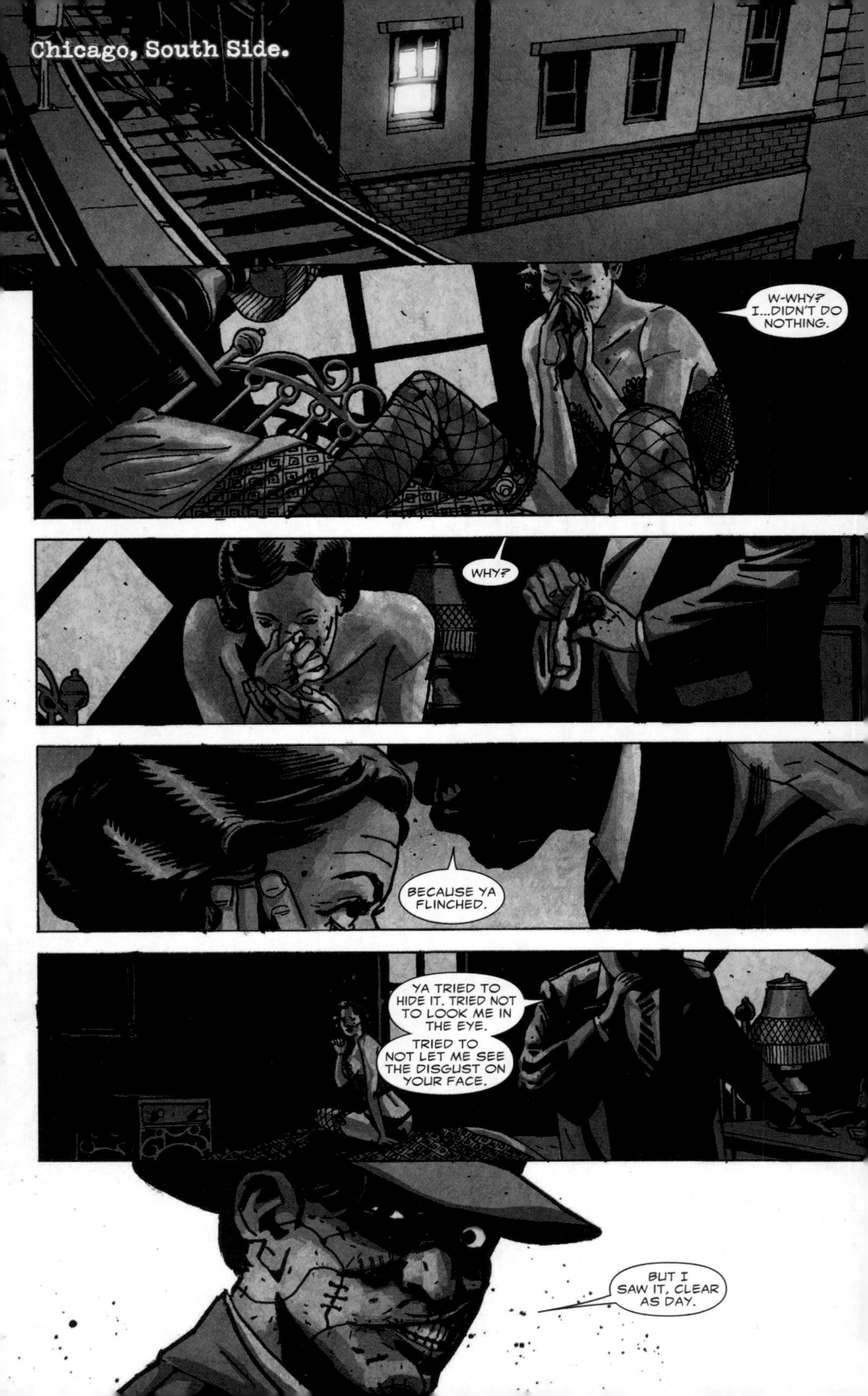
Chicago, South Side.
W-WHY? I...DIDN'T DO NOTHING.
WHY?
BECAUSE YA FLINCHED.
YA TRIED TO HIDE IT. TRIED NOT TO LOOK ME IN THE EYE.
TRIED TO NOT LET ME SEE THE DISGUST ON YOUR FACE.
BUT I SAW IT, CLEAR AS DAY.

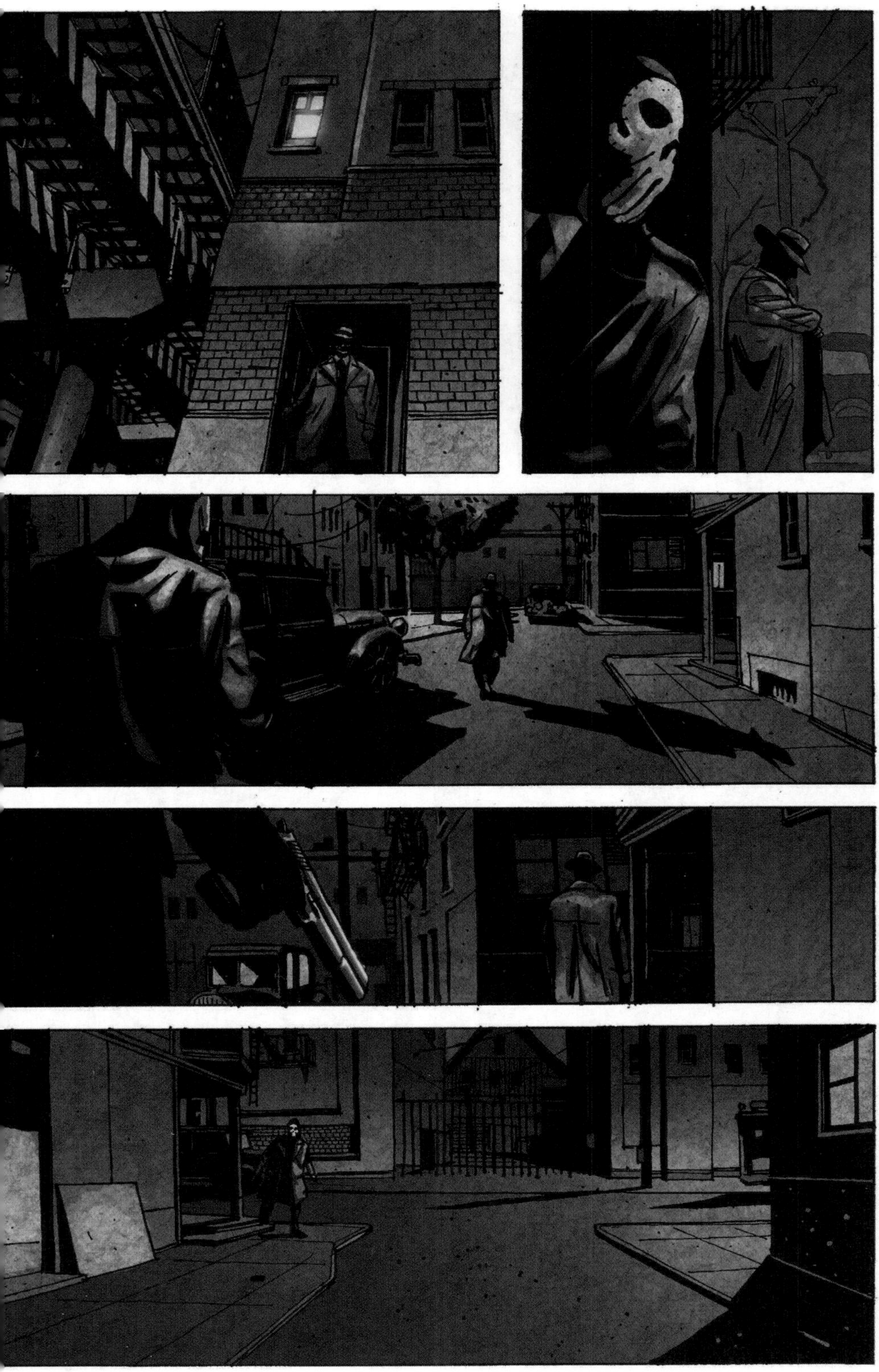

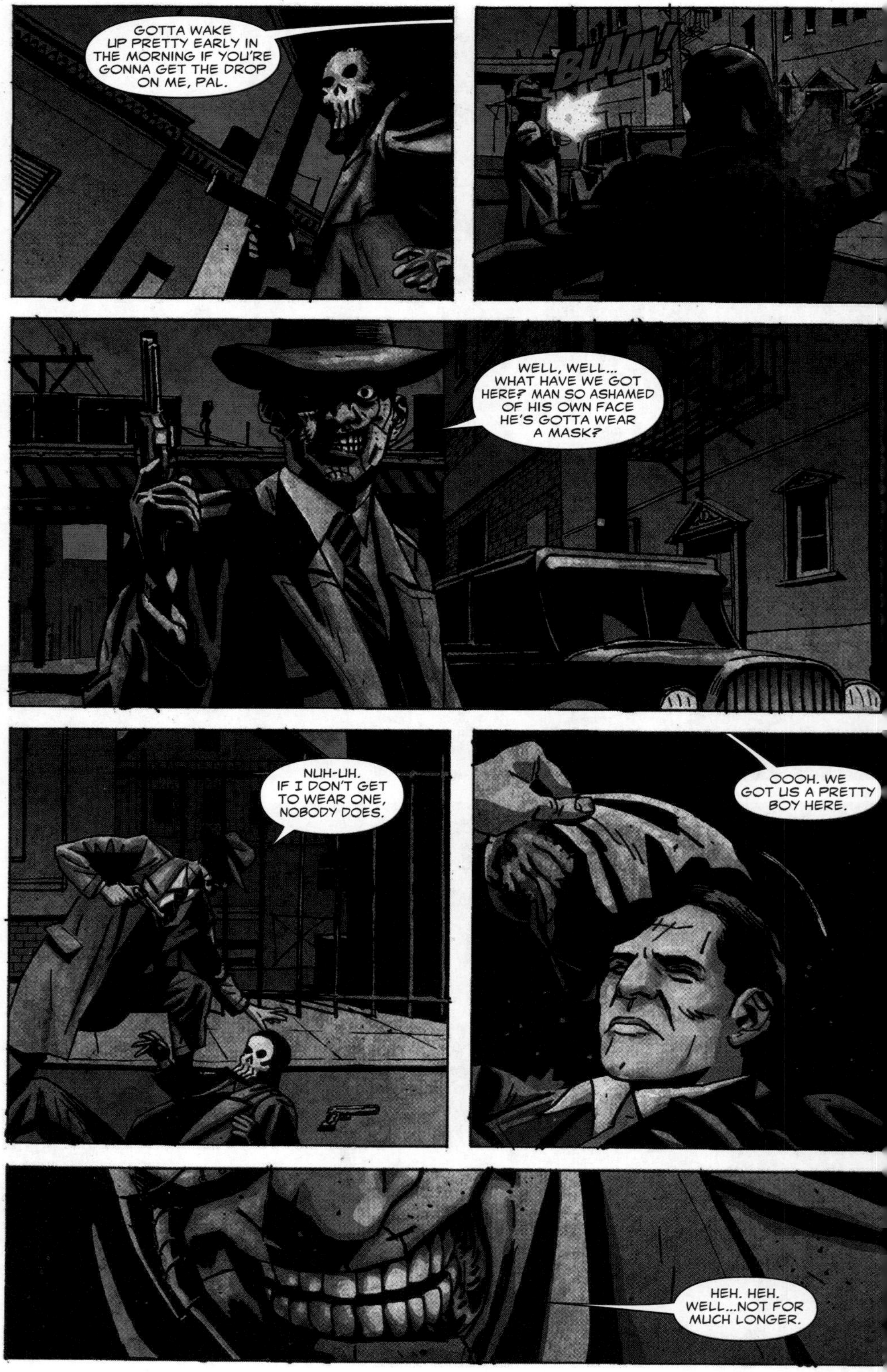
GOTTA WAKE UP PRETTY EARLY IN THE MORNING IF YOU'RE GONNA GET THE DROP ON ME, PAL.
BLAM!
WELL, WELL... WHAT HAVE WE GOT HERE? MAN SO ASHAMED OF HIS OWN FACE HE'S GOTTA WEAR A MASK?
NUH-UH. IF I DON'T GET TO WEAR ONE, NOBODY DOES.
OOOH. WE GOT US A PRETTY BOY HERE.
HEH. HEH. WELL...NOT FOR MUCH LONGER.

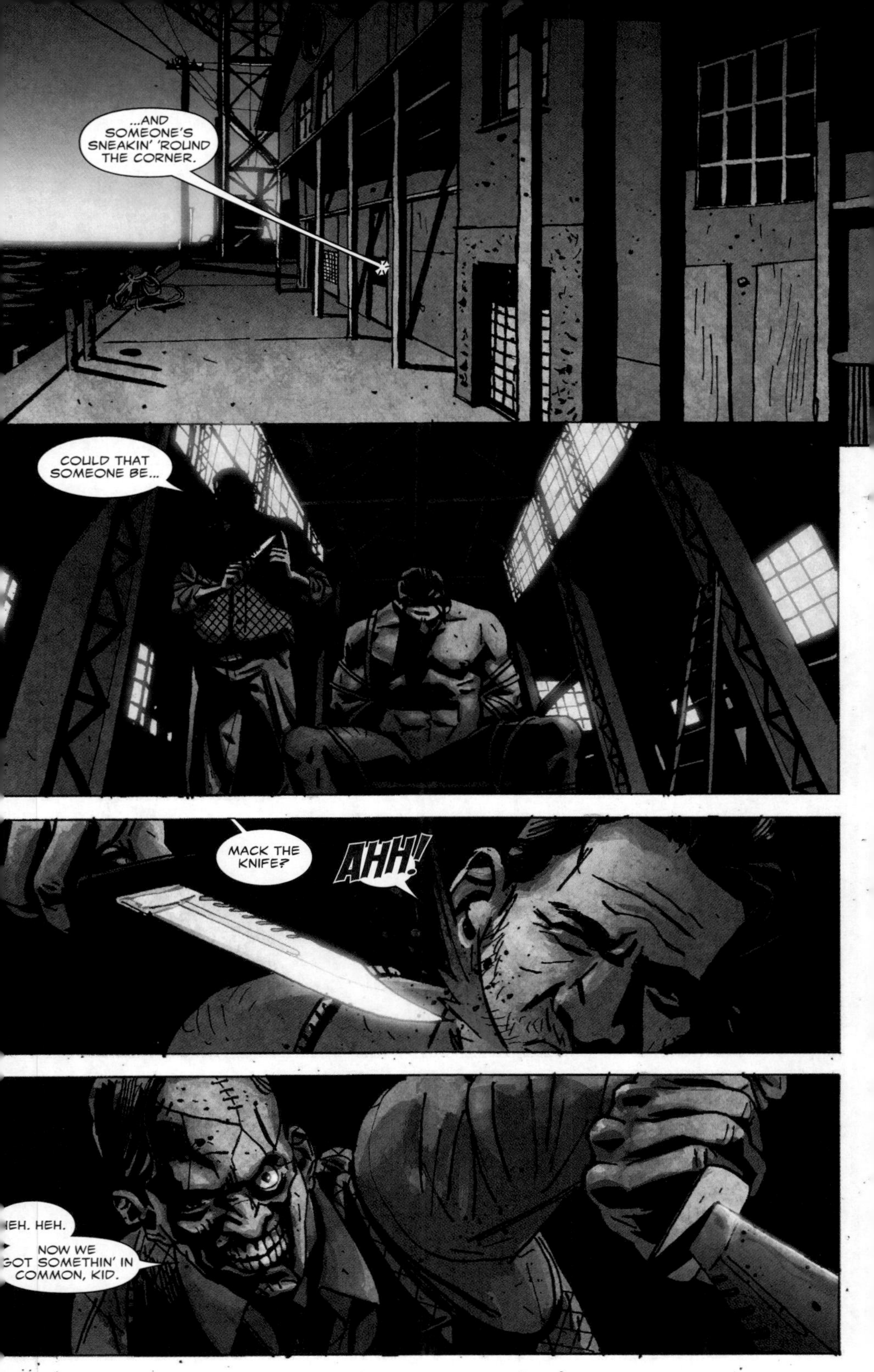
...AND SOMEONE'S SNEAKIN' 'ROUND THE CORNER.
COULD THAT SOMEONE BE...
MACK THE KNIFE?
AHH!
HEH. HEH.
NOW WE GOT SOMETHIN' IN COMMON, KID.

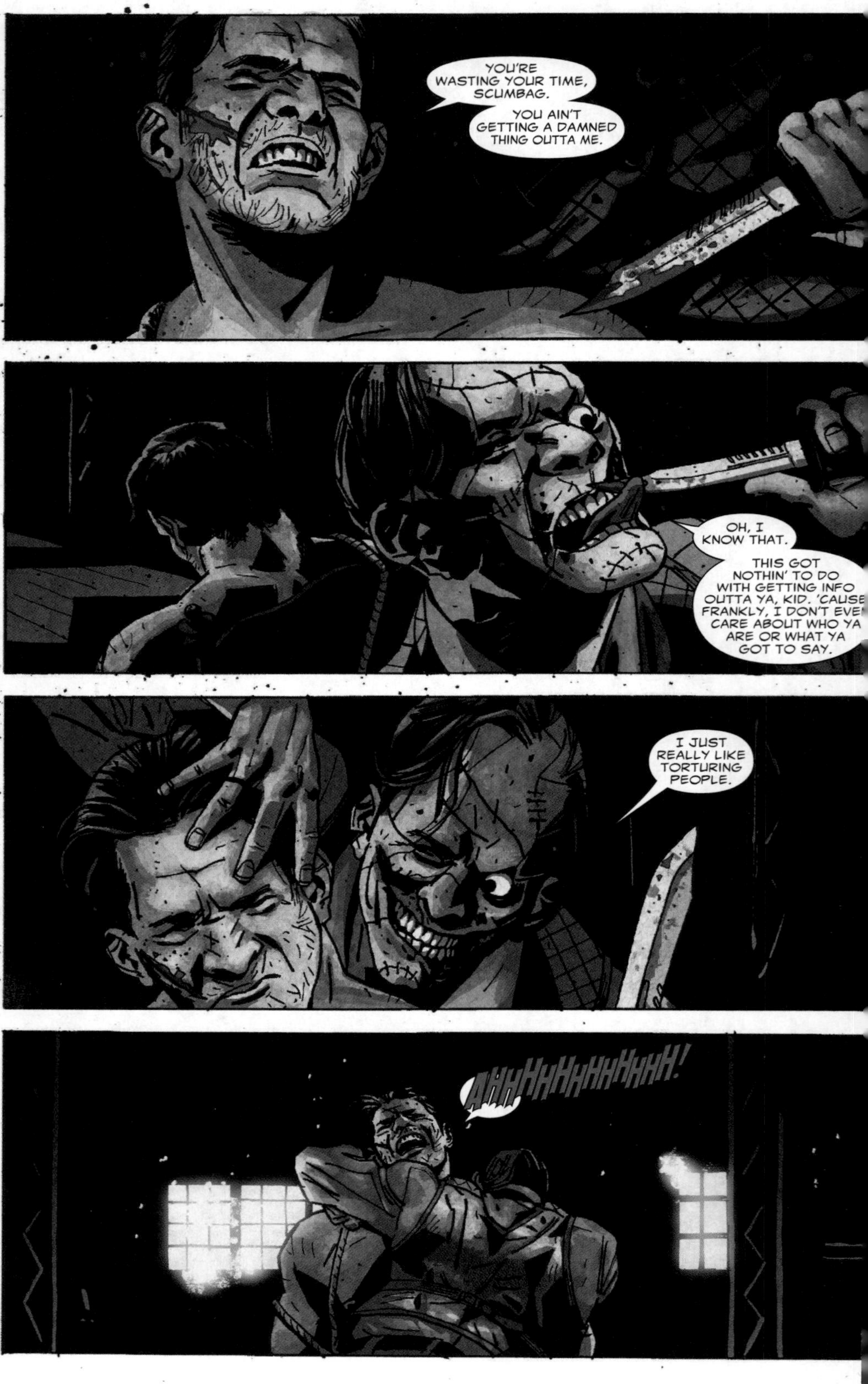
YOU'RE WASTING YOUR TIME, SCUMBAG.
YOU AIN'T GETTING A DAMNED THING OUTTA ME.
OH, I KNOW THAT.
THIS GOT NOTHIN' TO DO WITH GETTING INFO OUTTA YA, KID. 'CAUSE FRANKLY, I DON'T EVEN CARE ABOUT WHO YA ARE OR WHAT YA GOT TO SAY.
I JUST REALLY LIKE TORTURING PEOPLE.
AHHHHHHHHHHHH!

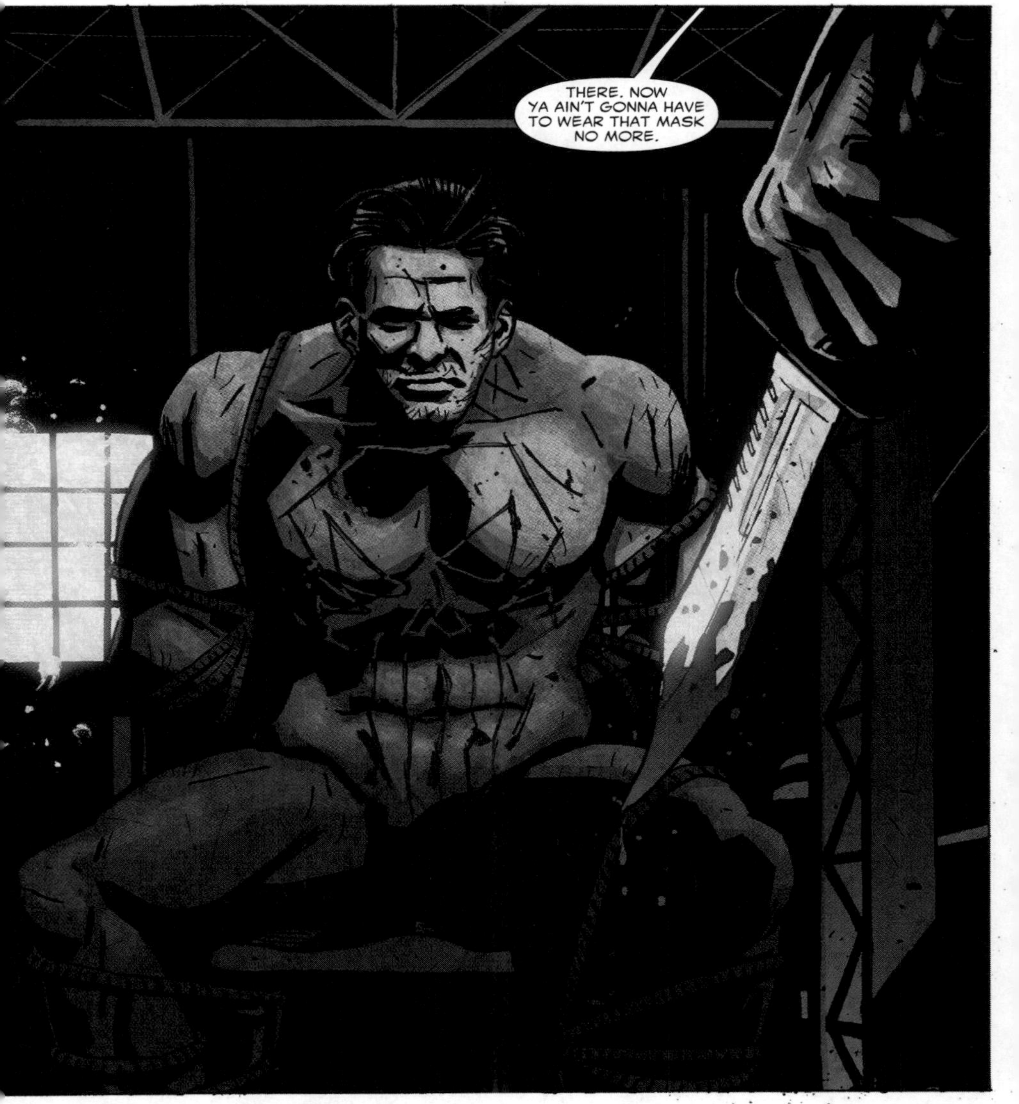
THERE. NOW YA AIN'T GONNA HAVE TO WEAR THAT MASK NO MORE.

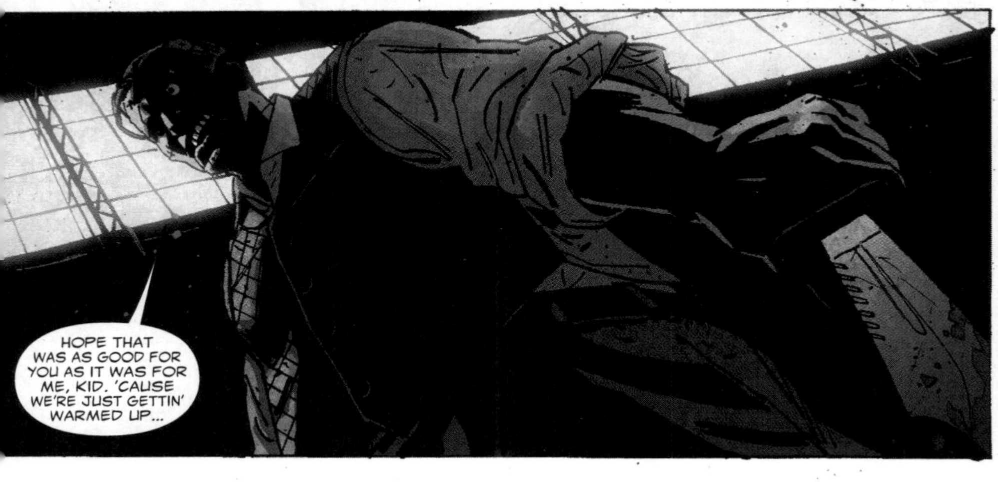
HOPE THAT WAS AS GOOD FOR YOU AS IT WAS FOR ME, KID. 'CAUSE WE'RE JUST GETTIN' WARMED UP...

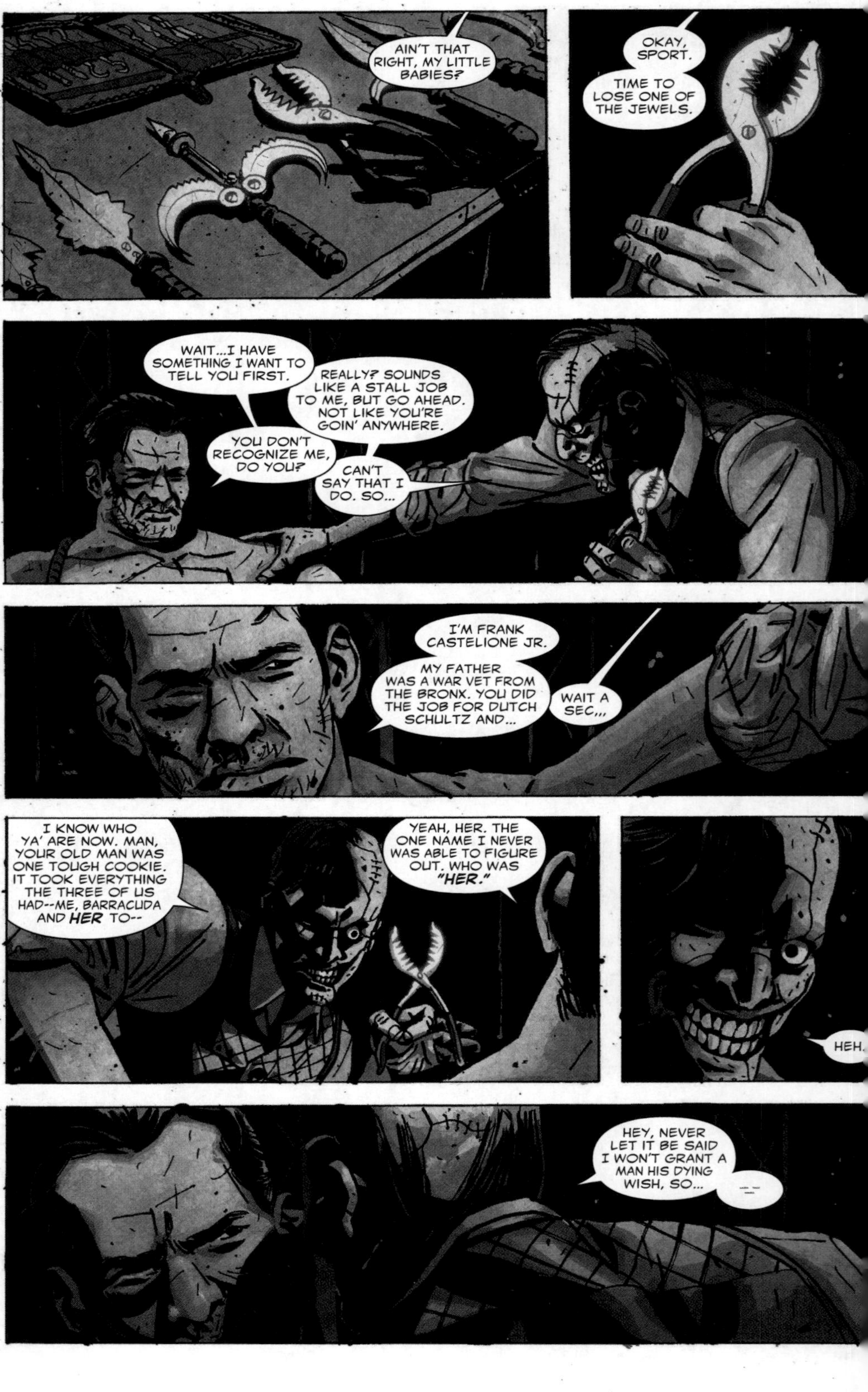
AIN'T THAT RIGHT, MY LITTLE BABIES?
OKAY, SPORT.
TIME TO LOSE ONE OF THE JEWELS.
WAIT...I HAVE SOMETHING I WANT TO TELL YOU FIRST.
REALLY? SOUNDS LIKE A STALL JOB TO ME, BUT GO AHEAD. NOT LIKE YOU'RE GOIN' ANYWHERE.
YOU DON'T RECOGNIZE ME, DO YOU?
CAN'T SAY THAT I DO. SO...
I'M FRANK CASTELIONE JR.
MY FATHER WAS A WAR VET FROM THE BRONX. YOU DID THE JOB FOR DUTCH SCHULTZ AND...
WAIT A SEC,,,
I KNOW WHO YA' ARE NOW. MAN, YOUR OLD MAN WAS ONE TOUGH COOKIE. IT TOOK EVERYTHING THE THREE OF US HAD--ME, BARRACUDA AND HER TO--
YEAH, HER. THE ONE NAME I NEVER WAS ABLE TO FIGURE OUT. WHO WAS "HER."
HEH.
HEY, NEVER LET IT BE SAID I WON'T GRANT A MAN HIS DYING WISH, SO...

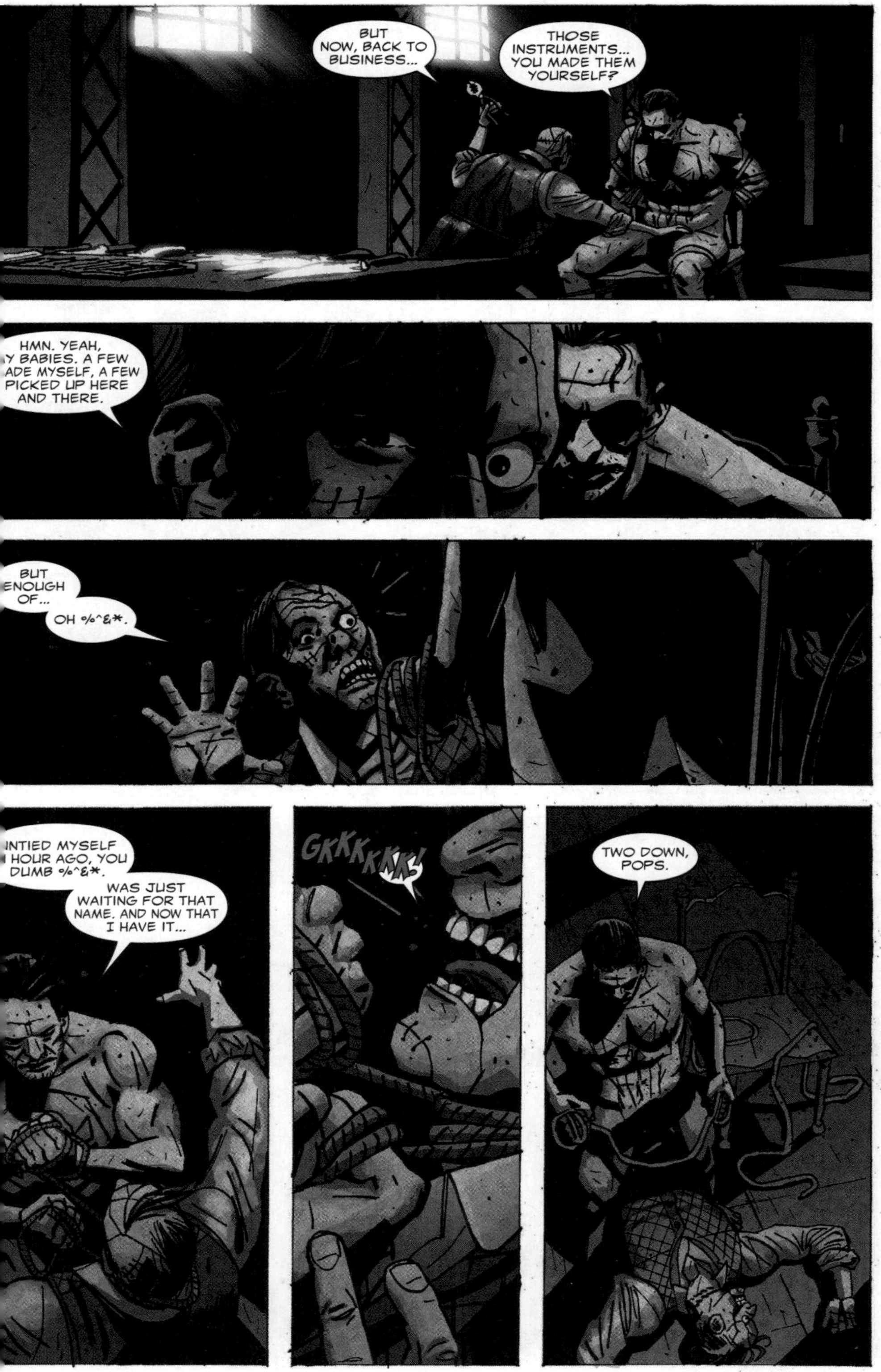
BUT NOW, BACK TO BUSINESS...
THOSE INSTRUMENTS... YOU MADE THEM YOURSELF?
HMN. YEAH, Y BABIES. A FEW ADE MYSELF, A FEW PICKED UP HERE AND THERE.
BUT ENOUGH OF...
OH %^&*.
NTIED MYSELF HOUR AGO, YOU DUMB %^&*.
WAS JUST WAITING FOR THAT NAME. AND NOW THAT I HAVE IT...
GKKKKKK!
TWO DOWN, POPS.

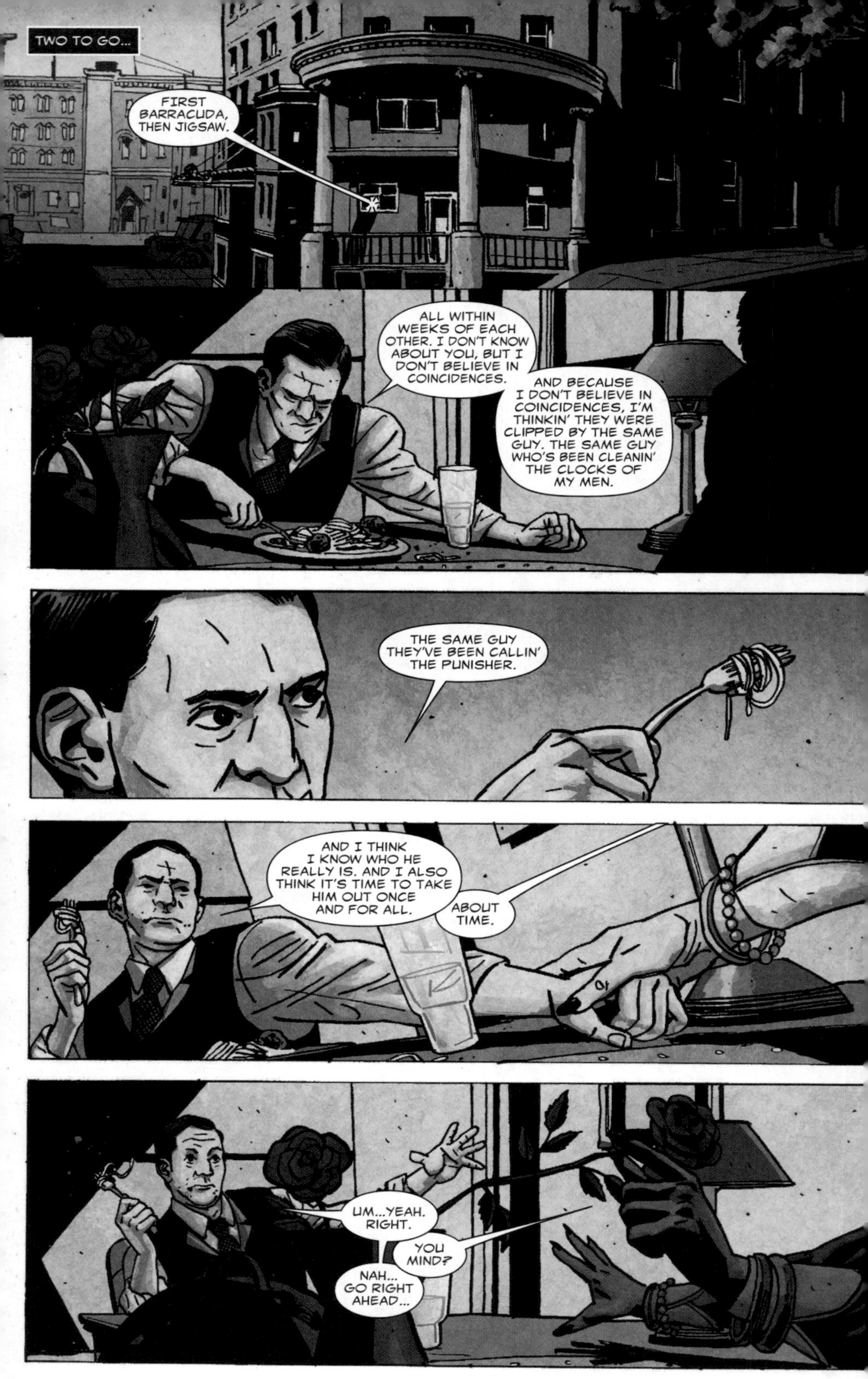
TWO TO GO...
FIRST BARRACUDA, THEN JIGSAW.
ALL WITHIN WEEKS OF EACH OTHER. I DON'T KNOW ABOUT YOU, BUT I DON'T BELIEVE IN COINCIDENCES.
AND BECAUSE I DON'T BELIEVE IN COINCIDENCES, I'M THINKIN' THEY WERE CLIPPED BY THE SAME GUY. THE SAME GUY WHO'S BEEN CLEANIN' THE CLOCKS OF MY MEN.
THE SAME GUY THEY'VE BEEN CALLIN' THE PUNISHER.
AND I THINK I KNOW WHO HE REALLY IS. AND I ALSO THINK IT'S TIME TO TAKE HIM OUT ONCE AND FOR ALL.
ABOUT TIME.
UM...YEAH. RIGHT.
YOU MIND?
NAH... GO RIGHT AHEAD...

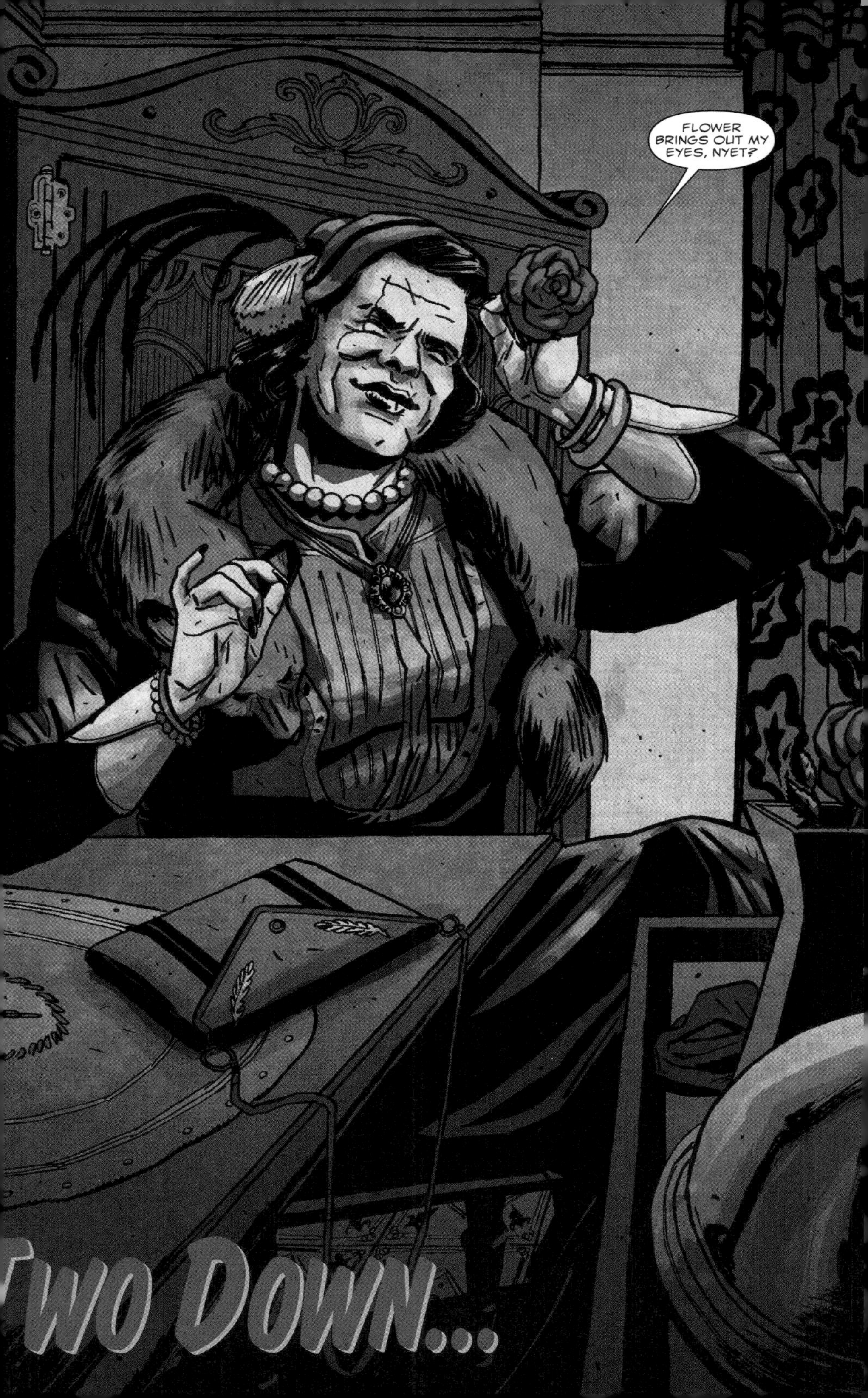
FLOWER BRINGS OUT MY EYES, NYET?
TWO DOWN...

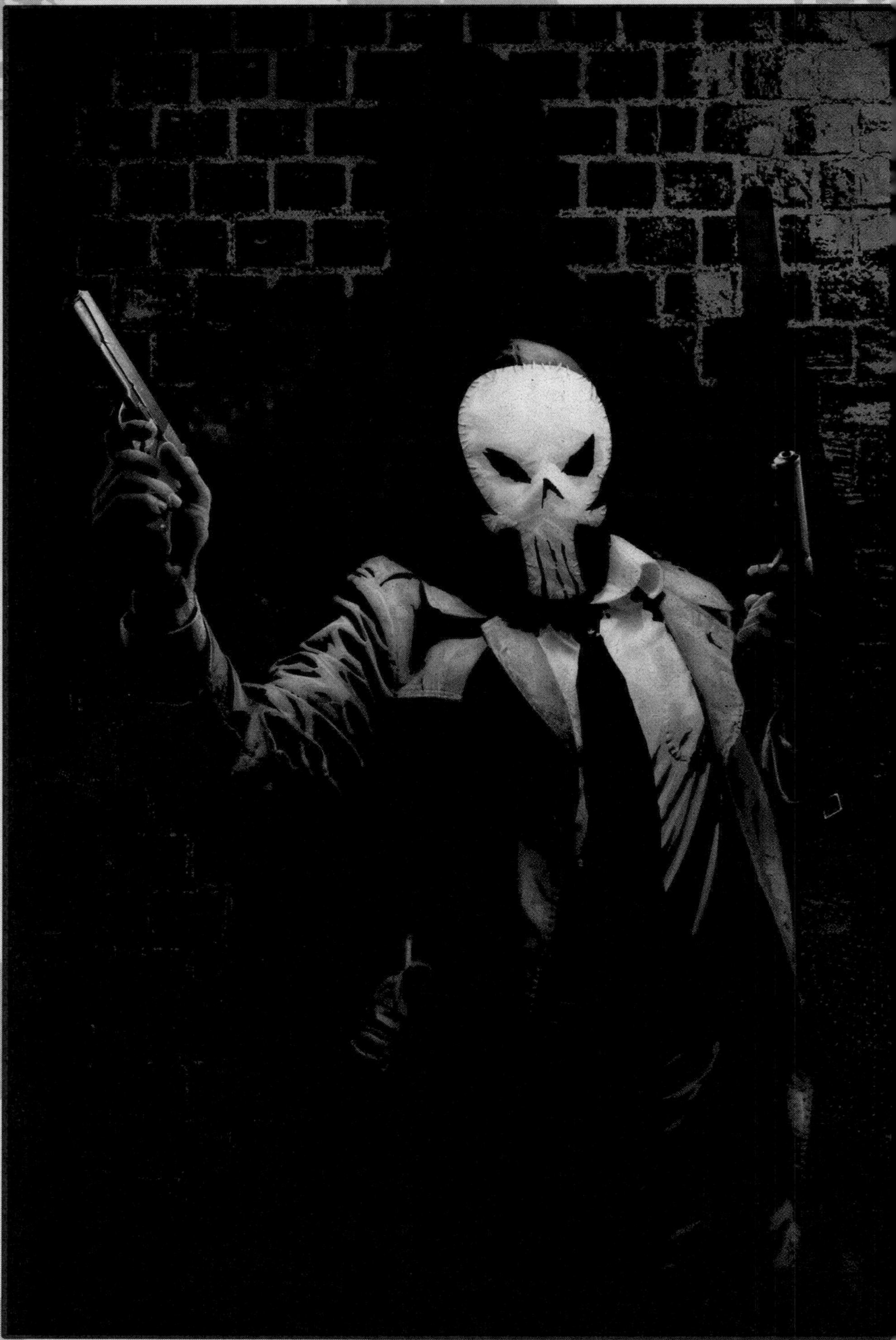

FOUR

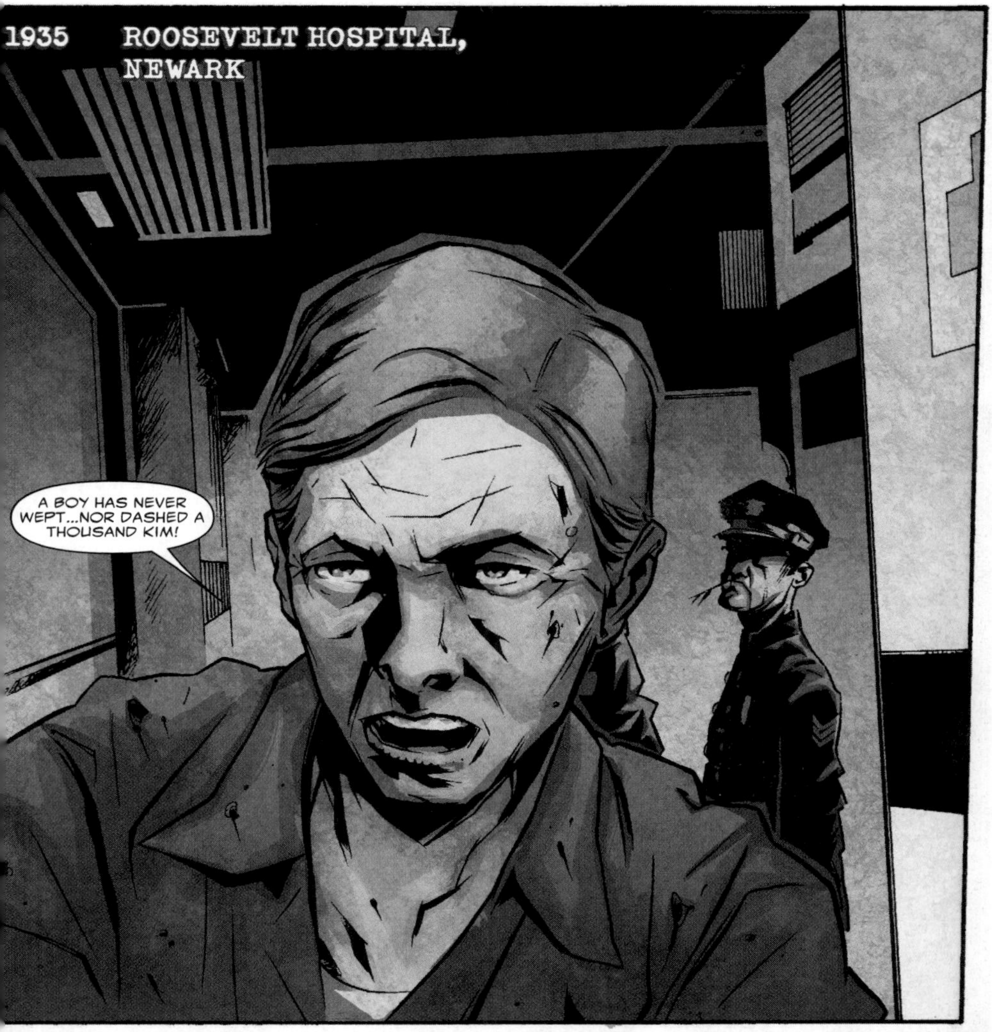
1935 ROOSEVELT HOSPITAL, NEWARK
A BOY HAS NEVER WEPT...NOR DASHED A THOUSAND KIM!

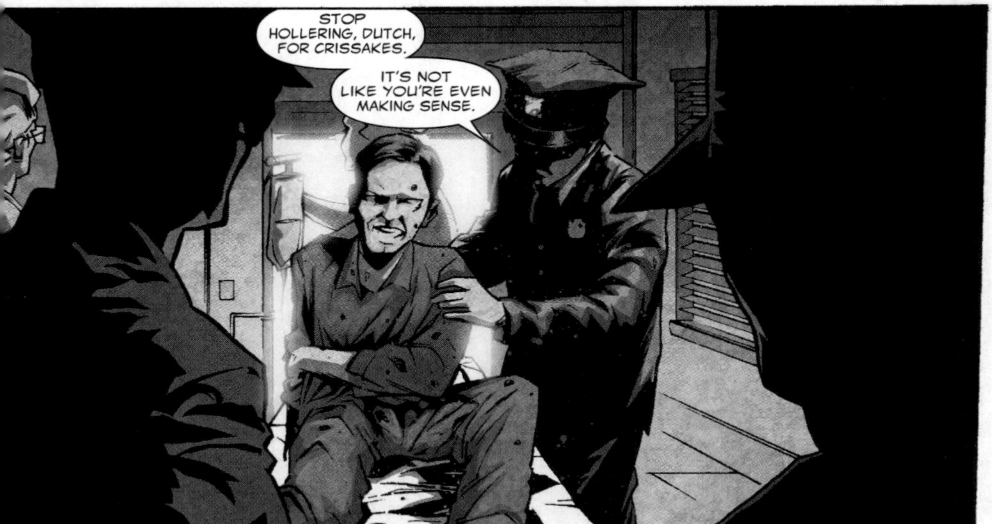
STOP HOLLERING, DUTCH, FOR CRISSAKES.
IT'S NOT LIKE YOU'RE EVEN MAKING SENSE.

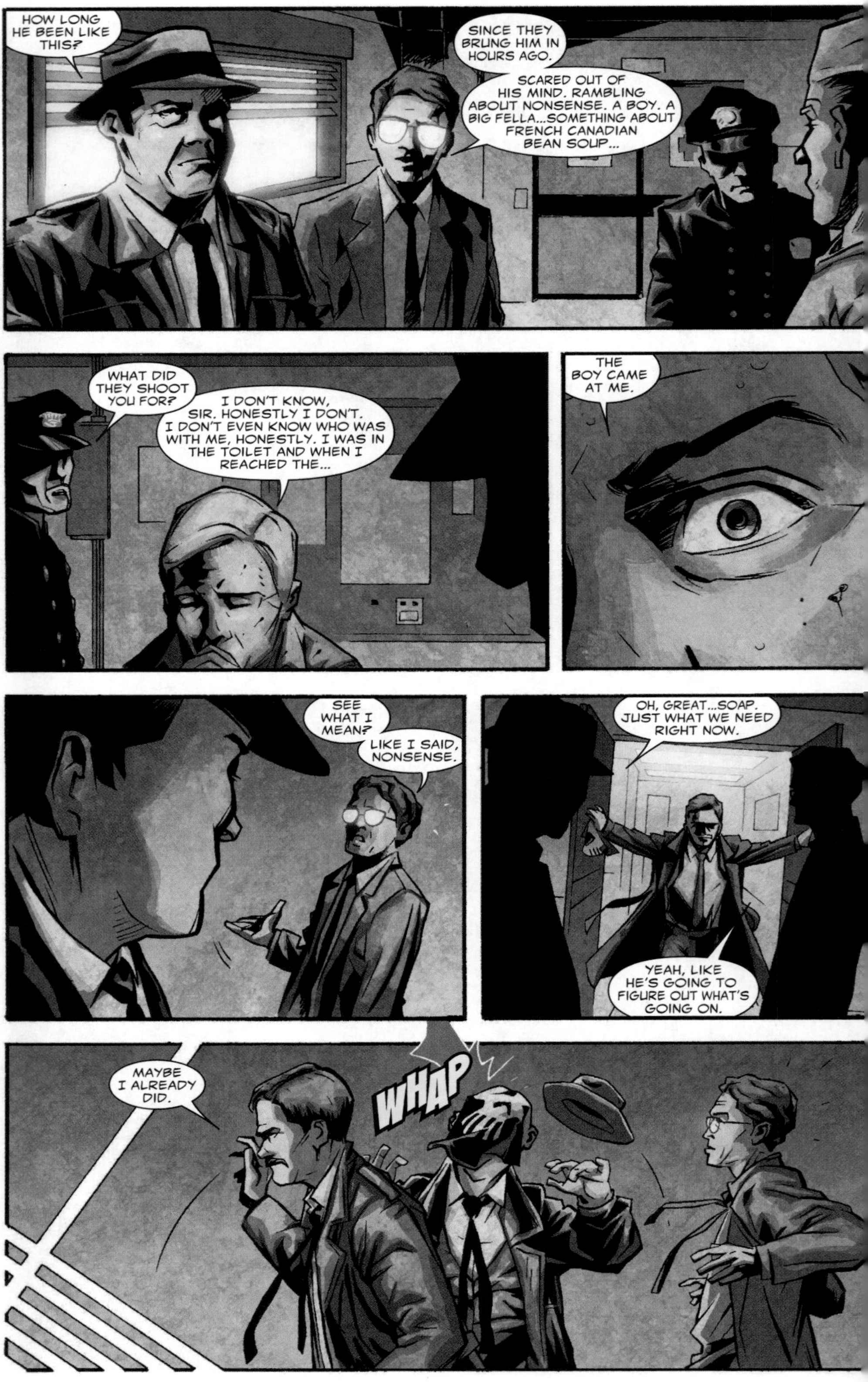
HOW LONG HE BEEN LIKE THIS?
SINCE THEY BRUNG HIM IN HOURS AGO.
SCARED OUT OF HIS MIND. RAMBLING ABOUT NONSENSE. A BOY. A BIG FELLA...SOMETHING ABOUT FRENCH CANADIAN BEAN SOUP...
WHAT DID THEY SHOOT YOU FOR?
I DON'T KNOW, SIR. HONESTLY I DON'T. I DON'T EVEN KNOW WHO WAS WITH ME, HONESTLY. I WAS IN THE TOILET AND WHEN I REACHED THE...
THE BOY CAME AT ME.
SEE WHAT I MEAN?
LIKE I SAID, NONSENSE.
OH, GREAT...SOAP. JUST WHAT WE NEED RIGHT NOW.
YEAH, LIKE HE'S GOING TO FIGURE OUT WHAT'S GOING ON.
MAYBE I ALREADY DID.
WHAP

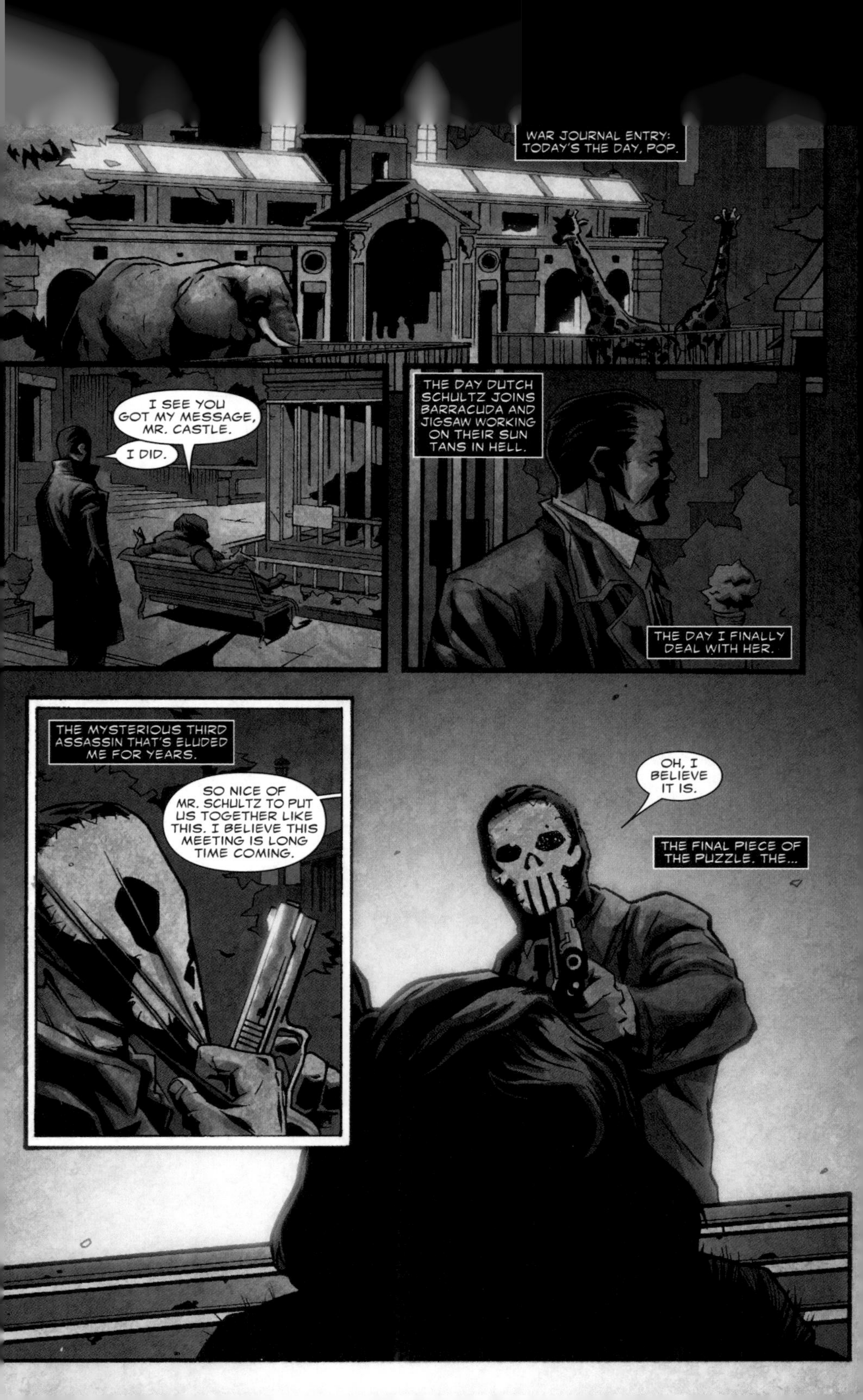

WAR JOURNAL ENTRY: TODAY'S THE DAY, POP.
I SEE YOU GOT MY MESSAGE, MR. CASTLE.
I DID.
THE DAY DUTCH SCHULTZ JOINS BARRACUDA AND JIGSAW WORKING ON THEIR SUN TANS IN HELL.
THE DAY I FINALLY DEAL WITH HER.
THE MYSTERIOUS THIRD ASSASSIN THAT'S ELUDED ME FOR YEARS.
SO NICE OF MR. SCHULTZ TO PUT US TOGETHER LIKE THIS. I BELIEVE THIS MEETING IS LONG TIME COMING.
OH, I BELIEVE IT IS.
THE FINAL PIECE OF THE PUZZLE. THE...

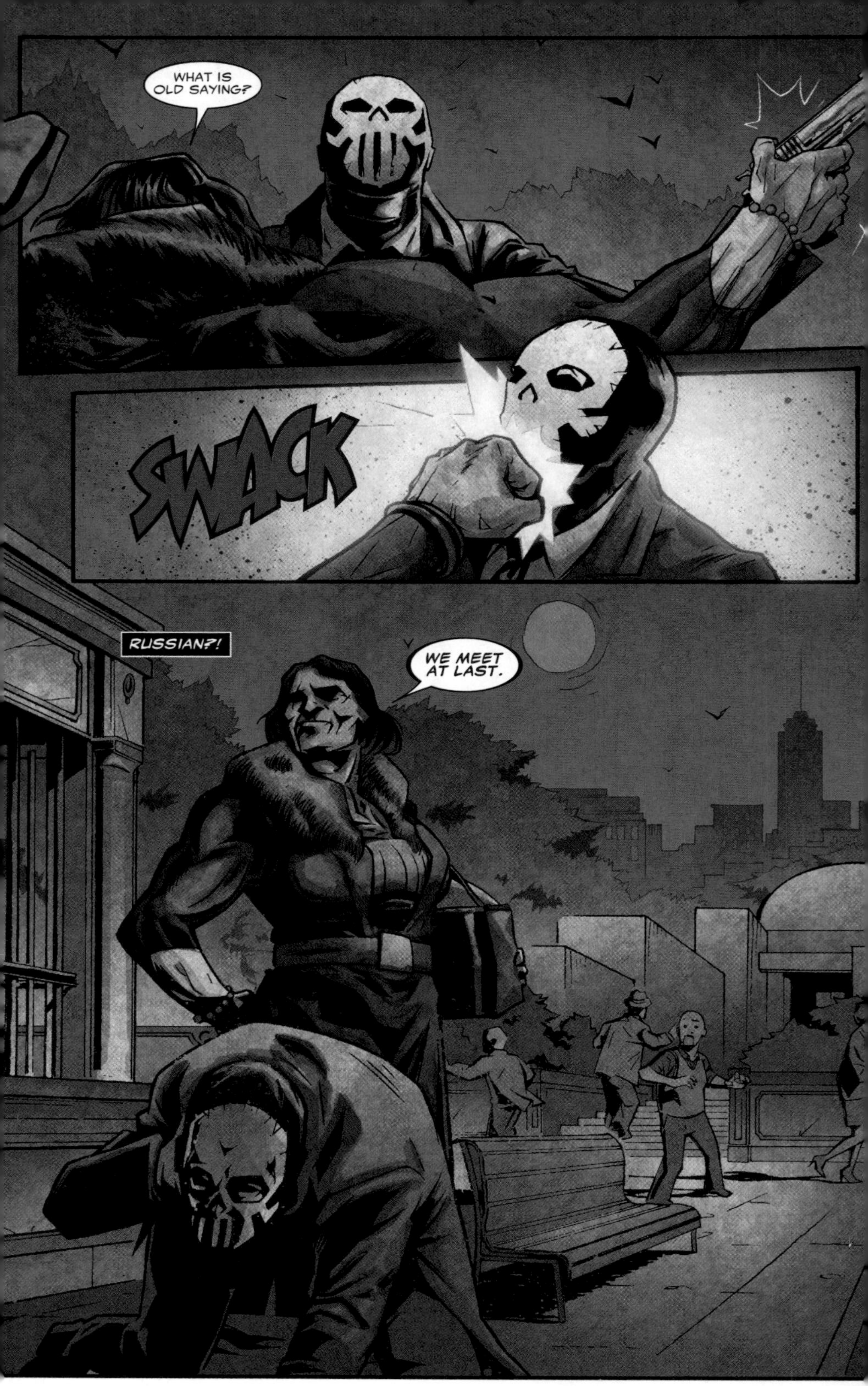
WHAT IS OLD SAYING?
SWACK
RUSSIAN?!
WE MEET AT LAST.

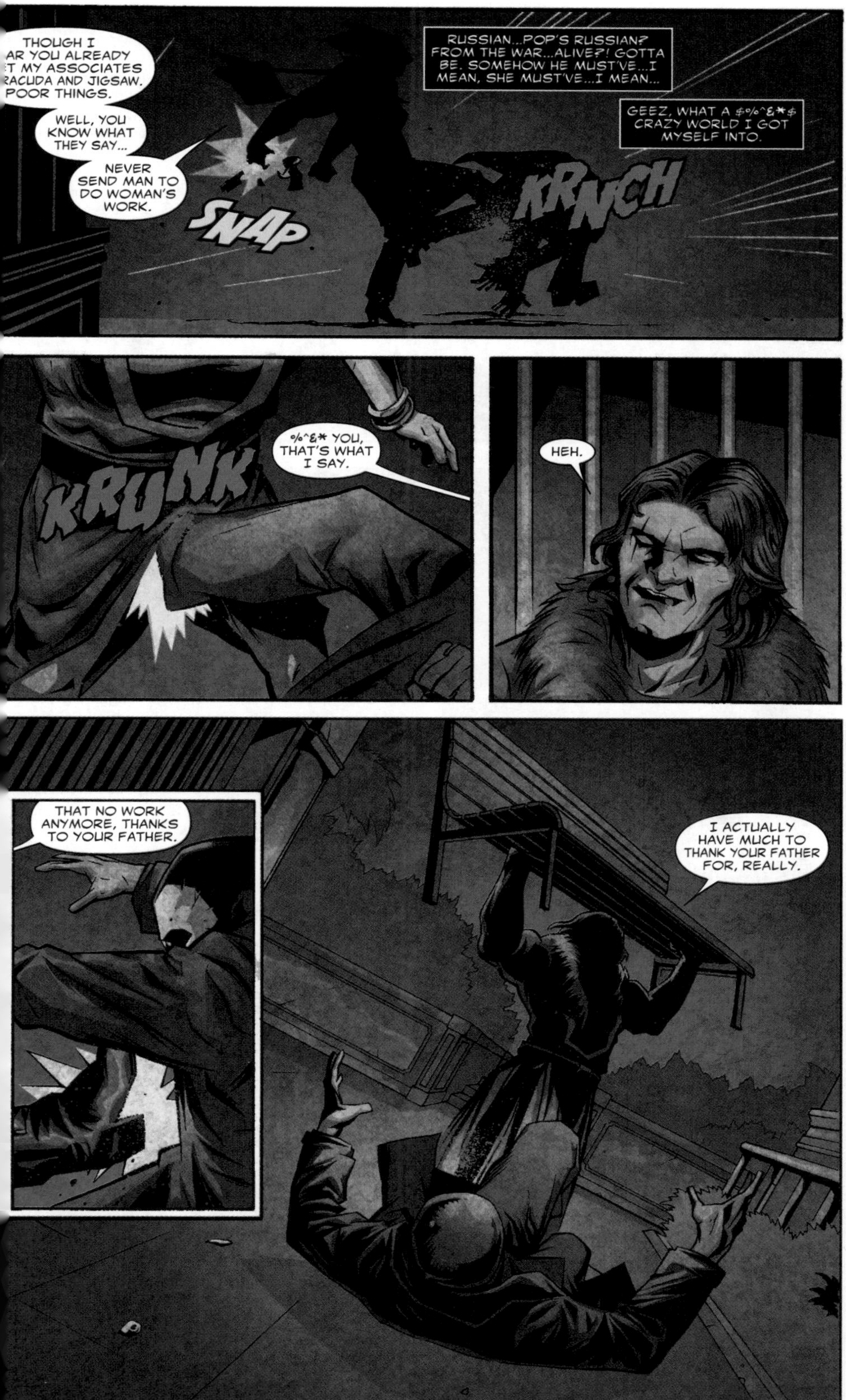
THOUGH I AR YOU ALREADY ET MY ASSOCIATES RACUDA AND JIGSAW. POOR THINGS.
WELL, YOU KNOW WHAT THEY SAY...
NEVER SEND MAN TO DO WOMAN'S WORK.
RUSSIAN...POP'S RUSSIAN? FROM THE WAR...ALIVE?! GOTTA BE. SOMEHOW HE MUST'VE...I MEAN, SHE MUST'VE...I MEAN...
GEEZ, WHAT A $%^&*$ CRAZY WORLD I GOT MYSELF INTO.
SNAP
KRNCH
KRUNK
%^&* YOU, THAT'S WHAT I SAY.
HEH.
THAT NO WORK ANYMORE, THANKS TO YOUR FATHER.
I ACTUALLY HAVE MUCH TO THANK YOUR FATHER FOR, REALLY.

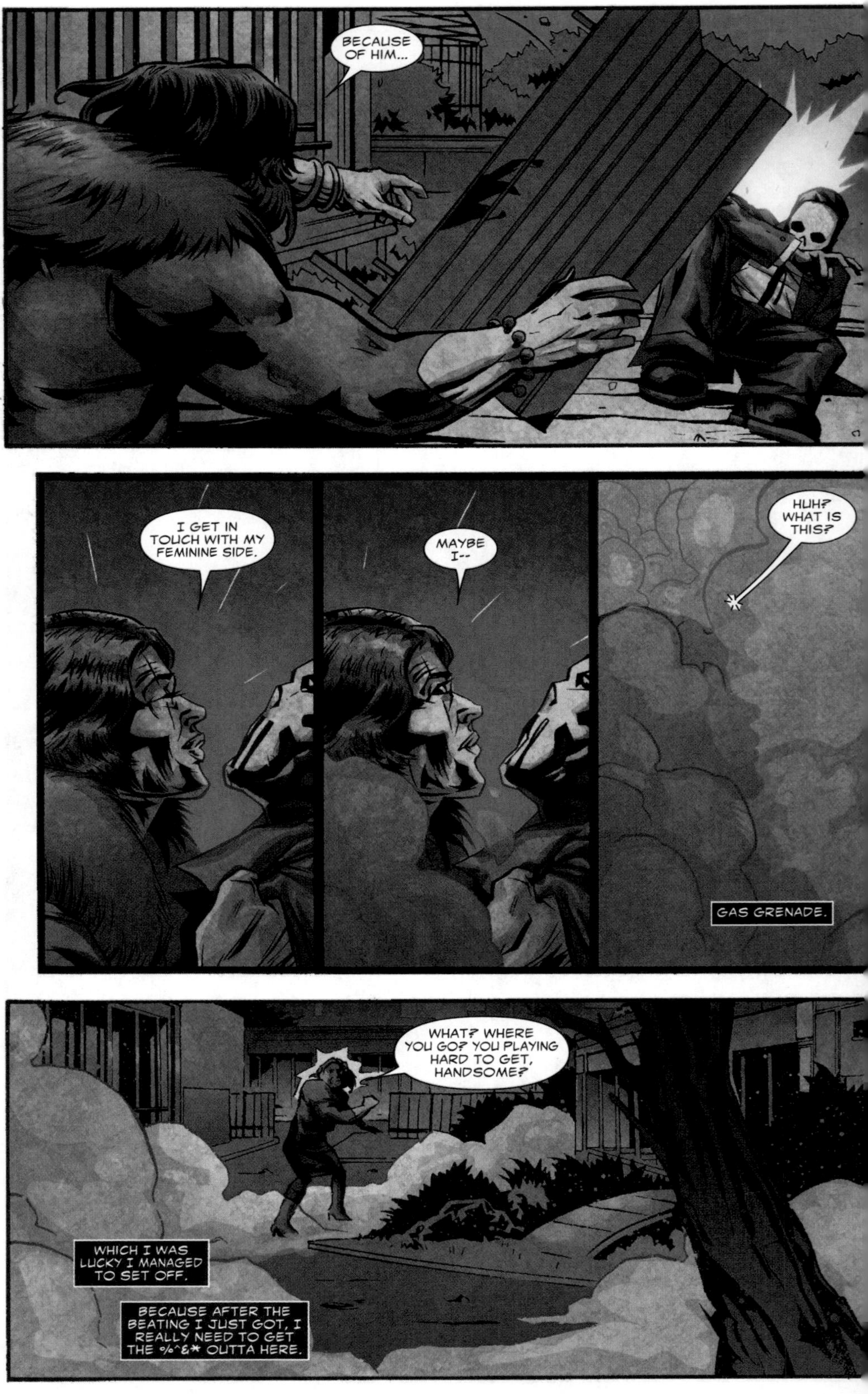
BECAUSE OF HIM...
I GET IN TOUCH WITH MY FEMININE SIDE.
MAYBE I--
HUH? WHAT IS THIS?
GAS GRENADE.
WHAT? WHERE YOU GO? YOU PLAYING HARD TO GET, HANDSOME?
WHICH I WAS LUCKY I MANAGED TO SET OFF.
BECAUSE AFTER THE BEATING I JUST GOT, I REALLY NEED TO GET THE %^&* OUTTA HERE.

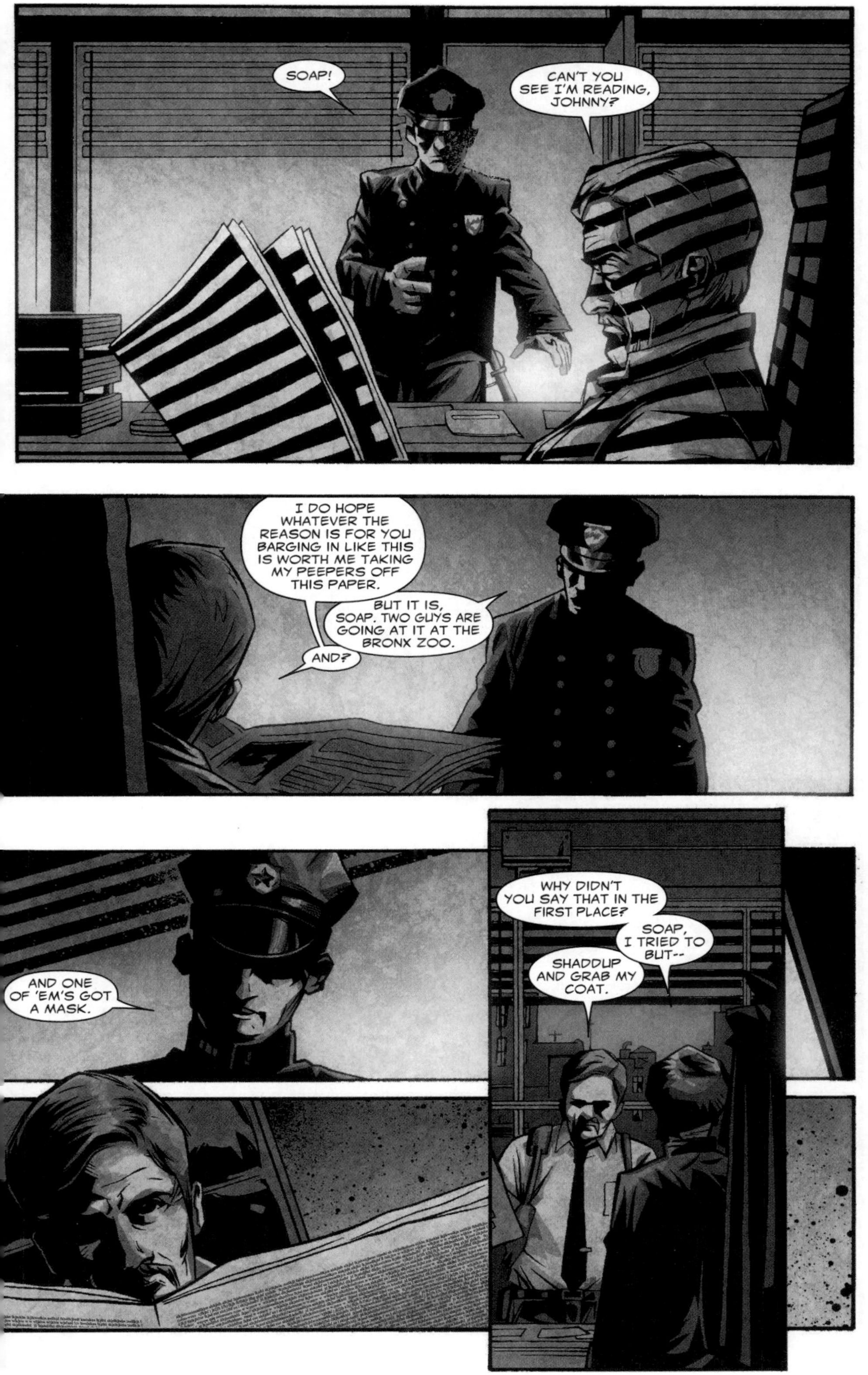
SOAP!
CAN'T YOU SEE I'M READING, JOHNNY?
I DO HOPE WHATEVER THE REASON IS FOR YOU BARGING IN LIKE THIS IS WORTH ME TAKING MY PEEPERS OFF THIS PAPER.
BUT IT IS, SOAP. TWO GUYS ARE GOING AT IT AT THE BRONX ZOO.
AND?
AND ONE OF 'EM'S GOT A MASK.
WHY DIDN'T YOU SAY THAT IN THE FIRST PLACE?
SOAP, I TRIED TO BUT--
SHADDUP AND GRAB MY COAT.

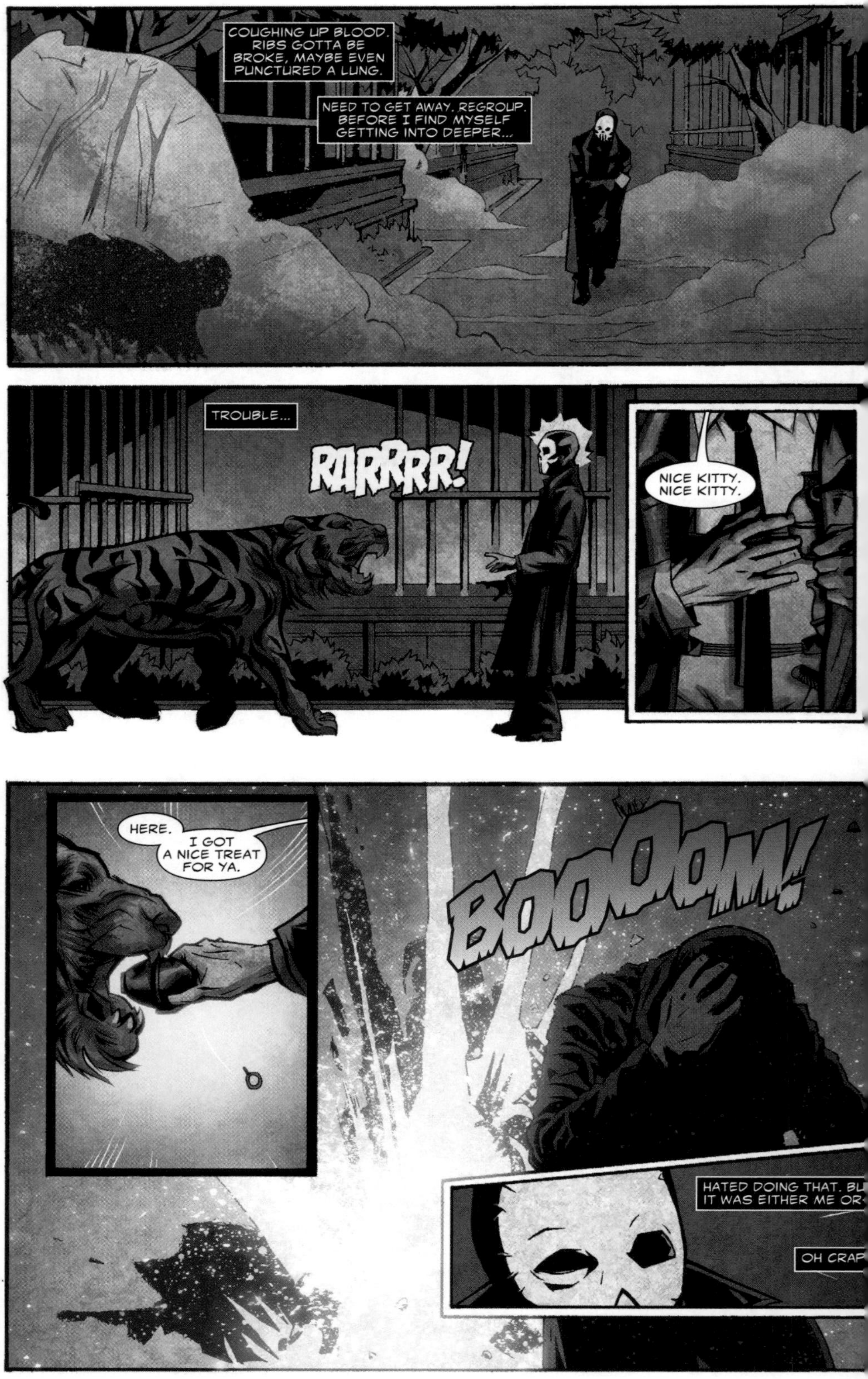
COUGHING UP BLOOD. RIBS GOTTA BE BROKE, MAYBE EVEN PUNCTURED A LUNG.
NEED TO GET AWAY. REGROUP. BEFORE I FIND MYSELF GETTING INTO DEEPER...
TROUBLE...
RARRRR!
NICE KITTY. NICE KITTY.
HERE.
I GOT A NICE TREAT FOR YA.
BOOOOM!
HATED DOING THAT. BU
IT WAS EITHER ME OR
OH CRAP

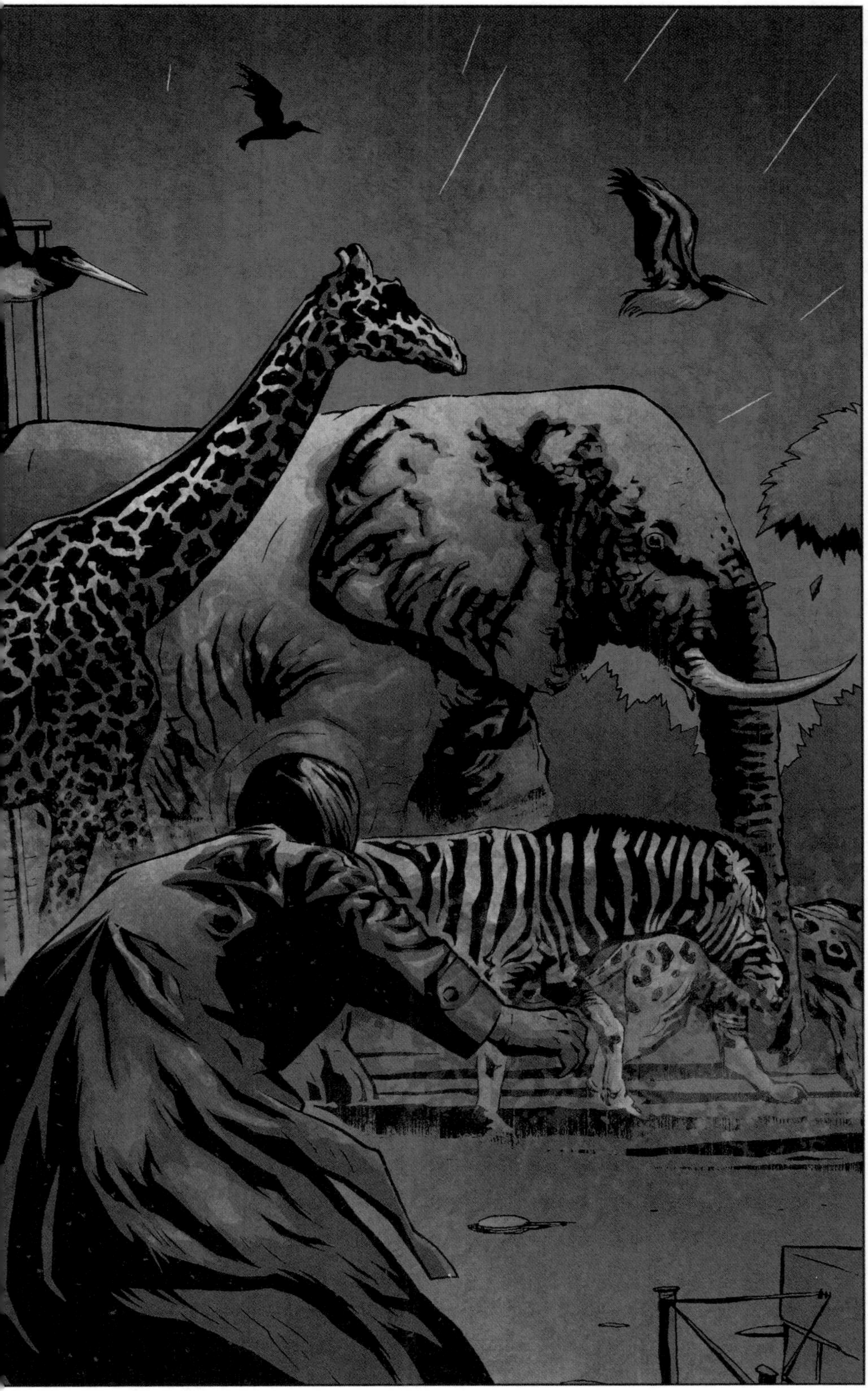

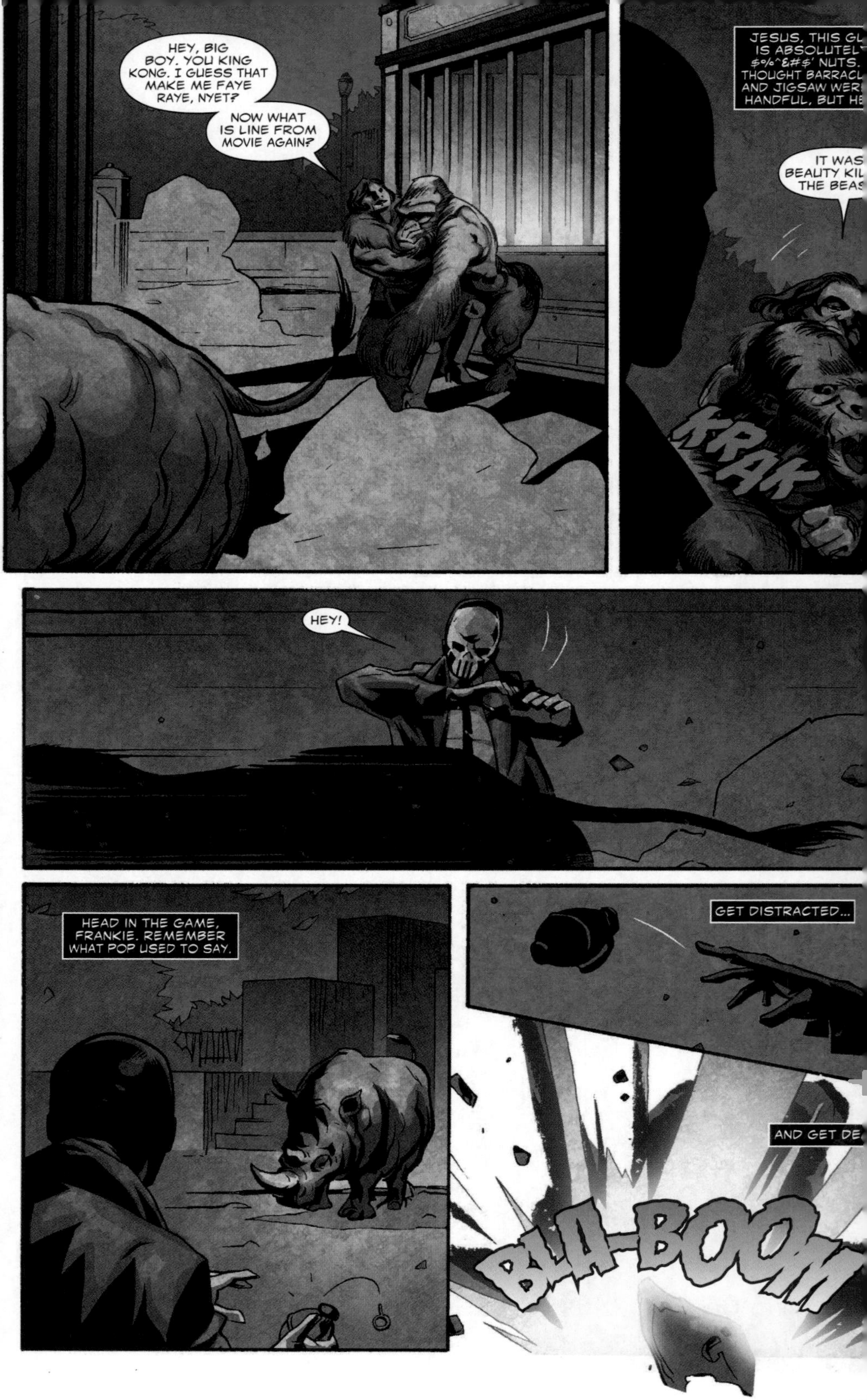
HEY, BIG BOY. YOU KING KONG. I GUESS THAT MAKE ME FAYE RAYE, NYET?
NOW WHAT IS LINE FROM MOVIE AGAIN?
JESUS, THIS GL IS ABSOLUTEL $%^&#$' NUTS. THOUGHT BARRACL AND JIGSAW WER HANDFUL, BUT HE
IT WAS BEAUTY KIL THE BEAS
KRAK
HEY!
HEAD IN THE GAME, FRANKIE. REMEMBER WHAT POP USED TO SAY.
GET DISTRACTED...
AND GET DE
BLA-BOOM

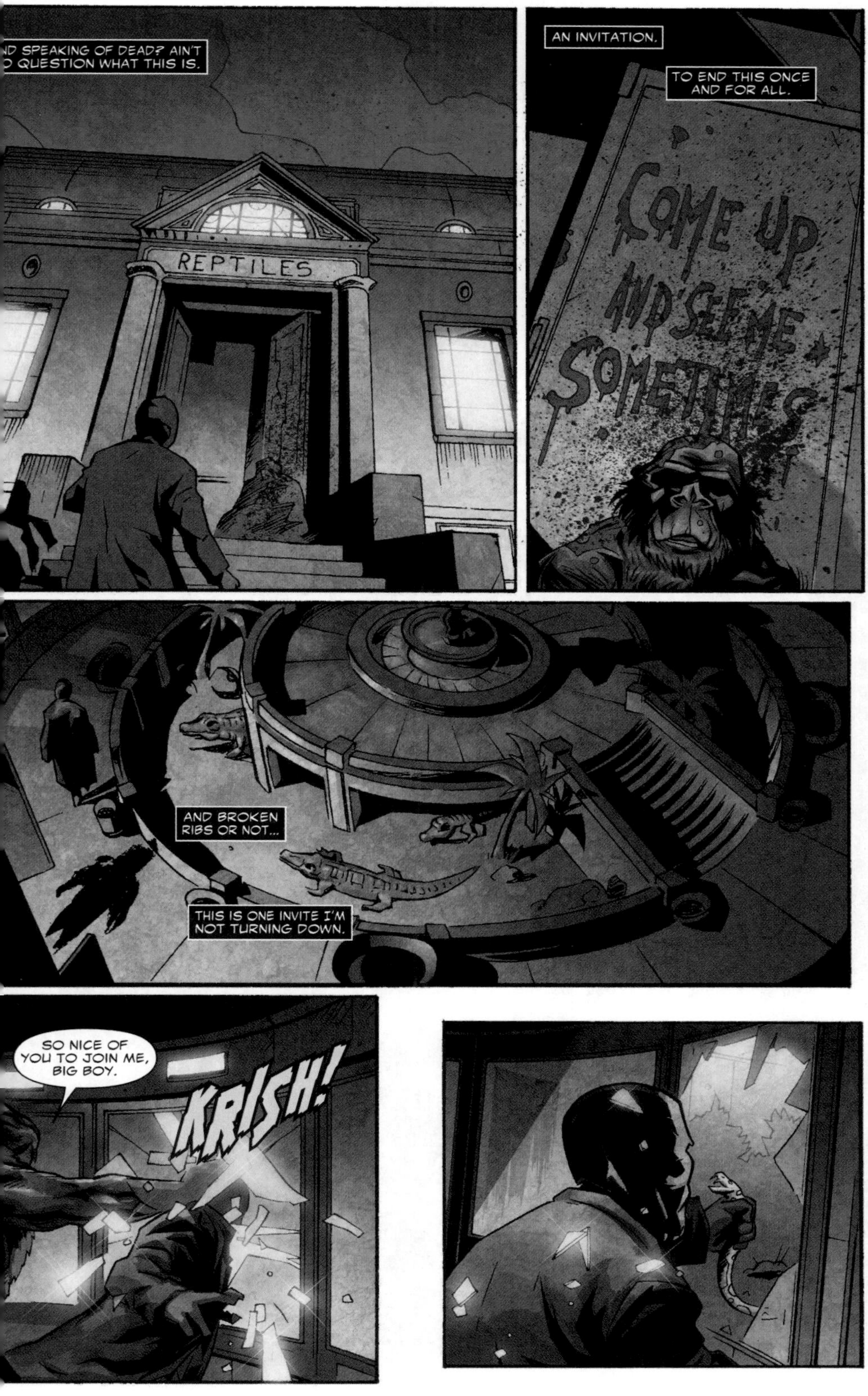
ND SPEAKING OF DEAD? AIN'T
O QUESTION WHAT THIS IS.
REPTILES
AN INVITATION.
TO END THIS ONCE AND FOR ALL.
COME UP AND SEE ME SOMETIMES
AND BROKEN RIBS OR NOT...
THIS IS ONE INVITE I'M NOT TURNING DOWN.
SO NICE OF YOU TO JOIN ME, BIG BOY.
KRISH!

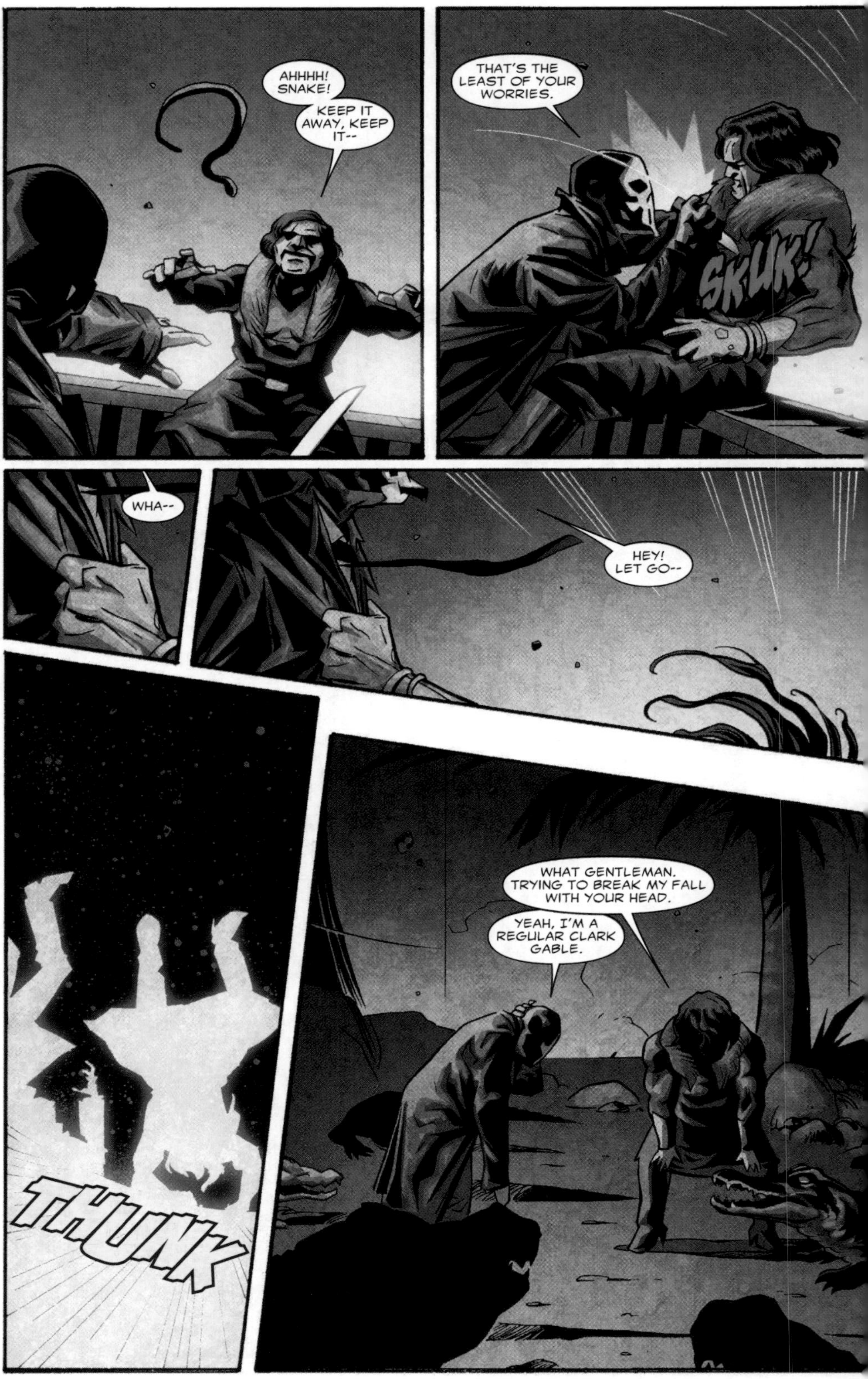
AHHHH! SNAKE!
KEEP IT AWAY, KEEP IT--
THAT'S THE LEAST OF YOUR WORRIES.
SKUK!
WHA--
HEY! LET GO--
THUNK
WHAT GENTLEMAN. TRYING TO BREAK MY FALL WITH YOUR HEAD.
YEAH, I'M A REGULAR CLARK GABLE.

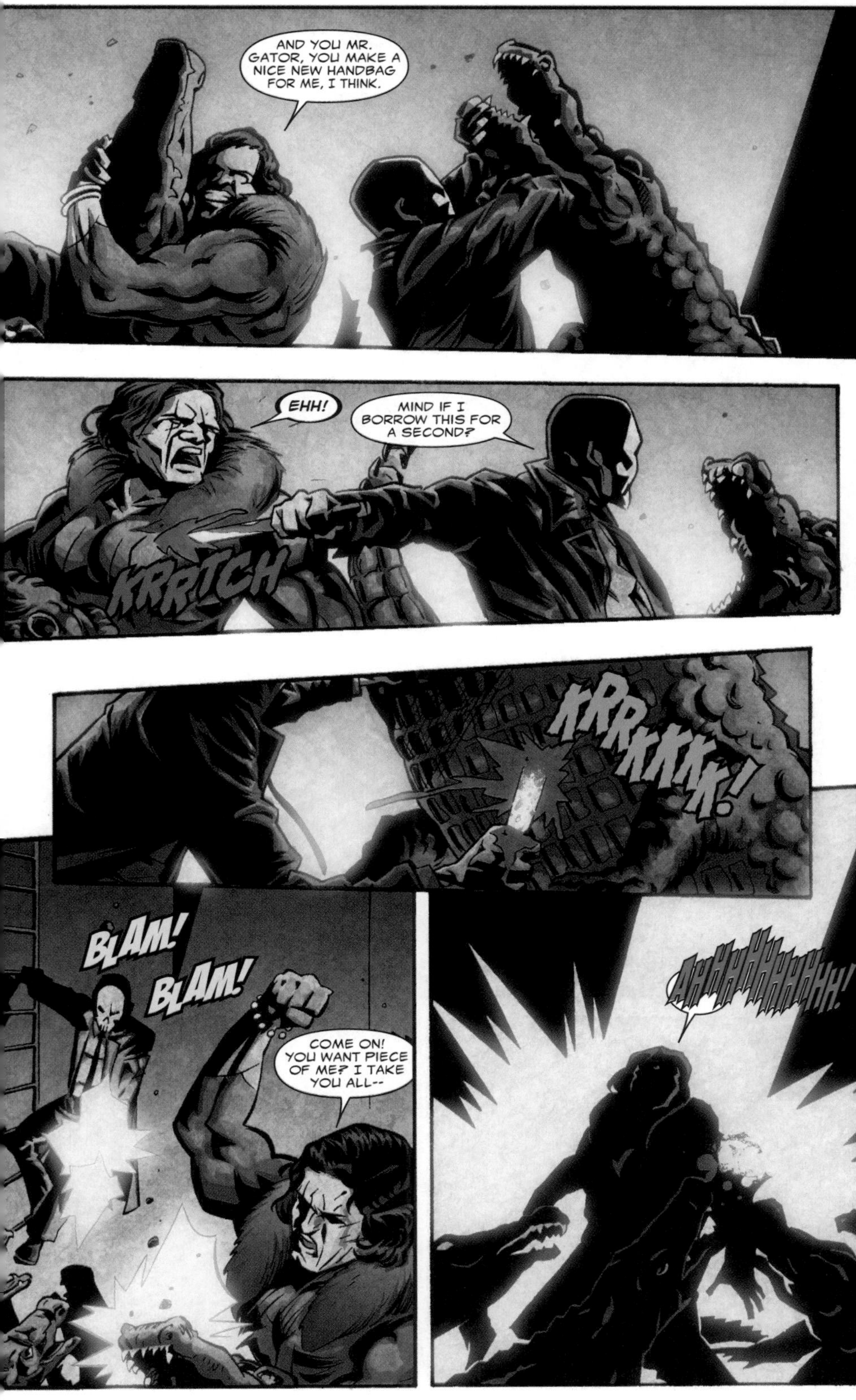
AND YOU MR. GATOR, YOU MAKE A NICE NEW HANDBAG FOR ME, I THINK.
EHH!
MIND IF I BORROW THIS FOR A SECOND?
KRRITCH
KRRKKKK!
BLAM!
BLAM!
COME ON! YOU WANT PIECE OF ME? I TAKE YOU ALL--
AHHHHHHHHHH!

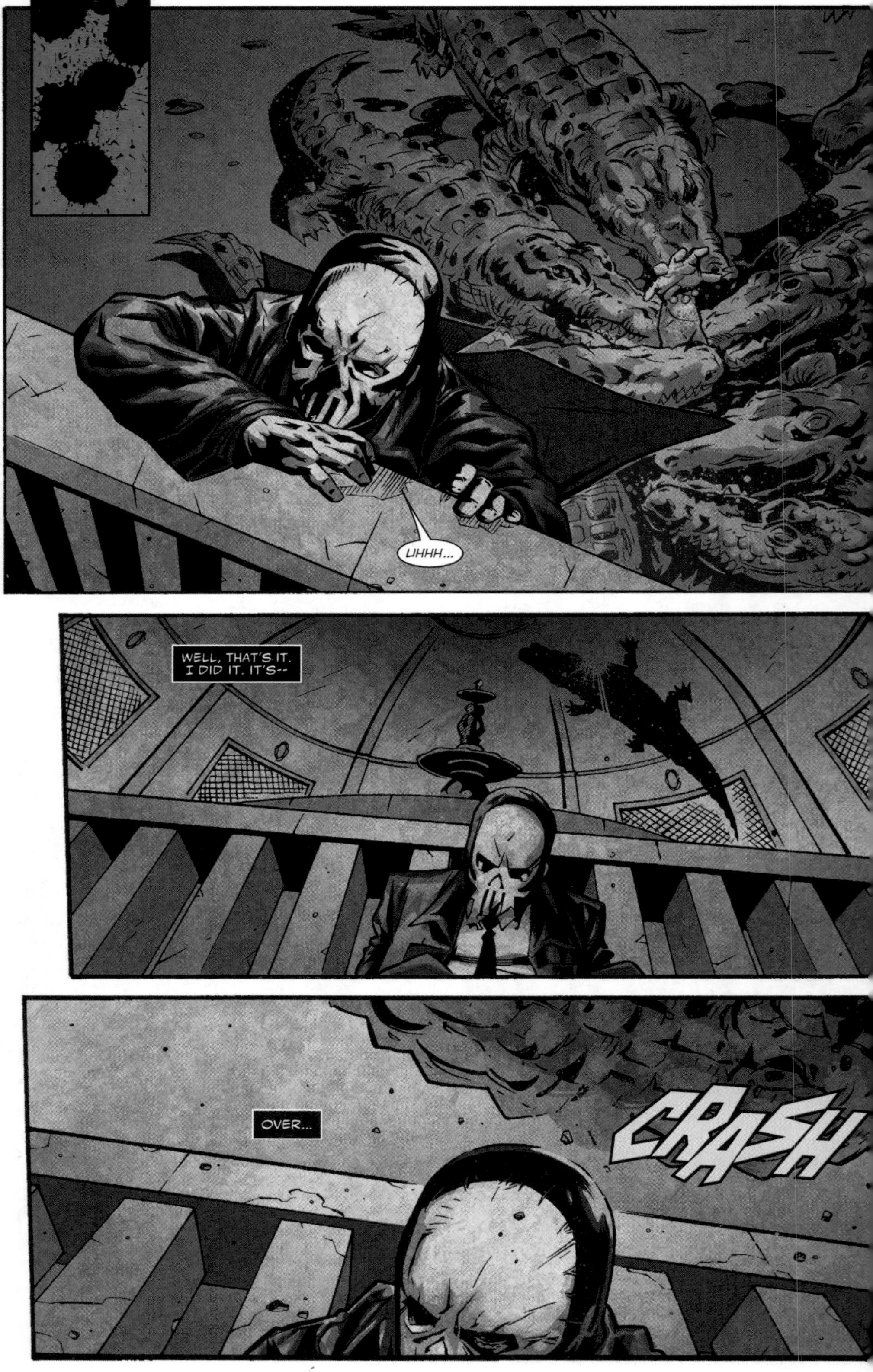
UHHH...
WELL, THAT'S IT. I DID IT. IT'S--
OVER...
CRASH

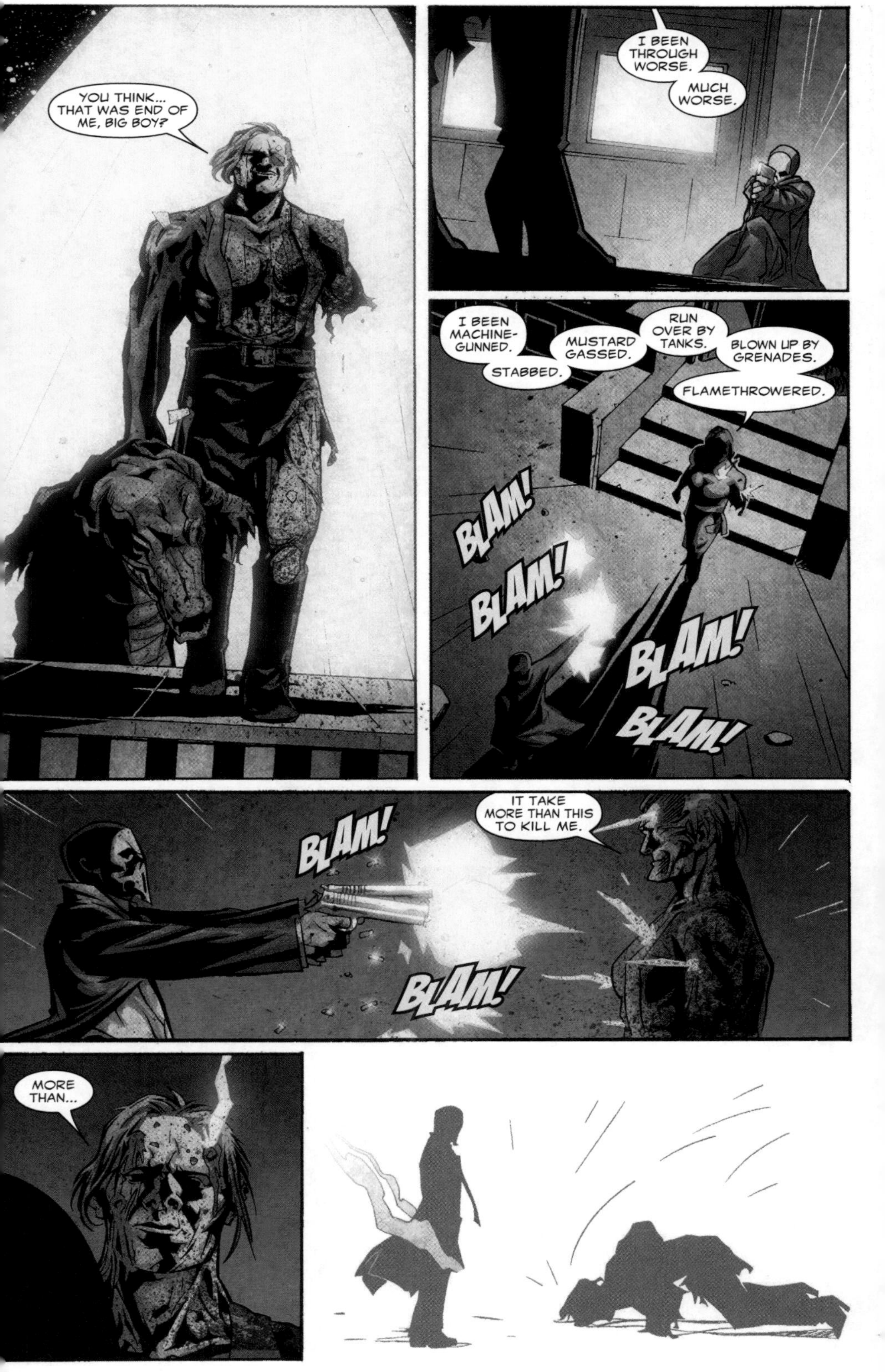

YOU THINK... THAT WAS END OF ME, BIG BOY?
I BEEN THROUGH WORSE.
MUCH WORSE.
I BEEN MACHINE-GUNNED.
STABBED.
MUSTARD GASSED.
RUN OVER BY TANKS.
BLOWN UP BY GRENADES.
FLAMETHROWERED.
BLAM!
BLAM!
BLAM!
BLAM!
BLAM!
IT TAKE MORE THAN THIS TO KILL ME.
BLAM!
MORE THAN...

JESUS. THIS IS LIKE WHAT HAPPENED TO ALL THE ANIMALS THAT *DIDN'T* MAKE IT TO NOAH'S ARK.

YOU KNOW WHAT HAPPENED HERE, SOAP?

NO I DON'T, JOHNNY.

BUT I CERTAINLY SUSPECT.

SOAP!

YOU GOTTA SEE THIS! YOU...WELL, YA AIN'T GONNA BELIEVE THIS, IT'S...

WELL, YOU WAS RIGHT.

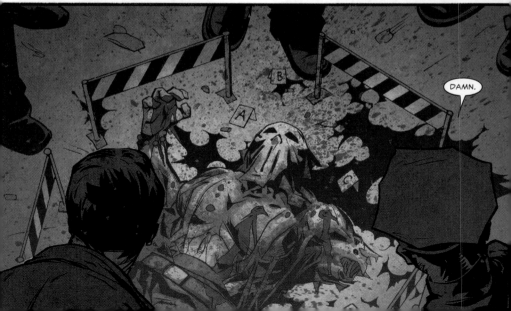

DAMN.

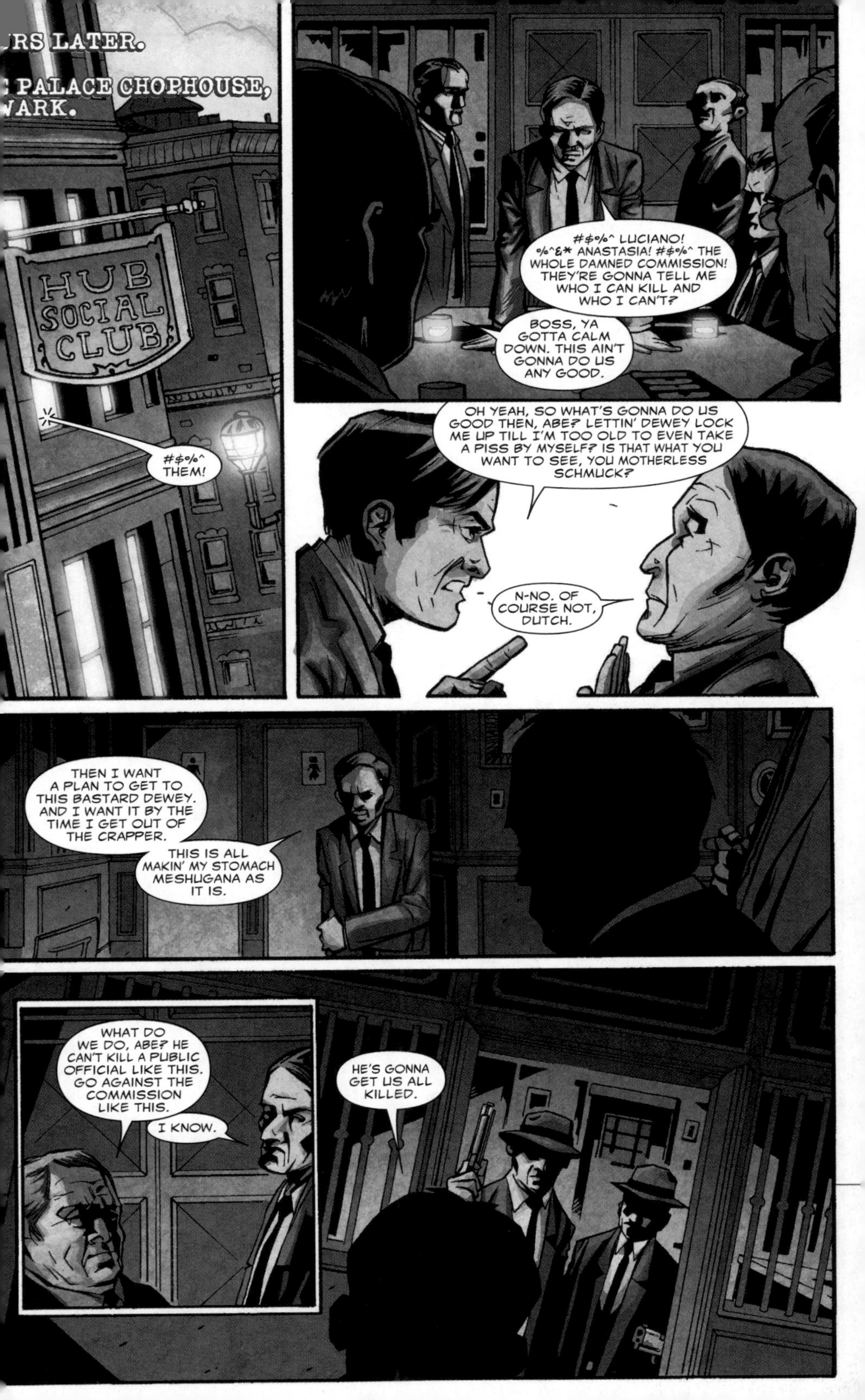

RS LATER.
PALACE CHOPHOUSE,
ARK.
HUB SOCIAL CLUB
#$%^ THEM!
#$%^ LUCIANO! %^&* ANASTASIA! #$%^ THE WHOLE DAMNED COMMISSION! THEY'RE GONNA TELL ME WHO I CAN KILL AND WHO I CAN'T?
BOSS, YA GOTTA CALM DOWN. THIS AIN'T GONNA DO US ANY GOOD.
OH YEAH, SO WHAT'S GONNA DO US GOOD THEN, ABE? LETTIN' DEWEY LOCK ME UP TILL I'M TOO OLD TO EVEN TAKE A PISS BY MYSELF? IS THAT WHAT YOU WANT TO SEE, YOU MOTHERLESS SCHMUCK?
N-NO. OF COURSE NOT, DUTCH.
THEN I WANT A PLAN TO GET TO THIS BASTARD DEWEY. AND I WANT IT BY THE TIME I GET OUT OF THE CRAPPER.
THIS IS ALL MAKIN' MY STOMACH MESHUGANA AS IT IS.
WHAT DO WE DO, ABE? HE CAN'T KILL A PUBLIC OFFICIAL LIKE THIS. GO AGAINST THE COMMISSION LIKE THIS.
I KNOW.
HE'S GONNA GET US ALL KILLED.

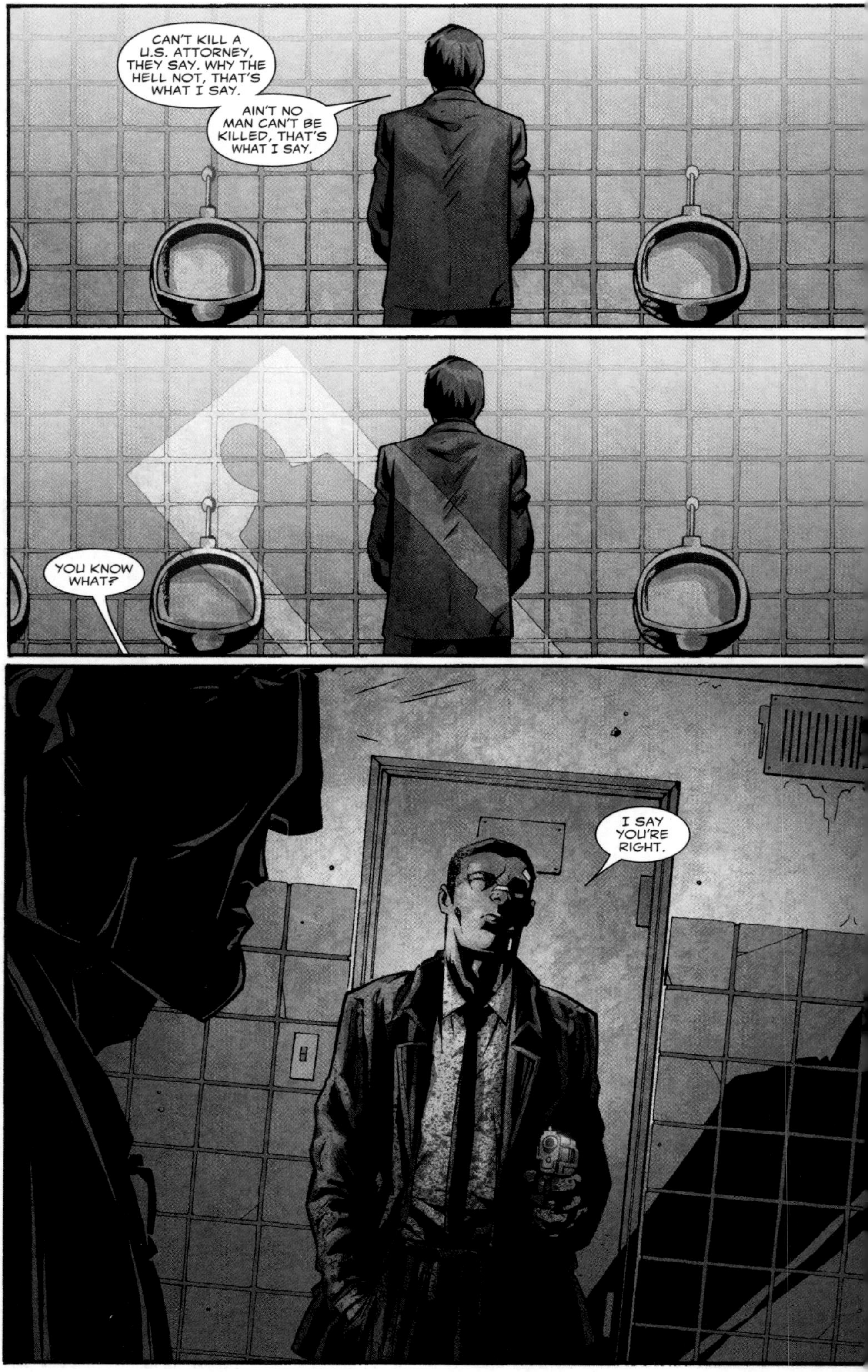
CAN'T KILL A U.S. ATTORNEY, THEY SAY. WHY THE HELL NOT, THAT'S WHAT I SAY.
AIN'T NO MAN CAN'T BE KILLED, THAT'S WHAT I SAY.
YOU KNOW WHAT?
I SAY YOU'RE RIGHT.

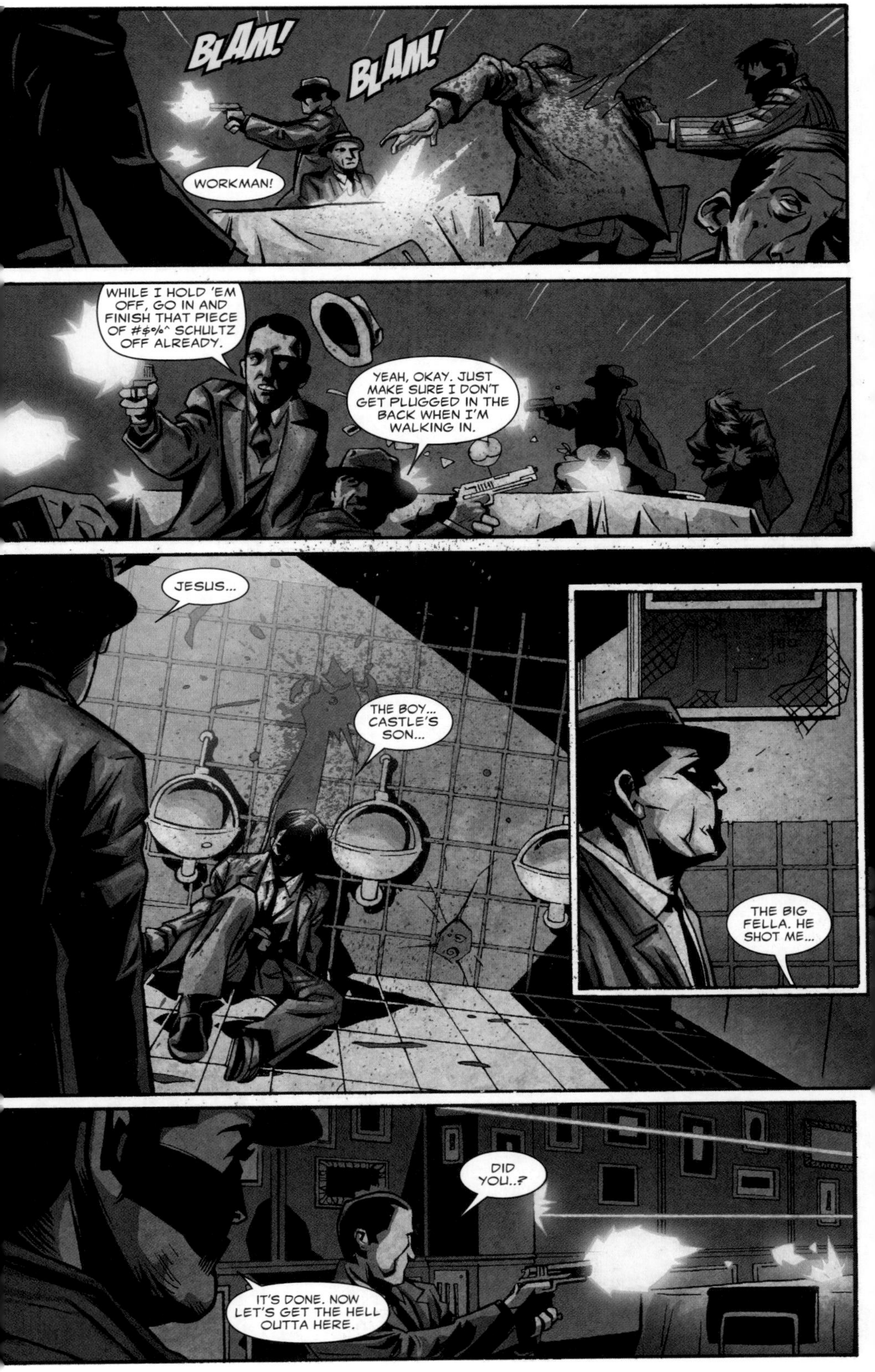
BLAM!
BLAM!
WORKMAN!
WHILE I HOLD 'EM OFF, GO IN AND FINISH THAT PIECE OF #$%^ SCHULTZ OFF ALREADY.
YEAH, OKAY. JUST MAKE SURE I DON'T GET PLUGGED IN THE BACK WHEN I'M WALKING IN.
JESUS...
THE BOY... CASTLE'S SON...
THE BIG FELLA. HE SHOT ME...
DID YOU..?
IT'S DONE. NOW LET'S GET THE HELL OUTTA HERE.

I WOULDN'T BE SURPRISED IF THE SHOW SERVED AS SOME KIND OF INSPIRATION FOR THE MAN, MR. DEWEY, SIR.

WHO WOULD'VE EVER DREAMED...A RUSSIAN WAR VET--A TRANSVESTITE ONE AT THAT--WHO WAS TERRORIZING THE UNDERWORLD FOR YEARS RIGHT UNDER OUR NOSES. AND WHO WAS ULTIMATELY RESPONSIBLE FOR DOING WHAT I NEVER COULD...

TAKING OUT DUTCH SCHULTZ.

SO...THE PUNISHER? NAMED HIM AFTER THE RADIO SHOW, HUH?

WELL, I GUESS YOU DREAMED IT, DETECTIVE, AS YOU'VE BEEN FOLLOWING THIS CASE FOR YEARS, SO I'M TOLD.

JUST DOING M JOB, SIR

WELL, I'LL SEE YOU GET A COMMENDATION FOR THIS, DOING YOUR JOB OR NOT. OF COURSE...

WE CAN'T POSSIBLY TELL THE GENERAL PUBLIC ABOUT THIS PUNISHER, YOU UNDERSTAND? IMAGINE THE REACTION IF THEY KNEW THE LIKES OF HIM WAS RUNNING AROUND. YOU'D THINK WE WERE GETTING INVADED BY MEN FROM MARS OR SOMETHING.

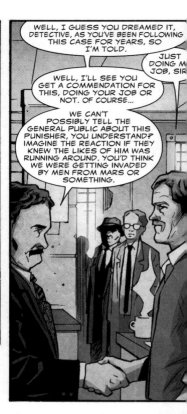

NO, I'M TOLD WE'VE GOT WORKMAN IN CUSTODY SO WE'LL BE PINNING DUTCH'S DEATH ON HIM. GET ME, DETECTIVE?

I GOT YOU.

WELL, MIKE, LOOK WHAT WE GOT HERE. A GENUINE HERO, DON'T YA KNOW.

FELLAS, EVEN YOU TWO COULDN'T SPOIL MY MOOD ON A DAY LIKE THIS.

OH REALLY? THEN LET ME ASK YA THIS ABOUT THAT LITTLE FAIRY TALE YA JUST LAID ON DEWEY, HERO...

HOW IS IT POSSIBLE THAT THE RUSSIAN GUY WAS THIS SO-CALLED PUNISHER OF YOURS, KILLING DUTCH AND EVERYTHING, WHEN HE WAS FOUND DEAD IN THE BRONX HOURS EARLIER? OR DON'T YOU WANT YOUR NEW ADORING FANS TO KNOW ABOUT THAT LITTLE MORSEL?

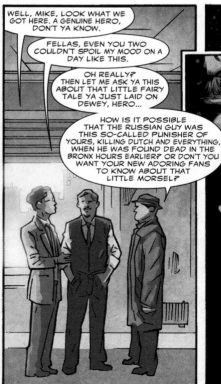

HEH.

C'MON BOYS, WE'RE GOING OUT TO CELEBRATE.

OR HAVEN'T YOU HEARD? TH CASE IS CLOSEC

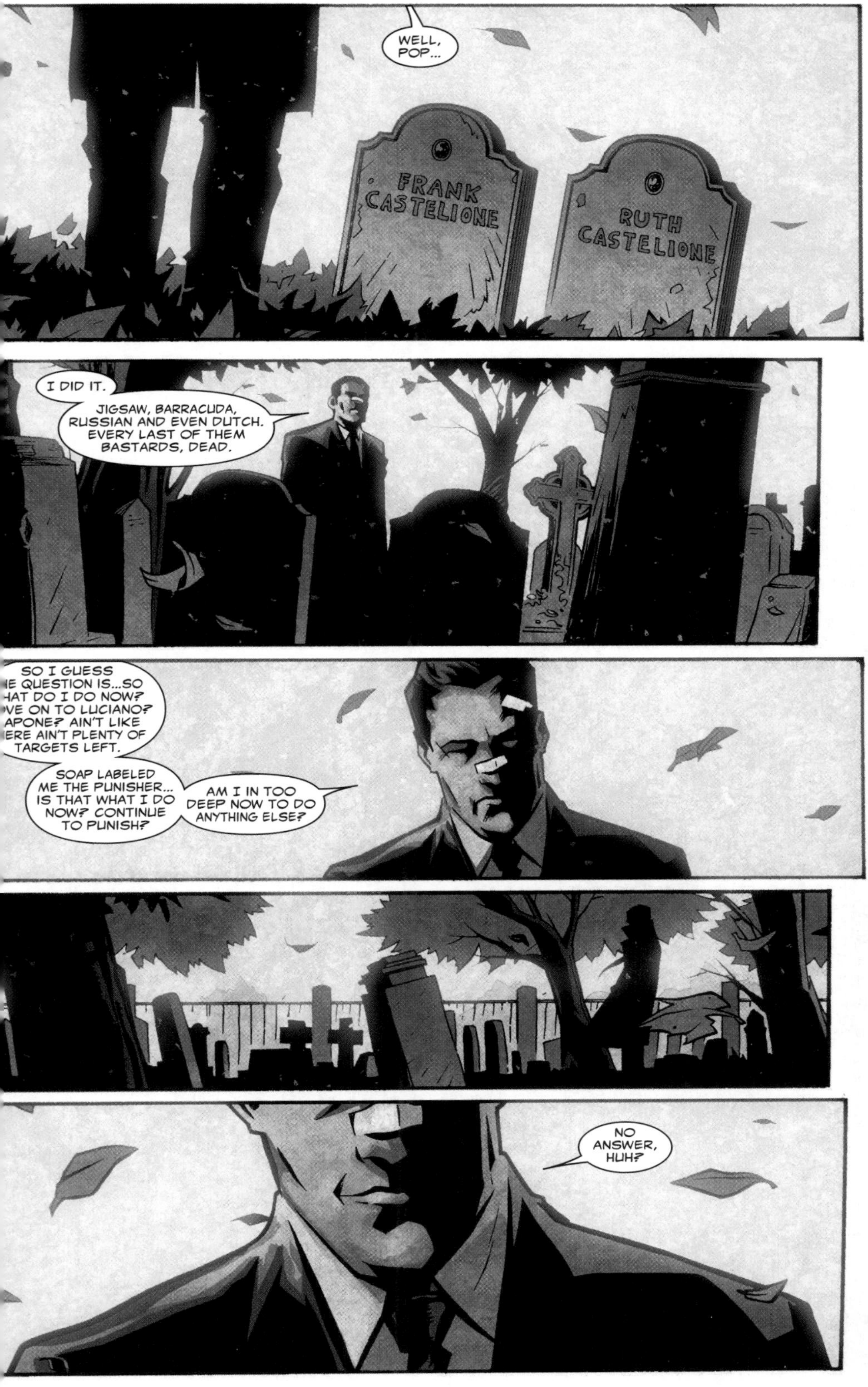
WELL, POP...
FRANK CASTELIONE
RUTH CASTELIONE
I DID IT.
JIGSAW, BARRACUDA, RUSSIAN AND EVEN DUTCH. EVERY LAST OF THEM BASTARDS, DEAD.
SO I GUESS
QUESTION IS...SO
DO I DO NOW?
ON TO LUCIANO?
APONE? AIN'T LIKE
AIN'T PLENTY OF
TARGETS LEFT.
SOAP LABELED ME THE PUNISHER... IS THAT WHAT I DO NOW? CONTINUE TO PUNISH?
AM I IN TOO DEEP NOW TO DO ANYTHING ELSE?
NO ANSWER, HUH?

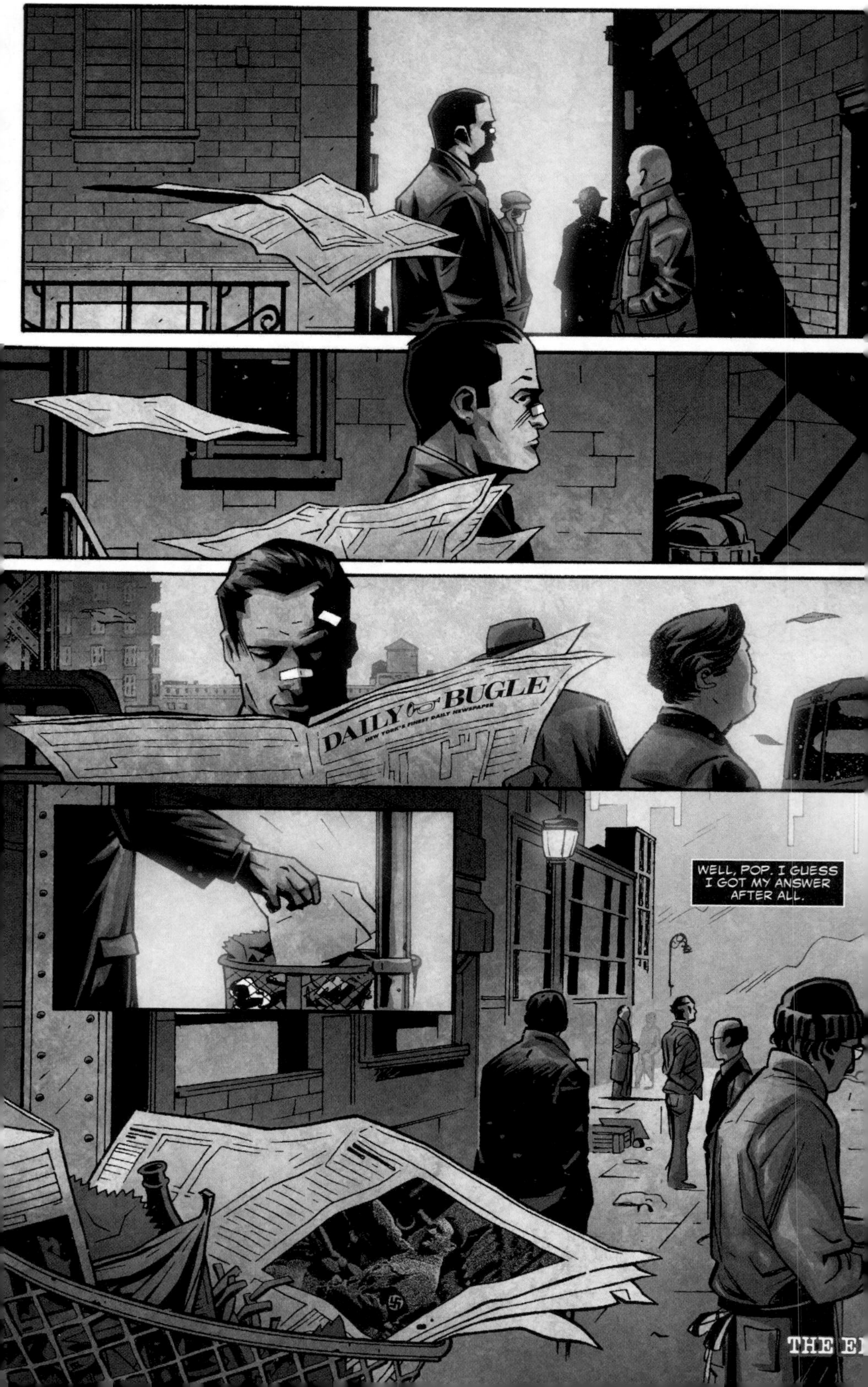
DAILY BUGLE
NEW YORK'S FINEST DAILY NEWSPAPER
WELL, POP. I GUESS I GOT MY ANSWER AFTER ALL.
THE E

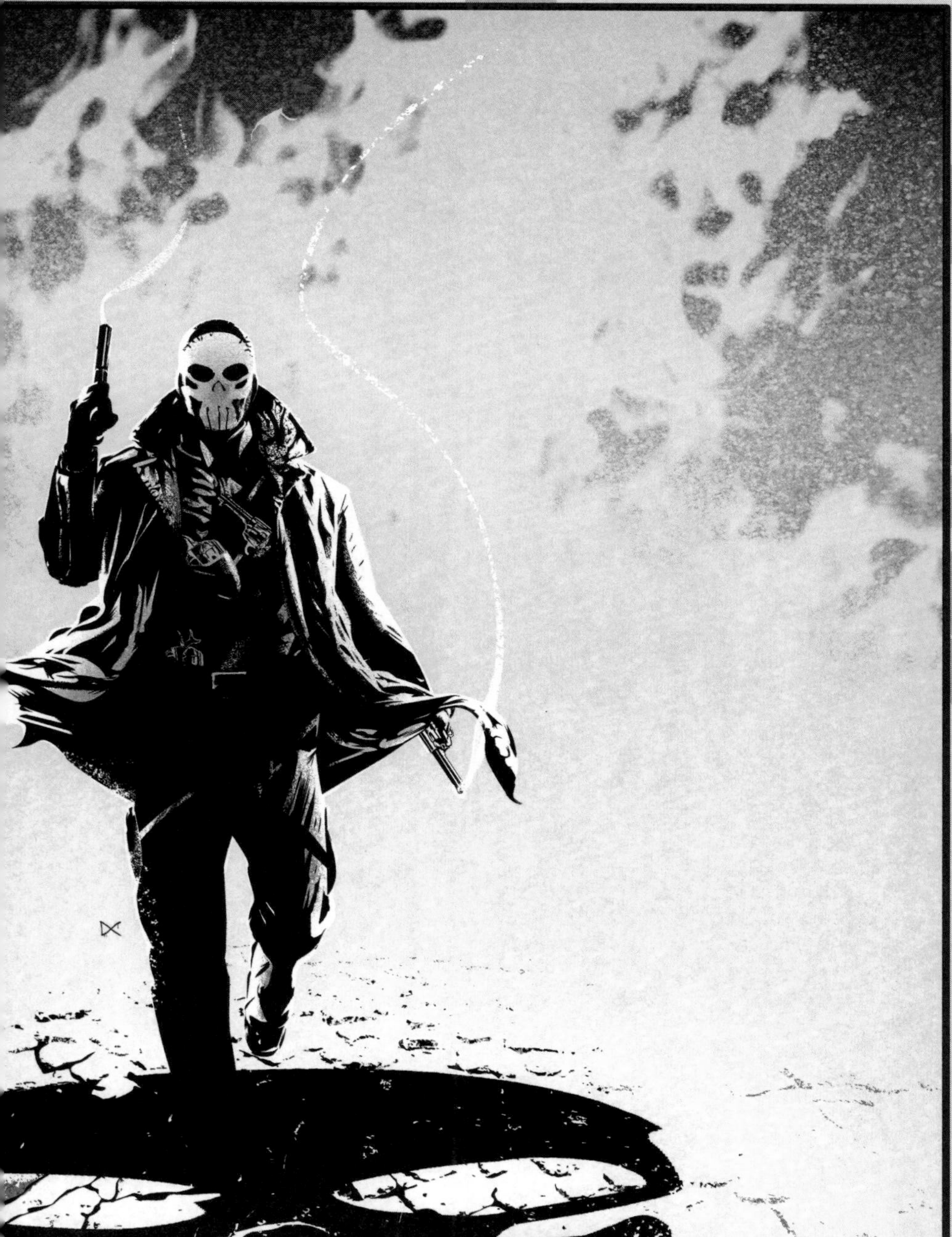

#1 VARIANT BY DENNIS CALERO

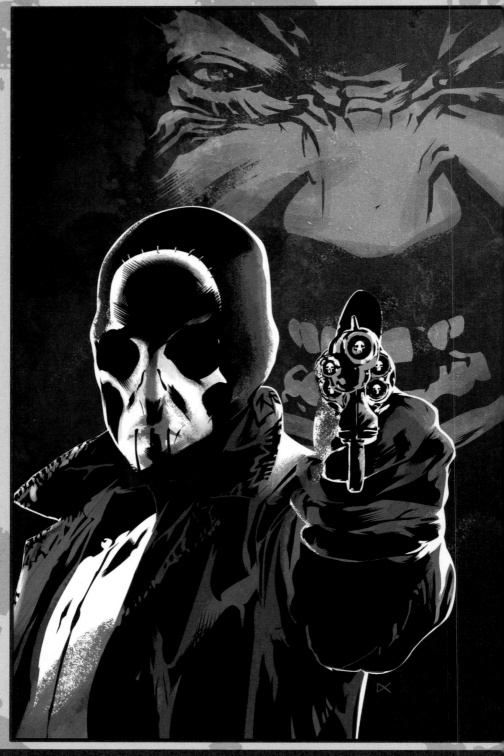

#2 VARIANT BY DENNIS CALERO

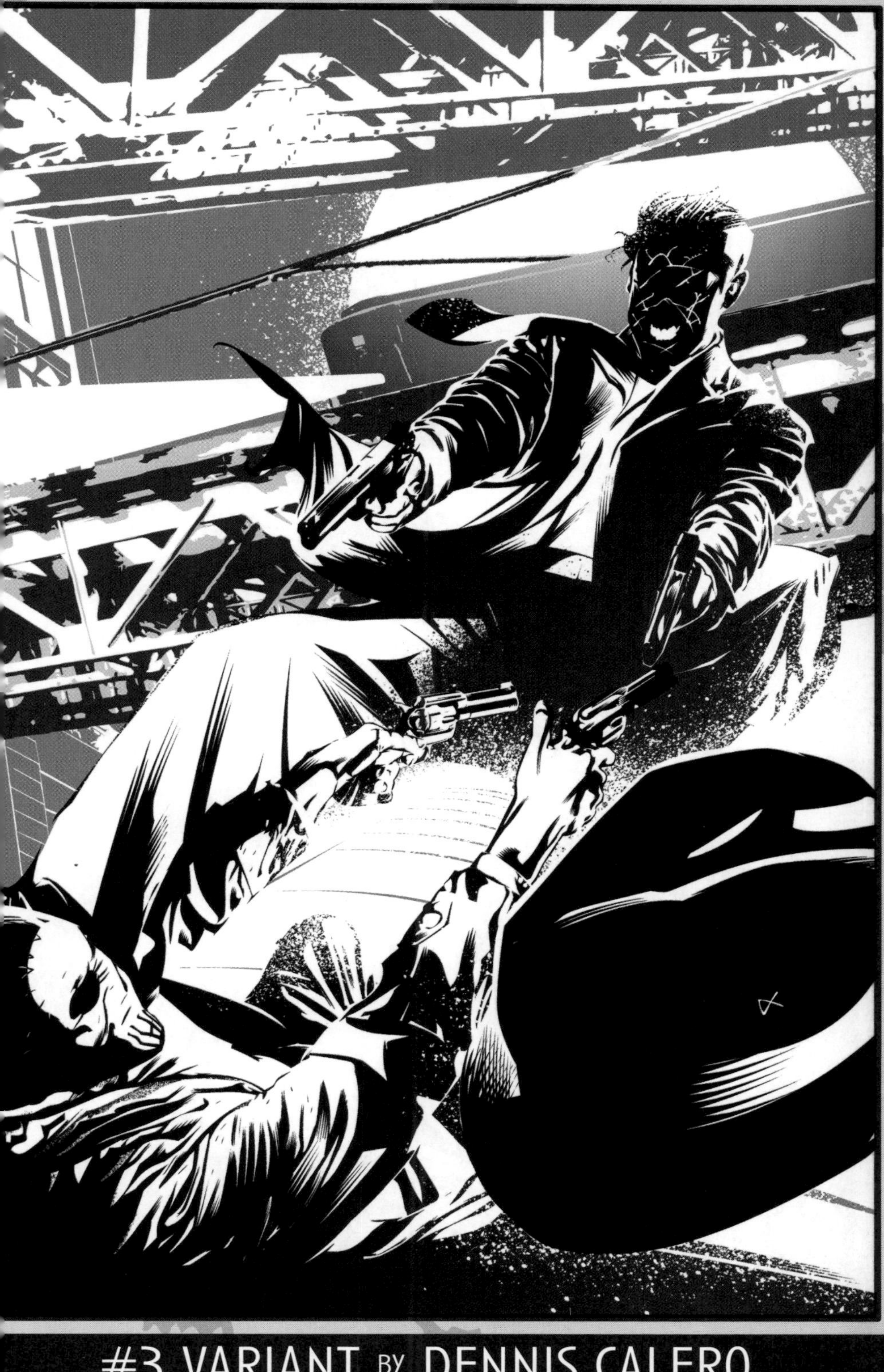

#3 VARIANT BY DENNIS CALERO

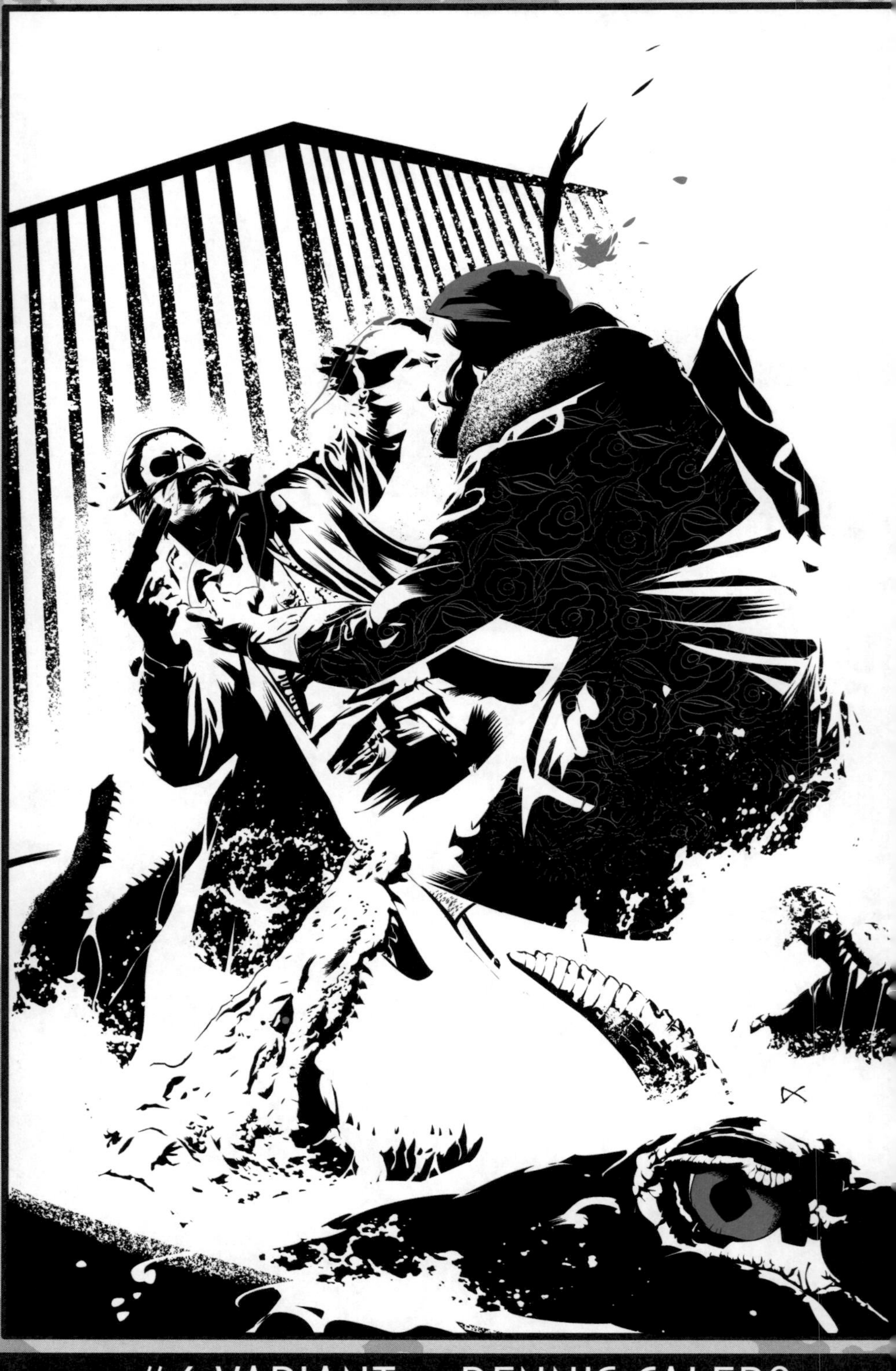

#4 VARIANT BY DENNIS CALERO

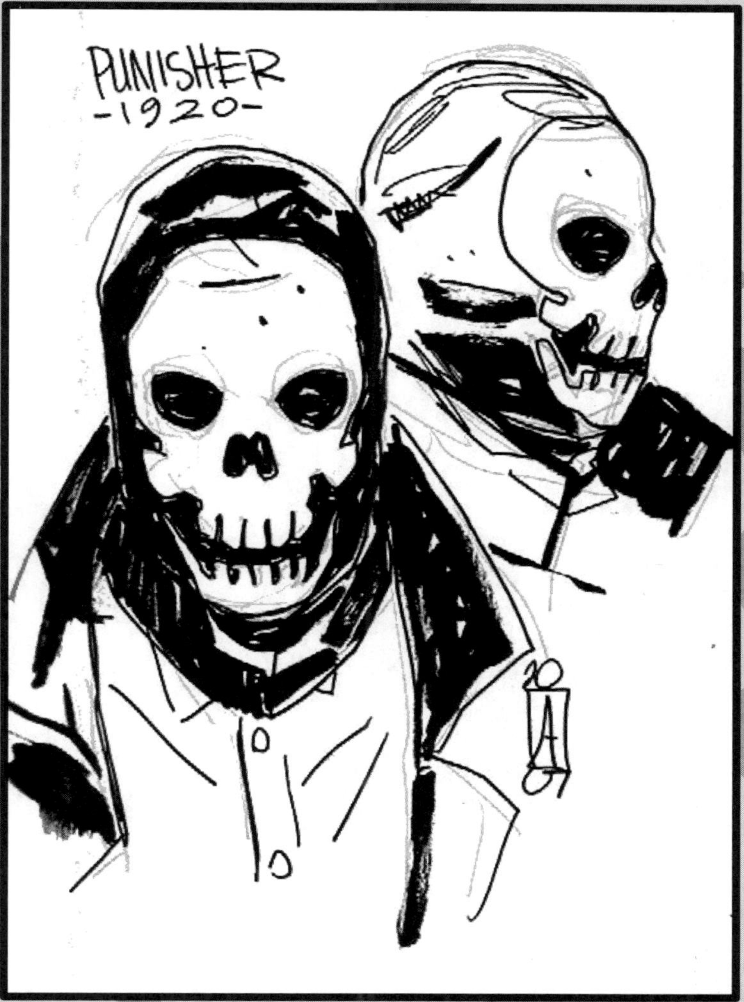
PUNISHER
-1920-

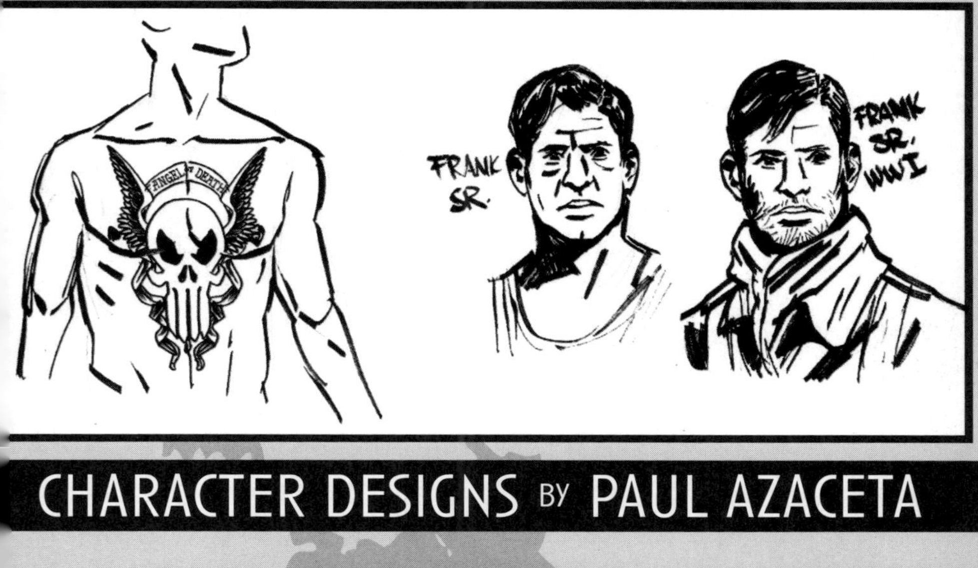
ANGEL OF DEATH
FRANK SR.
FRANK SR. WWI

CHARACTER DESIGNS BY PAUL AZACETA

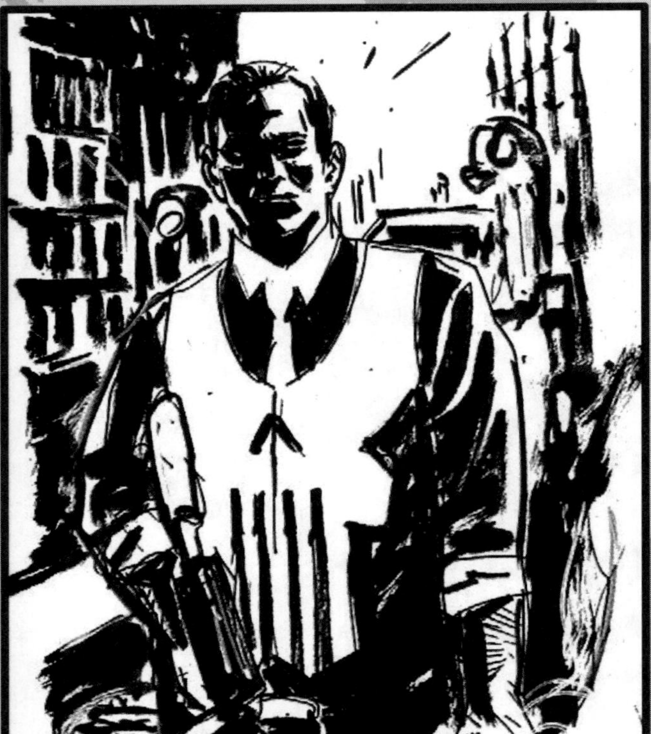
PUNISHER
1930

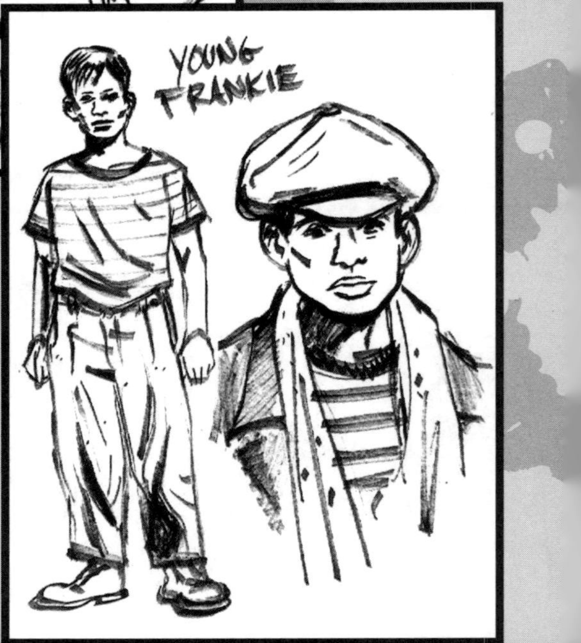
YOUNG
FRANKIE

CHARACTER DESIGNS BY PAUL AZACETA

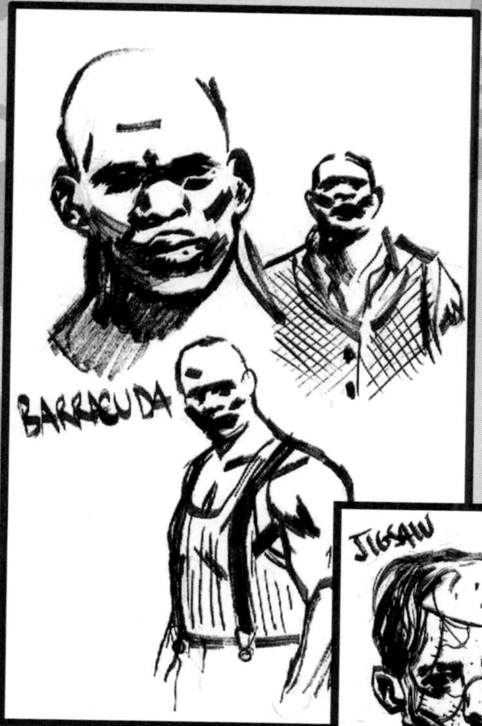
BARRACUDA

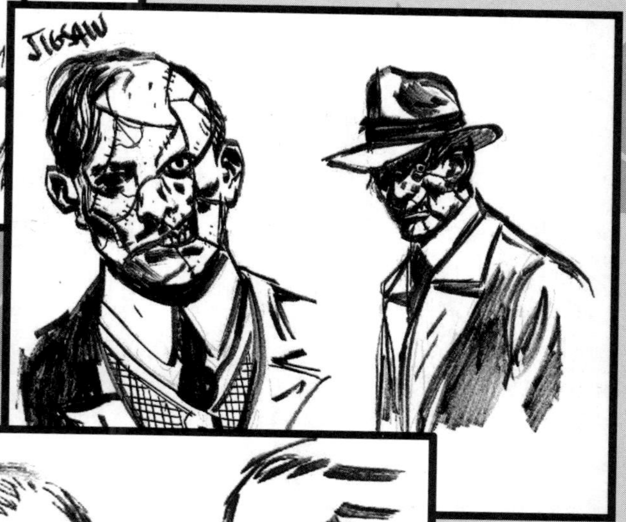
JIGSAW

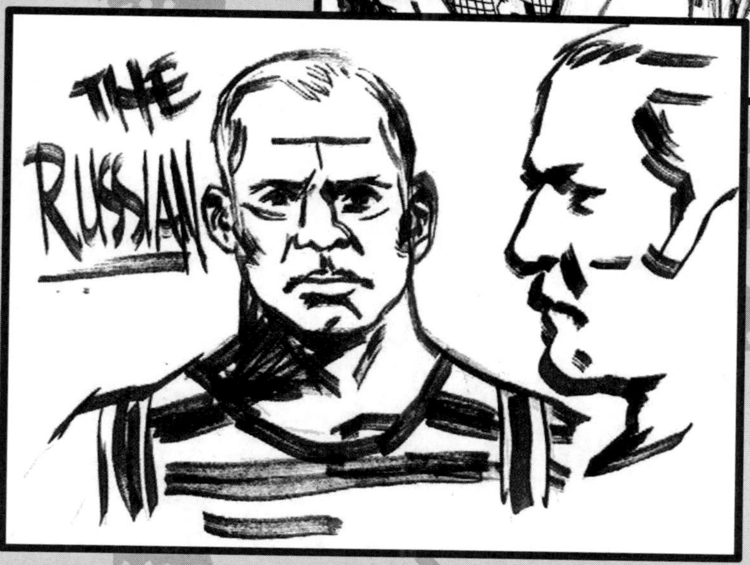
THE
RUSSIAN

CHARACTER DESIGNS BY PAUL AZACETA

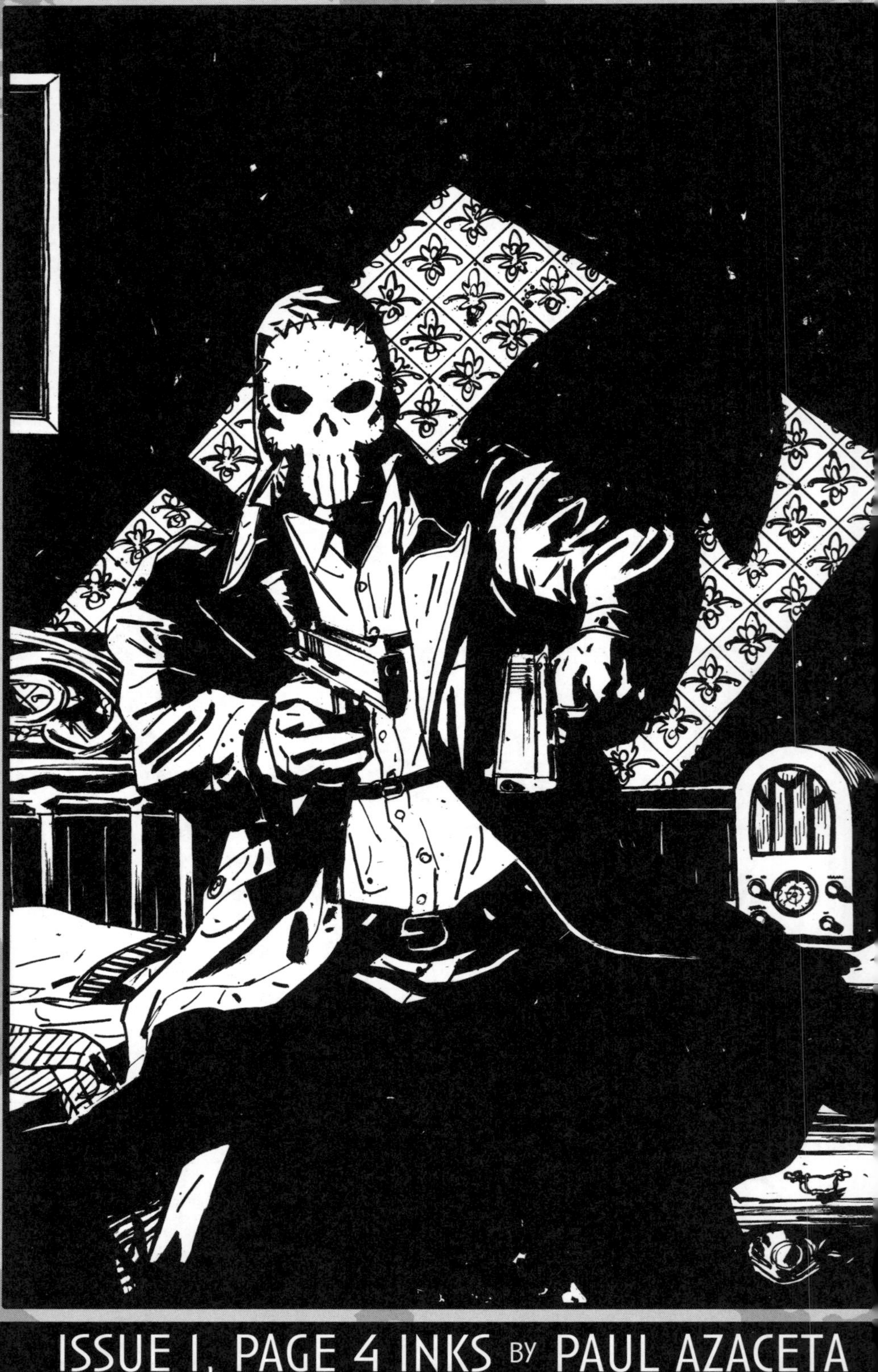

ISSUE 1, PAGE 4 INKS BY PAUL AZACETA

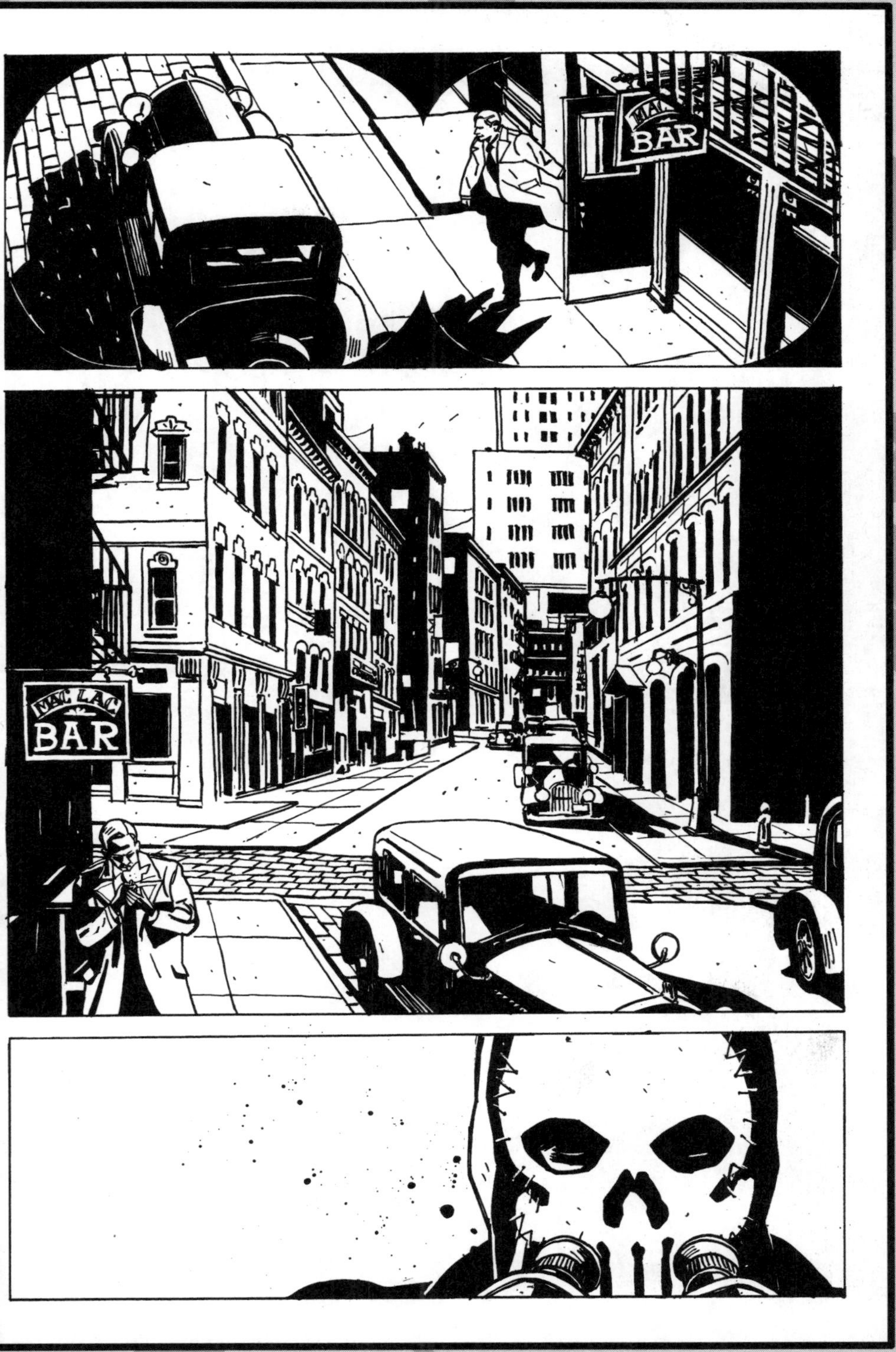
BAR
MAC LAC
BAR

ISSUE 2, PAGE 4 INKS BY PAUL AZACETA

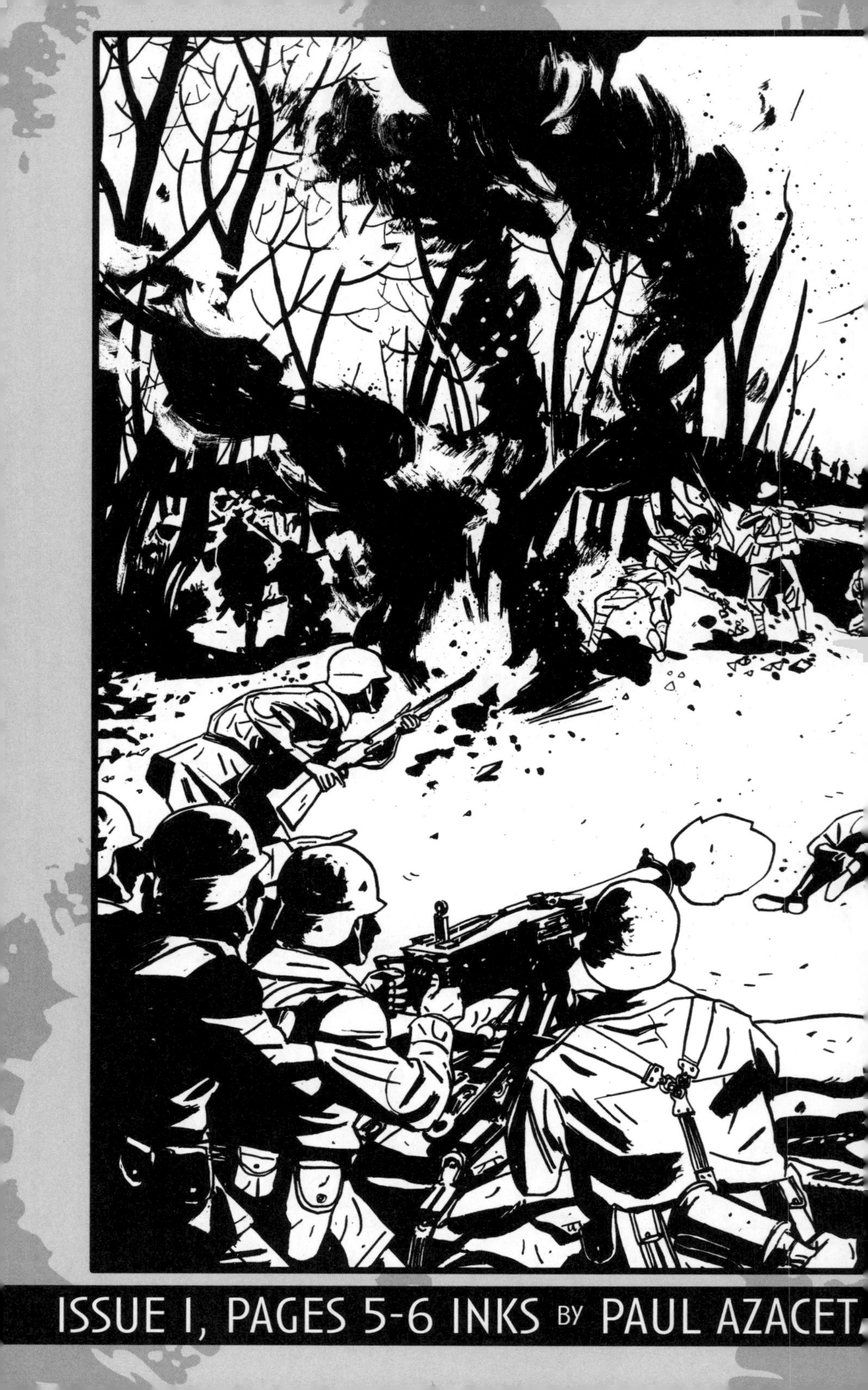

ISSUE 1, PAGES 5-6 INKS BY PAUL AZACETA

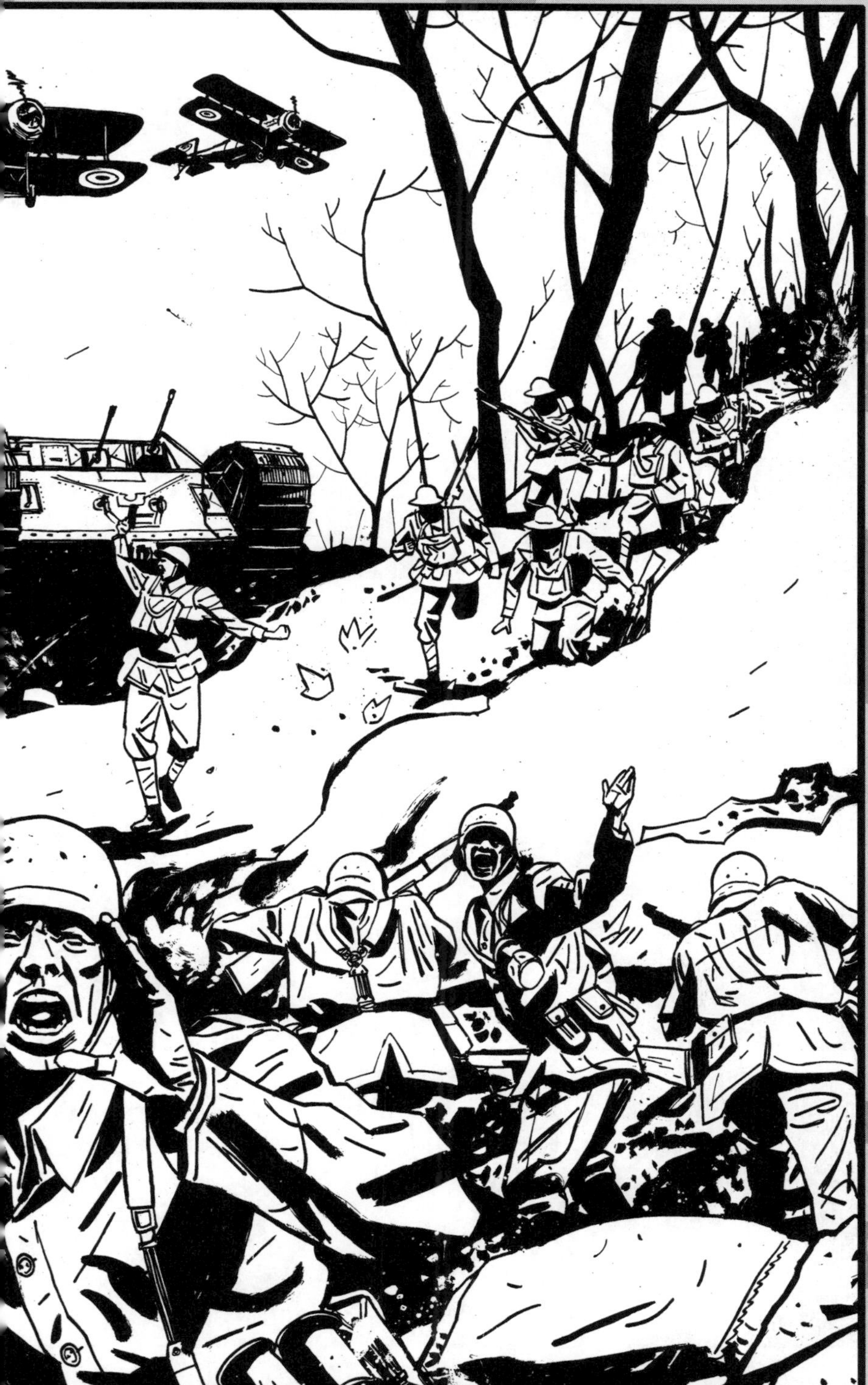

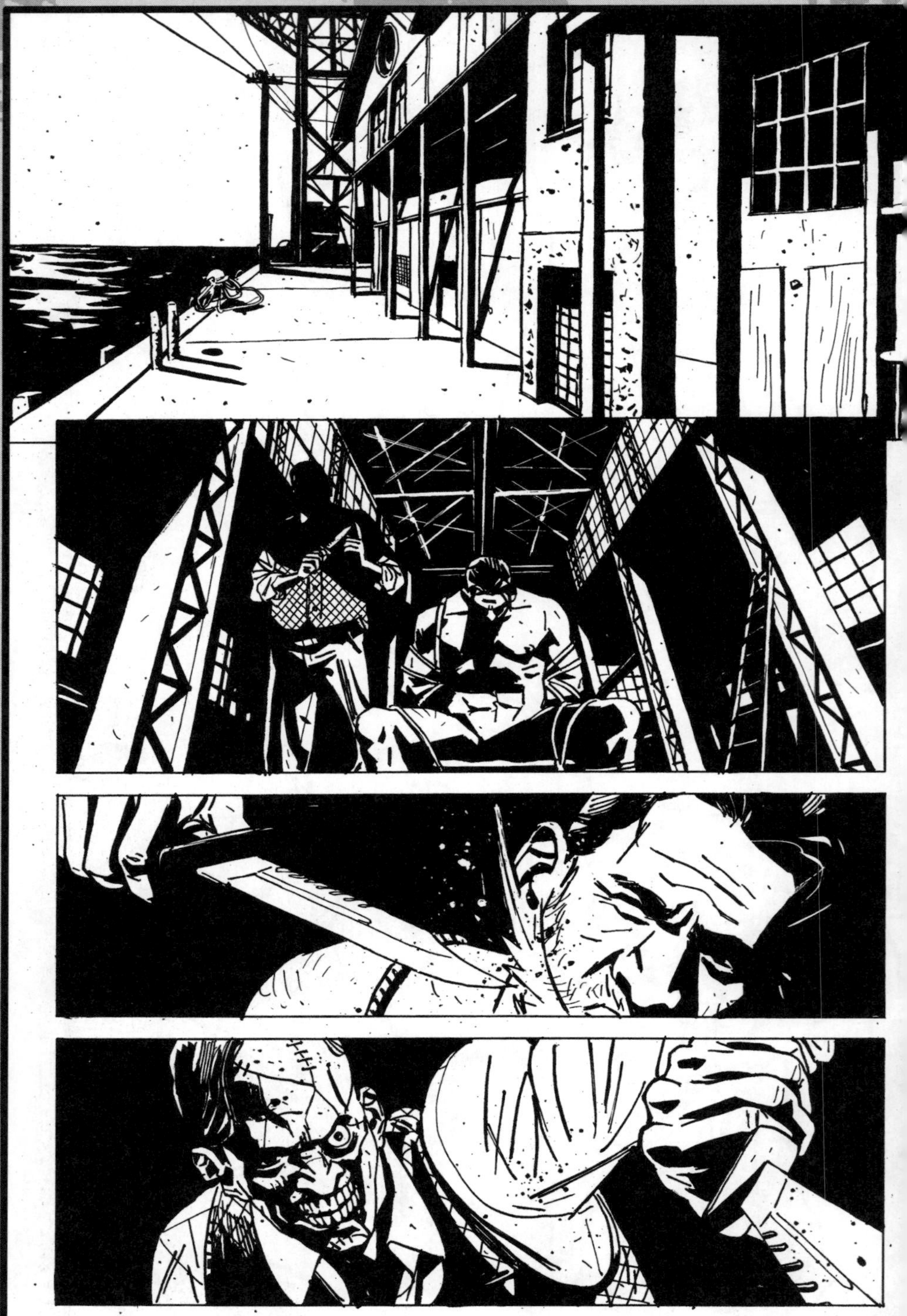

ISSUE 3, PAGE 16 INKS BY PAUL AZACETA

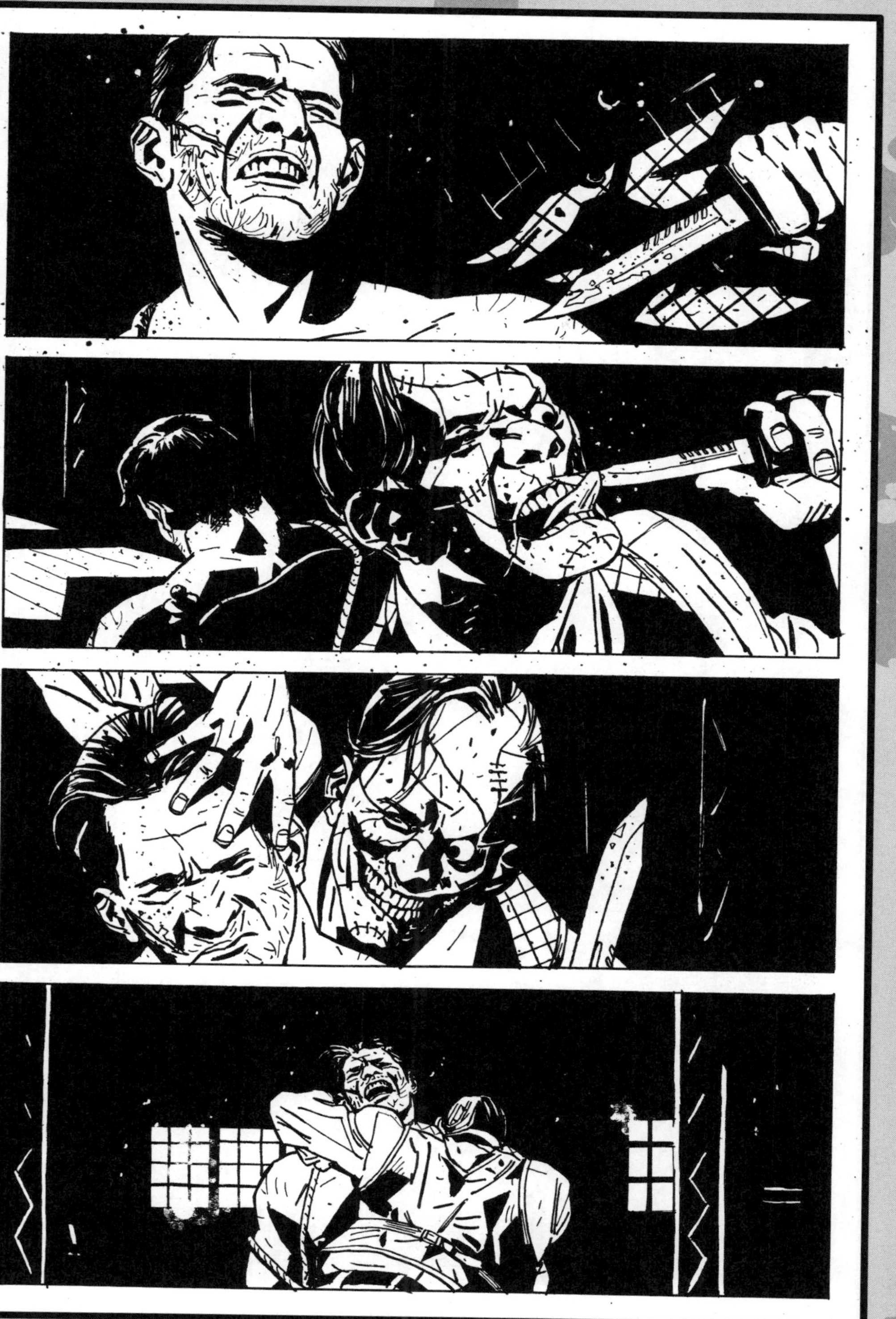

ISSUE 3, PAGE 17 INKS BY PAUL AZACETA

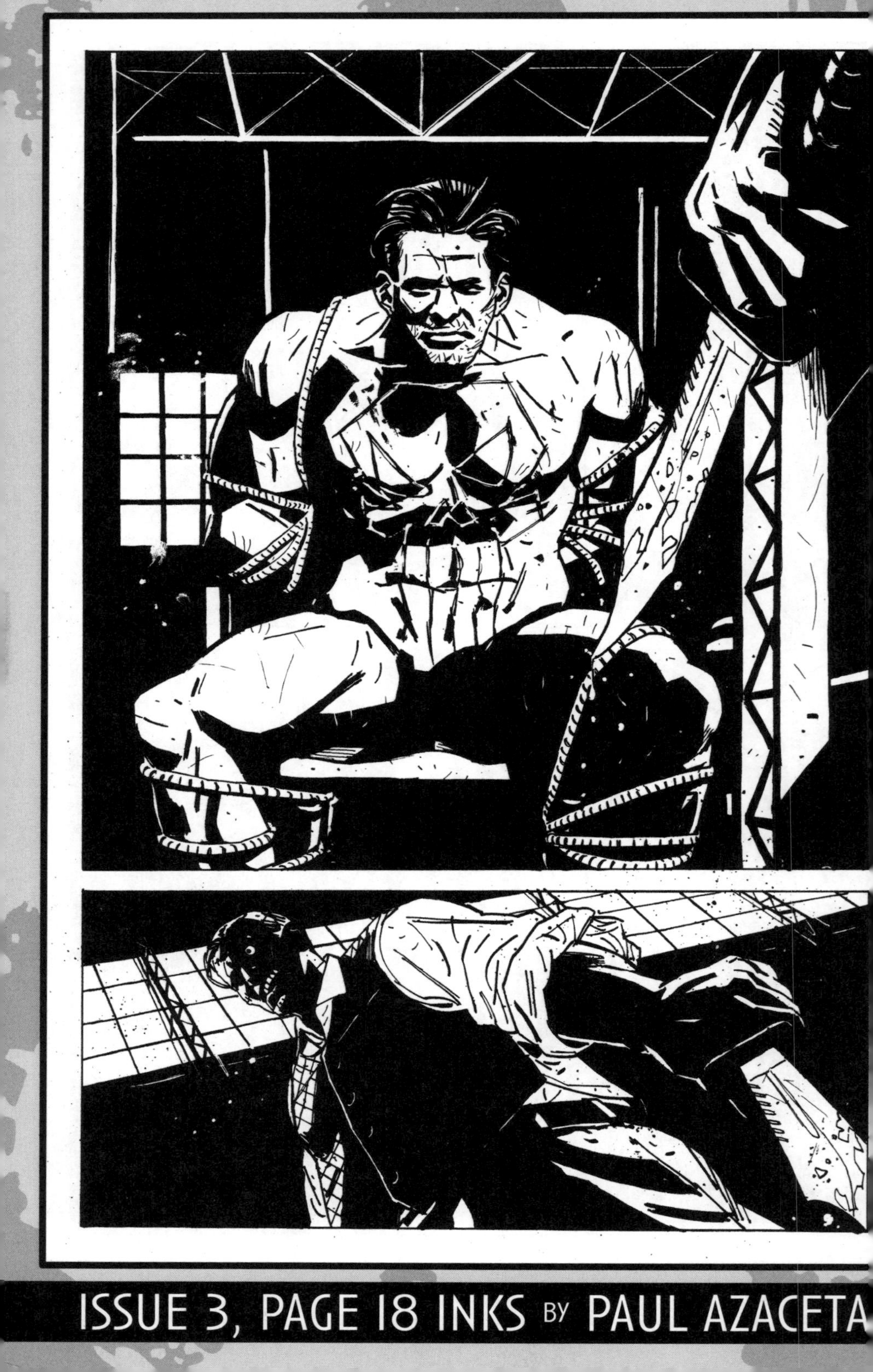

ISSUE 3, PAGE 18 INKS BY PAUL AZACETA

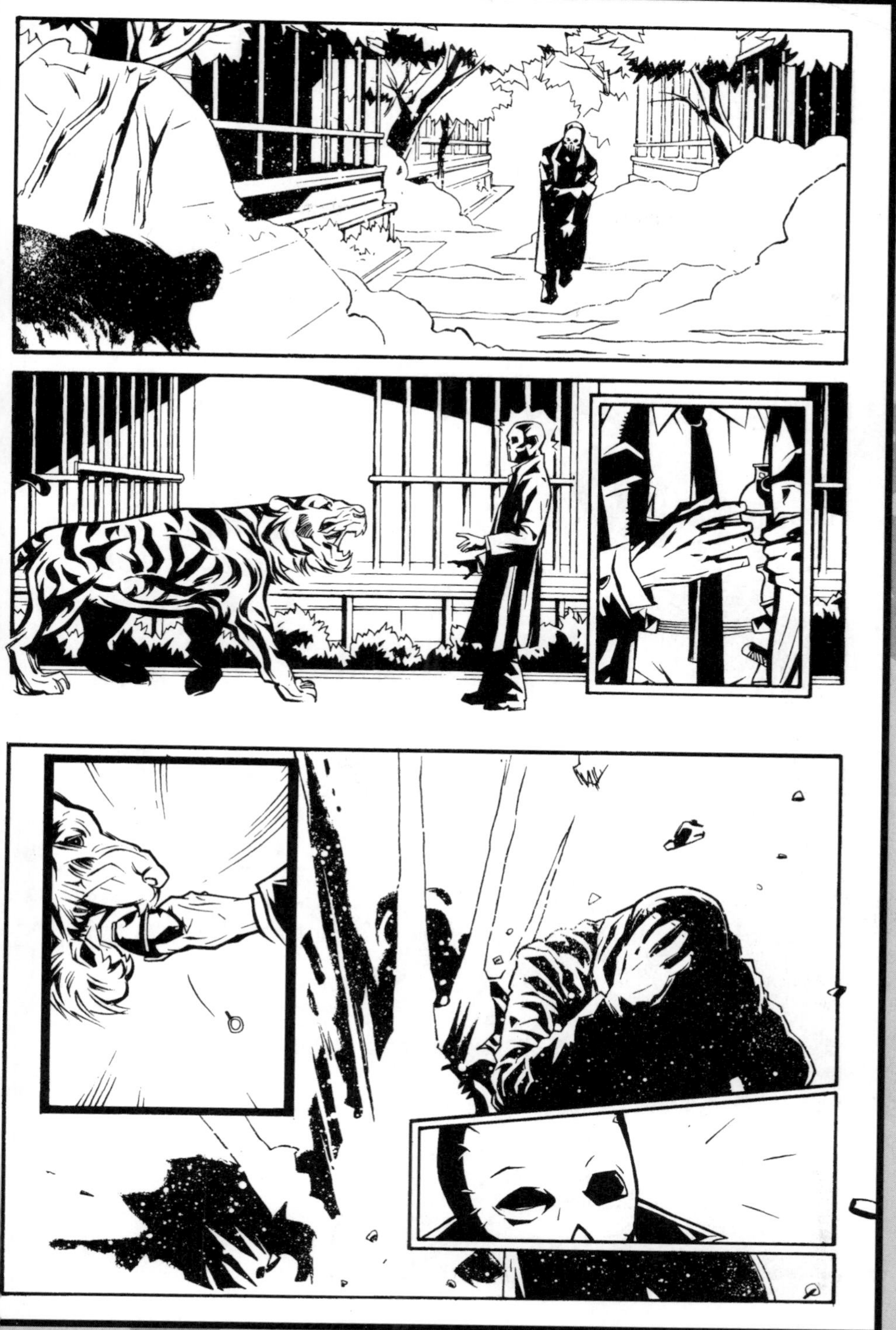

ISSUE 4, PAGE 8 INKS BY ANTONIO FUSO

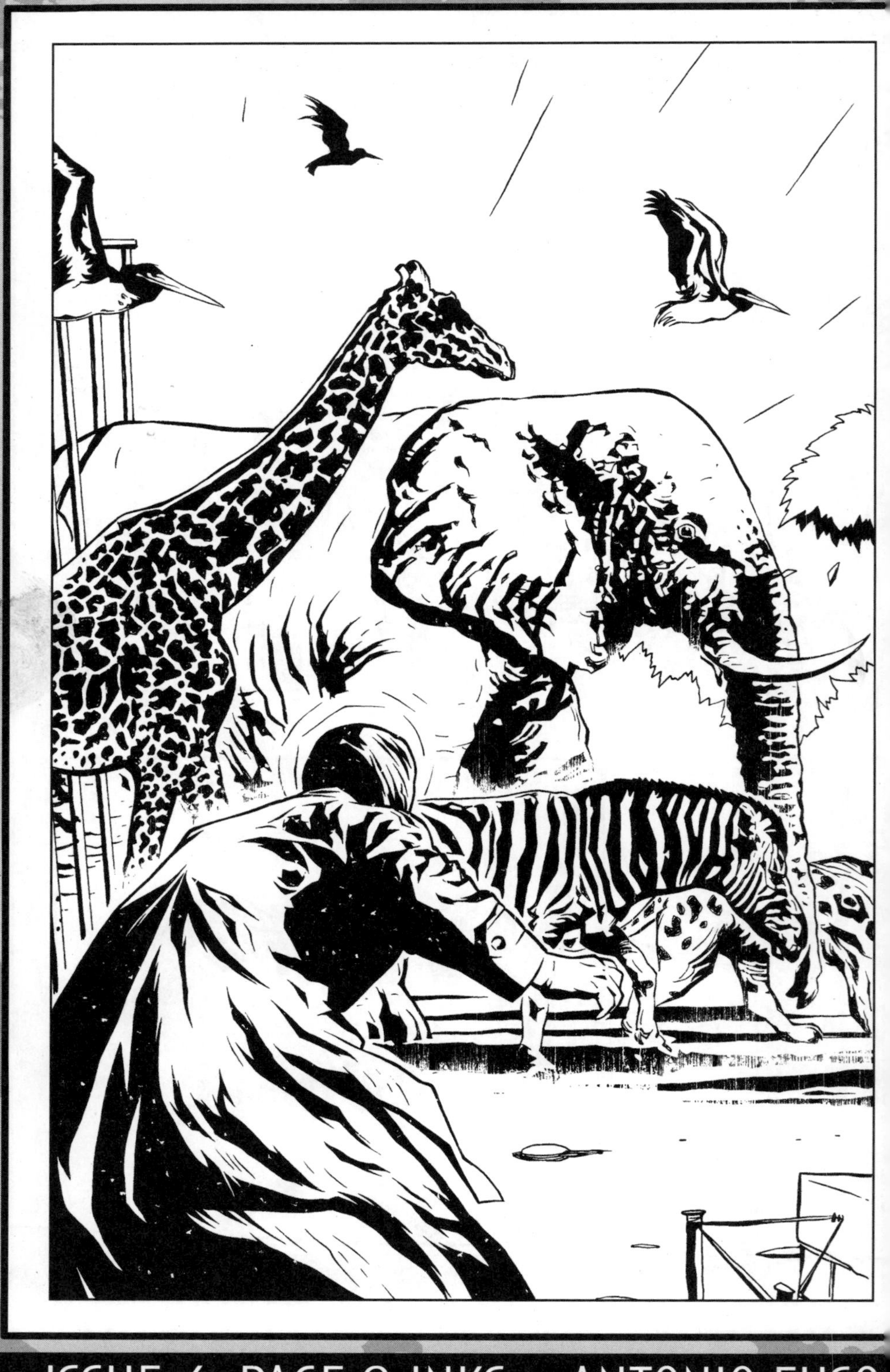

ISSUE 4, PAGE 9 INKS BY ANTONIO FUSO